Haut-Brion

Asa Briggs, who was created a life peer in 1976, is one of Britain's most eminent historians and the author of many books, including one on the history of wine. From 1967 to 1976 he was Vice-Chancellor of the University of Sussex and from 1976 to 1991 Provost of Worcester College, Oxford. He has been Chancellor of the Open University since 1978. He is a frequent broadcaster and has written five volumes on the history of British broadcasting.

D1572005

HAUT-BRION

An Illustrious Lineage

═══

ASA BRIGGS

═══

faber and faber
LONDON · BOSTON

First published in 1994
by Faber and Faber Limited
3 Queen Square, London, WC1N 3AU

Phototypeset by Intype, London
Printed by Clays Ltd, St Ives plc

© Domaine Clarence Dillon SA, 1994
Maps © John Flower, 1994

Asa Briggs is hereby identified as the author of this work in
accordance with Section 77 of the Copyright, Designs and Patents Act 1988.

A CIP record for this book
is available from the British Library
ISBN 0–571–16927–9 (cased)
0–571–17118–4 (pbk)

1 3 5 7 9 10 8 6 4 2

Contents

List of Illustrations

Old Bordeaux
The château at Haut-Brion seen through the arch
The park at Haut-Brion
The vineyards
Gathering the grapes
Sorting
A crate of grapes
The arrival of the grapes at the chais
M. Delmas tasting in the laboratory
The computer screen
The cuvier
Wine in the barrel
Haut-Brion labels

Photographs by Burdin

MAPS

The historian is not the man who knows,
but the man who seeks to find out.

Lucien Febvre

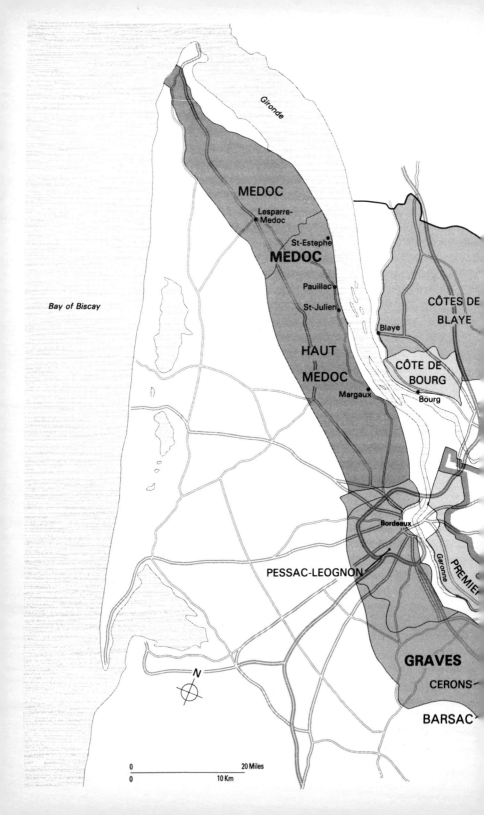

Gironde

MEDOC

Lesparre-
Medoc

St-Estephe

MEDOC

Pauillac

St-Julien

Bay of Biscay

HAUT

MEDOC

Margaux

CÔTES DE
BLAYE

Blaye

CÔTE DE
BOURG

Bourg

Bordeaux

Garonne

PESSAC-LEOGNON

PREMIER

N

GRAVES

CERONS

BARSAC

0   20 Miles
0   10 Km

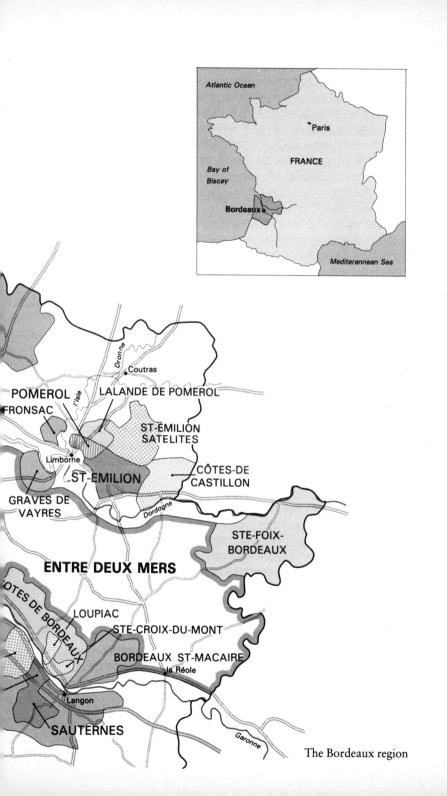

Atlantic Ocean

Paris

FRANCE

Bay of
Biscay

Bordeaux

Mediterannean Sea

Dronne

Coutras

l'Isle

POMEROL

FRONSAC

LALANDE DE POMEROL

ST-ÉMILION
SATELITES

Limborne

ST-EMILION

CÔTES-DE
CASTILLON

GRAVES DE
VAYRES

Dordogne

STE-FOIX-
BORDEAUX

ENTRE DEUX MERS

ÔTES DE BORDEAUX

LOUPIAC

STE-CROIX-DU-MONT

BORDEAUX ST-MACAIRE

la Réole

Langon

SAUTERNES

Garonne

The Bordeaux region

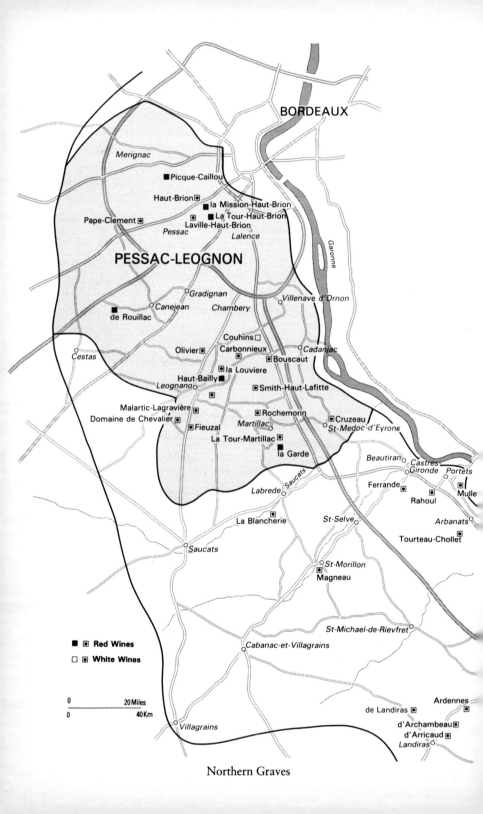

BORDEAUX

Merignac

■ Picque-Caillou

Haut-Brion◉ ■ la Mission-Haut-Brion

■ La Tour-Haut-Brion

Pape-Clement◉   Laville-Haut-Brion

Pessac   Lalence

PESSAC-LEOGNON

Garonne

○Gradignan

○Canejean   Chambery   ○Villenave d'Ornon

■ de Rouillac

○Cestas   Couhins□

Olivier◉   Carbonnieux   ○Cadanjac

◉Bouscaut

◉la Louviere

Haut-Bailly■

Leognan○   ◉Smith-Haut-Lafitte

Malartic-Lagravière ◉

Domaine de Chevalier◉   ◉Rochemorin   ◉Cruzeau

■Fieuzal   Martillac   St-Medoc-d'Eyrons

La Tour-Martillac

■la Garde

Beautiran   Castres

Labrede○   Saucats   Gironde○   Portets

Ferrande◉   ○

Rahoul   ◉Mulle

La Blancherie◉   St-Selve○

Arbanats○

Tourteau-Chollet

○Saucats

○St-Morillon
Magneau◉

St-Michael-de-Rievfret○

■ ◉ Red Wines
□ ◉ White Wines

Cabanac-et-Villagrains○

0 _____ 20 Miles
0 _____ 40 Km

Ardennes○
de Landiras◉   ◉
○Villagrains   d'Archambeau◉
d'Arricaud◉
Landiras○

Northern Graves

Preface

This is the first book to deal in detail with Haut-Brion, one of the oldest of the wines of Bordeaux and the first of the wines to be given a name of its own. It tells the story of a great wine and of a great vineyard.

The approach is my own. I have told the story as a historian who believes that the history of wine should be fully integrated into economic, social, political and, not least, cultural history. Spanning the centuries, it is a distinctive book among my own writings, although I have written one other book on the recent history of the retailing of wine in Britain, *Wine for Sale*, which appeared in 1985. I would not have written this book, however, had I not been invited to do so by the Duc and Duchesse de Mouchy, and they, along with other members of the Dillon family (who now own the vineyard) on both sides of the Atlantic, have given me great encouragement – and offered me memorable hospitality – throughout the inevitably protracted period of my research. So, too, has Jean-Bernard Delmas, pioneering manager of Haut-Brion, whose profound knowledge of all aspects of viniculture and wine-making has been indispensable to me.

I was heartened at an early stage of my delving into the Haut-Brion archives when I fell upon a highly relevant letter written in December 1963 by Clarence Dillon, the first Dillon to acquire the vineyard, to his nephew, Seymour Weller, under whose overseeing it was managed. In it he stated that he would like to have prepared – and to see published – a history of Haut-Brion that 'would be of interest to anyone, whether he was particularly concerned with wine or not'. 'My only thought,' he added, 'is that you should consider someone other than a wine enthusiast for preparing this volume.'

Dillon, an American businessman of very wide experience, feared that a 'wine enthusiast' – others might have talked of a 'wine buff' – would tell only part of the story and that he or she might tell it in the then distinctive language of 'wine enthusiasts', usually replete with conventional, if often lush, adjectives, for a specialist, though growing audience. As I have pursued my researches, I have come to appreciate fully the work of 'wine enthusiasts' and could not have written my book without drawing upon their experience and knowledge. Yet I have drawn heavily, too, on the work of French social and cultural historians – and geographers – who have revolutionized the study of the history of wine in recent years, aware both of the specific detail in different periods of history and of the need to establish a perspective that spans them.

Already by 1963 Henri Enjalbert's first article on *'la révolution des boissons'* had appeared, explaining why the late seventeenth and eighteenth centuries stand out in the development of the concept of the *grand cru*, the quality wine that lasts. Not surprisingly, the article which forecast the thesis to be set out fully in Enjalbert's *Histoire de la Vigne* (1975) was published in the pioneering historical French journal *Annales* in 1953 under the title *'Comment naissent les grands crus – Bordeaux, Porto, Cognac'*. *Annales* has been as innovatory in historical studies as Haut-Brion itself in the making of wine, and its reputation has been just as international.

Professor Enjalbert and his pupil Professor René Pijassou have gone on to develop the field, turning in detail to Château Latour and to the wines of the Médoc, on the way frequently catching glimpses of Haut-Brion, which was renowned as a wine before the Médoc flourished. I owe a substantial debt to them as I do also to Professor P. Roudié, a careful scholar who, *inter alia*, has written about St-Émilion and who is deeply interested in Haut-Brion. He guided my early steps in France and provided me with essential leads into my subject. J.-P. Poussou, Lecturer in History at the University of Bordeaux, a specialist in the demography of the area, extended my researches, while Alain Puginier collected various historical source materials that I wished to consult, some relating to the Middle Ages (his own period), some to modern times, including the nineteenth century.

My sources were not only French. I have made more use of nineteenth-century and early twentieth-century British books on claret than do most contemporary British writers on wine, although

I imagine that many of them are now period pieces. I have also studied more recent books in English and French. My own account, which I hope will serve as a work of reference, includes an account of Haut-Brion as it is today.

An invaluable work of general reference is David Peppercorn's *Bordeaux*, first published in 1982 and fully revised in 1991. Peppercorn offers a different kind of perspective from that of French historians and geographers of wine. He himself comes from a wine trade family and studied history at Cambridge. He has visited Bordeaux regularly since 1952.

My bibliography, which is selective but comprehensive, is preceded by an introductory essay. It refers to a wide range of other books of different times and places, including books published in the United States where there is an intense interest in wine studies in general and in Haut-Brion in particular, as a wine to taste and enjoy. The literature of the subject is, indeed, international. One of the most agreeable books on the châteaux of Bordeaux is by a Dutch writer, Hubrecht Duijker. The illustrations that I have chosen, like his, not only illustrate the text but provide additional material in themselves. There are no footnotes in my book – these would be cumbrous – but the bibliography assembles the published references.

Because of my approach, which leads through history, I have chosen as a 'motto' of my book a key sentence of the great French historian Lucien Febvre, describing the role of the historian whether he is dealing with wine or with any other subject. It can be compared with a remark made by Dr Robert Druitt, an English writer on wine in mid-Victorian times, who was more concerned with health than with history: 'From the earliest ages of mankind wine has been drunk, and it is only reasonable to suppose that everything is known respecting it.'

In preparing my book for publication, both in English and in French, I have different debts – to librarians in a number of libraries, including the invaluable London Library, the Guildhall Library, and the Bibliothèque Municipal de Bordeaux; to Mme Thérèse Weller; to Mrs Burrell Hoffman, a great friend of Clarence Dillon; to Abdallah H. Simon and to John and Peter Brimelow for American material; for English material culled from different countries, to Susan Hard, not for the first or last time; to John O'Connor of Brookes University, Oxford; to Dr Bryan Wilson, Fellow and

Domestic Bursar of All Souls College, Oxford, himself both a scholar and a wine connoisseur, who has read the proofs; to Alain de Lyrot and Robert Silvers, who have assisted me at crucial points in the publication process; to Sarah Gleadell and Belinda Matthews of Faber and Faber; and, above all, to Julian Jeffs, my editor, who gave me extremely valuable advice that led me to a substantial reshaping of my first draft. He also gave me the rare pleasure of drinking with him Haut-Brion 1928, a wine which I had not previously tasted, and other Haut-Brions from his excellent cellar.

The first drafts of the book were word-processed by my then secretary, Jenny Blake, by Yvonne Collins, and by my daughter Judith Preston. Others, including Veronica Humphrey and Rosemary Cook, have coped with my manuscript as it has grown through several different versions – far less tidily than any vine, even the wildest, would have done. It often had to be lopped, even transplanted. Fortunately, to change the metaphors, at the end of my quest my book, like wine in the bottle, continues to develop in my mind.

Haut-Brion, the place, and its history are fascinating, and my book has a geographical as well as historical dimension. I have always been drawn to cities, and one of the attractions of Haut-Brion to me is that it is so near the great city of Bordeaux. Some of the people I have worked with at Haut-Brion itself are mentioned where they deserve to be – within the heart of the subsequent text. Alas, I cannot mention them all.

Asa Briggs
Lewes, Sussex, May 1993

I

Fact and Legend

―――――

Mankind is stubbornly curious of genealogy.

Evelyn Waugh

For centuries Haut-Brion has been renowned as one of the great wines of the world, and much has been written about its unique characteristics. 'No Château of the Médoc,' André Simon claimed, 'has a more illustrious lineage or a finer wine tradition than Château Haut-Brion.' The reputation is as old as the lineage. Indeed, both reputation and lineage preceded the development of the great châteaux of the Médoc. When 'the wines of Bordeaux' were formally classified in 1855 there was never any doubt that Haut-Brion would be included in the privileged top category, one of four – along with Lafite, Latour and Margaux.

It is perhaps surprising, therefore, that the history of Haut-Brion has never been told in full. It is a long history, and one rich in social and cultural associations. The legends of Haut-Brion are better known, however, than its history. In particular, Maurice Healy's legend of the origins of the name Haut-Brion, presented with charm in his *Claret and the White Wines of Bordeaux* (1934), has appealed to most lovers of wine, many of whom would like it to be true. According to Healy, who knew well that he was romancing, it could have been an Irish merchant, John O'Brien of Ross in County Cork – and this particular Irishman actually existed – who gave his name to the Château d'Aubrion. Haut-Brion was O'Brien.

The legend that Healy had created appealed so much to Healy himself that he asked to be pardoned if 'a theory' – it was really a fantasy – that he had first 'formulated in jest' had 'come to persuade' him that it might 'not be far removed from the truth'. Healy was a barrister, nephew of the great Tim Healy, first Governor-General in 1922 of the newly formed Irish Free State, the present Republic of Ireland, and he presented his case so persuasively that in the story of wine, a story in which legends abound, the Haut-Brion legend still carries weight.

In fact, the true story of the name of Haut-Brion, free from all speculation, begins in an age of legend, the middle ages, when wines from the Haut-Brion area, very different from the Haut-Brion of today, were already renowned not only in England, where kings commandeered them, but in Ireland, where seamen had braved the seas to deliver them. Healy himself noted, for example, that the *Book of Lismore* records that as early as the year 535 traders from southern Gaul sailed up the Shannon and sold wine in Saint Kieran's time at Clonmacnoise.

There was to be a strong Irish connection in the eighteenth-century age of enlightenment, too, for there were Irish *courtiers* – or brokers – in Bordeaux. There were Scots brokers there also, for at that time the Scots were drinking greater quantities of claret than the English, large numbers of whom had turned to port. The poet Thomas Campbell recalled how in the days of his grandfather, before Scotland 'had been reduced to degeneracy and corn spirits by wine duties and the Union', gardens, fields and paddocks had been fenced in with claret staves.

The detailed facts about Haut-Brion emerge long before the eighteenth century, in the late Middle Ages, when the name appears on legal documents concerning property and feudal rights. English kings were still in power in Bordeaux. They had acquired Aquitaine, including the whole of Gascony and within it Bordeaux, following Henry II's marriage to Eleanor of Aquitaine in 1152, one of the greatest dynastic marriages in history: Henry was then Duke of Normandy and Count of Anjou. The English were to be forced out, however, in 1453, the year of Constantinople's fall to the Turks. This was eighty years before the purchase of the Haut-Brion estate by Jean de Pontac, Civil and Criminal Registrar of the prestigious *Parlement* of Bordeaux. The seller came from the south, not from the north. He was a Basque about whom we know little, Jean Duhalde.

Jean de Pontac, born in 1488, four years before Columbus crossed the Atlantic, is a fascinating character who rose with the *Parlement* in Bordeaux and who is rightly recognized in the history books. In 1525, aged thirty-seven, he married Jeanne de Bellon, daughter of the Mayor of Libourne, a flourishing town and port north-east of Bordeaux, which in 1270 had been founded by and named after Roger de Leyburn, English Seneschal of Gascony. Jeanne brought with her on her marriage a dowry which included lands in the village of Pessac: '*au lieu dit Haut-Brion*' ('in the place called Haut-Brion'), a phrase the precise meaning of which was later to be caught up in dispute. That is how the true story of Haut-Brion begins. Jean de Pontac lived to be 101 and had fifteen children. When we have such genuine romance, we do not need legend. What true story of a vineyard could start as dramatically as that of Haut-Brion?

The name 'Au Brion' had been mentioned in a number of fifteenth-century documents before the estate was acquired by the Pontacs. In 1435, for example, there was a contemporary reference to vineyards which are in the Graves of Bordeaux in the place 'at Haut Mont, alias "Au Brion" ', and in 1472 the name was simplified to *au brion*. In 1474 we learn of '*la fon deubrion*' ('the fountain *debrion*'), later described by the Carmelites as 'the source of extraordinarily pure and abundant water'. In 1482 there were two contemporary references to *Haut Mont pres lo Brion*. Spelling was at least as variable as vintages during the fifteenth century – and it remained so much later.

The purchase of Haut-Brion by Jean de Pontac was only the first of a sequence of outstanding events in its history. It was not until the mid-seventeenth century that the wine produced by the Pontacs began to be known under its own name. In 1666, soon after the Great Fire of London, a later Pontac, François-Auguste, set up what soon became a famous tavern in Abchurch Street in the City of London which he called Pontacks and which bore on its sign a picture of his father's head. This was said to be the only sign in the City of London which depicted a French nobleman. Inside, François-Auguste served along with excellent French food pitchers of named 'Pontack wine'. His first customers included the distinguished Fellows of England's new Royal Society, founded six years earlier to promote 'by the authority of experiments the sciences of natural things and of useful arts'. Experiments in drinking wine promoted both.

Even before the Great Fire, the diarist Samuel Pepys had on 10

3

April 1663 drunk 'a sort of French wine called Ho-Bryan' that greatly pleased him. It had, he wrote, 'a good and most particular taste', He drank it at the Royal Oak Tavern in Lombard Street, very near to the present Bank of England. If the wine was new, so also was the name of the tavern where he drank it. The royal oak is the tree in which young Charles II had hidden himself away after the Battle of Worcester. Pepys was a wine lover whose cellar in 1665 included two tierces of claret, by modern measures two casks of forty gallons each. In 1663, two months after he had tasted Haut-Brion, Pepys went down to his cellar and found the door open and half his precious wine stolen.

The fact that 'Ho-Bryan' figured by name in Pepys's diary is of special importance. It was a genuine landmark. There are no fewer than four pages of references to taverns in the index volume to R. Latham's great edition of his diaries and no fewer than seventy-two references to wine. Twenty-two of them related to Rhenish wine: seventeen do not refer to any particular wine by name or by type. 'Clarets' were usually described in the plural. Ho-Bryan was singled out. Pepys continued to drink it too, for among the offices he held later was that of President of the Royal Society. He had been a member of a Gresham College group that was the forerunner of the Society, which became almost as renowned for its dinners as it was for its publications. For decades Pontacks was the scene of many of them. By a coincidence one of the last of its 'hostesses' to be mentioned, Mrs Susannah Austin, married a banker called William Pepys in 1736.

Aubryan, yet another early spelling of Haut-Brion, was drunk under its own name in the country as well as in the city. George Bell of the Montagu Arms Hotel at Beaulieu has drawn my attention to a reference to 'Aubryan wine' in the wine account of Lord Montagu with Richard Blatchford. In 1669 he purchased two hogsheads for £24 and six terses (tierces) of claret (unspecified) for £25, along with one hogshead of vinegar at £3.50. The account has been printed by the Sussex Archaeological Society.

In the early eighteenth century other great French clarets of the Médoc also came to be named after their estates – Lafite, Latour and Margaux – and as the century went by the different wines of Bordeaux became known for the first time in history both by their precise place of origin and by their year. Until then there were no clarets that could have survived. The wines of Bordeaux had to be drunk young – *de l'année*. There was no way of conserving them. Old wine was spoilt wine. Now with new techniques of wine-making – and with corks and bottles – *grands vins* began to be distinguished not only from *vins bourgeois* and *vins paysans* but from *seconds vins* from the same estate. Now also the great vintages of one year began to be distinguished from average or below average vintages in another year. *Vins bourgeois* and *vins paysans* themselves changed in appeal, with the newest wines losing their cachet. Precise age came to count. Wine was never the same product again.

Significantly, half-legendary stories began to be told in the early eighteenth century, as in the pages of a *Mémoire sur les vins de Bordeaux* (1720), of old wines that had been discovered in a cellar that tasted better than new ones. No one would have believed such stories in the Middle Ages, sometimes thought of as ages of credulity when anything could be believed. The seventeenth-century developments in the history of wine demonstrate that chronology matters as much in the narrative as in any other branch of history.

The *révolution viticole* that gave special significance to each year's vintage preceded the French Revolution by a hundred years and in some ways pointed in the opposite direction. The *premiers grands crus* were not for the *bourgeoisie* or for the masses, but for the élite. There was such a huge increase in the number of vines planted in France during the early eighteenth century that governmental action was taken to restrict it, but quality – not quantity – most concerned the owners of the vineyards that produced the *grands crus*. In the quest for quality, the owners and managers of Haut-Brion anticipated many of the changes in viticulture (the growing of vines), in vinification (the making of wines) and, not least, in the marketing of wines that transformed the eighteenth-century wine trade.

For this reason Haut-Brion, situated in the Graves region of Gascony, figures prominently in the two richly documented and footnoted, but unindexed and untranslated, volumes of Pijassou's *Un Grand Vignoble de Qualité, le Médoc* (1978), even though Haut-Brion is outside the geographical area of the Médoc. It had strong historical links, however, with Margaux and Lafite in the eighteenth century when the first stages in the transformation of winemaking were completed.

One key section of Pijassou's indispensable study, a great work of scholarship that goes deeply into the significant detail of history, is called 'the initiatives of the Pontac family at Haut-Brion'. It begins with land, *terroir*, difficult to translate adequately, not with people. A consciousness of the distinctiveness of the *terroir*, soil and climate, was crucial to the establishment of quality. Yet it needed a family of vision and drive to promote it. 'The success of the Pontac family at Haut-Brion', Pijassou remarks, 'opened the way to the future.' The future lay with the *'grands vins'*.

Because the opening up of the way led through London, it is appropriate that the first full history of Haut-Brion, that stands out as the first of the 'new French clarets', should be in English, not French. And in relating that history to the history of the Médoc Pepys's reference to the 'particular' taste of Haut-Brion now stands out also not as an interesting antiquarian curiosity but as a crucial reference. How best to describe the taste raised fundamental questions about taste and how it has changed over the years. Healy once generalized that 'taste in wine as in everything else is individual'. Yet collective as well as individual tastes have changed, and it is difficult to establish continuities over the centuries.

The approach to the subject has changed also. The verb *déguster* was not used in relation to wine-tasting until the early nineteenth century, but by the end of that century there was in Britain a cult of claret to which Healy adhered. George Saintsbury, a distinguished professor of English literature in Edinburgh, was the outstanding connoisseur, a man to be revered, even feared, although the author of his obituary in the *Dictionary of National Biography* refers only to literature and leaves out claret. In 1931, when he was living in retirement, having published his *Notes on a Cellar Book* in 1928, a club of connoisseurs was founded and given his name. Significantly, the inspiration for its founding was an Haut-Brion 1874, drunk at a London lunch where the guests included Healy and André Simon, greatest of twentieth-century connoisseurs and a prolific historian of both food and wine. Within the club Healy was the most eloquent spokesman of the merits of Haut-Brion. For him it was a claret that should be drunk kneeling.

Love of claret in general, and of Haut-Brion in particular, has long survived the Victorian preoccupation with what Simon called 'claret old and crusted'. It also survived the disappearance of many old houses with wine cellars, immortalized in Saintsbury's *Notes on a Cellar Book*. The biggest social and cultural changes have taken place during the last thirty years, when we have witnessed what has sometimes been described as the 'demystification' of claret. It can still carry with it an aura, but the cult of claret is now passing into legend. Nonetheless, as increased emphasis has been placed on critical discrimination, as much interest in what constitutes 'taste' remains as there was when the cult was at its height, or in the Age of Taste that preceded it.

In the late twentieth century Michael Broadbent, head of Christie's wine department, having noted that when he was a young wine merchant organizing tastings during the early 1950s there was no book on the subject, wrote first a pamphlet and then a book, *Wine Tasting, Enjoying, Understanding*, as comprehensive in its content as it was in its title. It rightly places 'enjoying' rather than reverencing in the middle of the action. Broadbent has also written an introduction to a fuller French study by Émile Peynaud, *Le Goût du Vin* (1983), translated into English in 1987 as *The Taste of wine*. It is a book for wine lovers, however, rather than for butlers – or investors.

Given all the layers of subsequent history (and science), it was just as important for the proprietors of Haut-Brion in the seventeenth and eighteenth centuries to establish the particular taste of the wine as it is for the proprietors today. It was a taste that was distinct not only from the taste of the *grands crus* of the Médoc, but from the wine of its neighbour La Mission, a wine produced under religious auspices from the seventeenth century onwards just across the road from Haut-Brion. Since 1983 the two have been operating under common ownership, but their separate identities are being carefully preserved.

Tastes go with names, and from the eighteenth century onwards a *marque vinicole* began to be thought of as constituting as individual a property as an author's copyright, another of the new concepts of the period. One wine could not just be substituted for another. Its distinctiveness was clearly related to the name and qualities of the particular place where the vines grew, to the enterprise of the named proprietors and to the skills of the *régisseur* or, in inadequate translation, manager. Nature and culture are seen as reacting upon each other.

One of the great eighteenth-century writers and philosophers who lived in the Graves district, Montesquieu, fully appreciated this. Unfortunately for him, the *terroir* on his own estate in the

southern Graves at La Brède offered no natural advantages. He
once said that as he wandered round his vineyard his 'fortune' was
under his feet, but *brède* meant swamp, and Montesquieu never
received 'substantial orders' for his wines from England. When he
tried to plant wines near Haut-Brion at Pessac he was appalled to
be told by the *intendant* that he could not do so. There had been
such a 'fury of planting' of vines that sustained – but ultimately
abortive – official attempts were made to limit production.

It was another philosopher, the Englishman John Locke, whose
influence on thinking was to be at least as great in the United States
as it was in England, who first noted particularity of place and its
influence on wine. When he visited Bordeaux in 1677–8, he had
recently left his post as Secretary of the Council of Trade and
Plantations, and he showed great interest in what he saw around
him. 'Pontac, so much esteemed in England,' Locke wrote, 'grows
on a rise of ground, openmost to the west', in 'pure white sand,
mixed with a little gravell . . . One would imagine it scarce fit to
bear anything.' But there was 'such a particularity in the soil that at
M. de Pontac's near Bordeaux [– and we are now indubitably in
Haut-Brion –] the merchants assured me that the wine growing in
the very next vineyard, where there was only a ditch between, and
the soil to appearance perfectly the same, was by no means so
good.'

Particular place, particular taste was the crucial correlation seen
clearly by Locke. Even though he was reporting what others said,
his reference to the ditch, which is still there, stands out, therefore
as a cultural as well as a topographical landmark. A similar point
was made, too, by the greatest American of the eighteenth century,
Thomas Jefferson, who visited Bordeaux and Haut-Brion for five
days in May 1787 when the revolution in wine-making and in
merchanting – although not in bottling – was complete. Later in life
he was to go on to taste, test and record no fewer than 200 wines,
white and red, cheap and expensive, from many different countries.

'The cantons [*sic*] in which the most celebrated wines of Bordeaux were made,' Jefferson wrote after his visit in 1787, were
Médoc, 'down the river', and 'Grave, adjoining the city, and the
parishes most above.' Among the four vineyards of the 'finest quality' in the latter area, he went on, Haut-Brion was pre-eminent.
And, like Locke, whose description he had not read, he added that

the soil there was 'a sand in which is near as much round gravel or small stone, and very little loam'.

A lover of good wine, Jefferson distinguished clearly between *vignobles* of first, second and third quality, with Haut-Brion taking its place along with Margau (*sic*), which belonged to 'the Marquis d'Agincourt' (*sic*), La Tour de Ségur and Château de la Fite. Haut-Brion, he had told the American agent in Bordeaux in 1784, 'is a wine of first rank and seems to please the American palate more than all the others that I have been able to taste in France'. This is a testimonial that has been quoted as frequently as that of Pepys, and, given the subsequent career of Jefferson, who became President of the United States in 1800, in itself it firmly places Haut-Brion not in legend but in history.

Many historians have laboured long in what a reviewer in the *Washington Post* in 1987 called in a delightful metaphor 'the Jeffersonian vineyards', the massive Jefferson archive, which covers the years before and after Jefferson became president. More than one of them has well appreciated, as did his biographer, Dumas Malone, the real vineyards that Jefferson studied so carefully, although Malone, who lived to the age of ninety-four, made few references to them. There are far more in the multi-volume *Papers of Thomas Jefferson* edited by Julian P. Boyd. Most recently, John Hailman has made the best use of the archives in his detailed study *The Wines of Thomas Jefferson*, which appeared appropriately in the bicentennial year of Jefferson's visit to Bordeaux. Among the key questions Hailman asked was 'What was wine like in Jefferson's time?' The most tantalizing of his questions was 'What if Jefferson returned?'

Because of the Jeffersonian connection with Bordeaux, it was appropriate that when his visit to Gascony was commemorated in 1987 there should be an American owner at Haut-Brion to welcome the visit of the American Ambassador to France, Joe Rogers, and a group of his fellow countrymen. He unveiled a marble plaque incorporating Jefferson's comments. An interesting exhibition, 'The Eye of Jefferson', was planned at the Departmental Archives of Bordeaux, where so much history, not least history of wine, is stored, and there was a great banquet at Haut-Brion.

The twentieth-century Franco-American connection at Haut-Brion began in 1935 when an American banker, Clarence Dillon, a successful businessman with a remarkable life story of his own, bought the Haut-Brion estate from André Gibert, who had owned it since 1923. 'As you can easily imagine,' Dillon wrote later, 'there was great interest in Bordeaux. An American had become proprietor of Haut-Brion.' Dillon was a very special American, however, for as early as 1929 he had rented an apartment in Paris, where he spent part of each year. Always proud of all his French connections, he went on to live to the great age of ninety-six – almost as long as Jean de Pontac – and in retrospect he was as much a man of his own age as Pontac had been in his. Certainly his own place in history is secure.

There can be more than a touch of legend, however, even in recent times, and there are as many stories about Dillon as there were about any Pontac. It is a fact that when he came to look at vineyards in the Bordeaux region in 1935 with the intention of buying one, it was not only Haut-Brion that was drawn to his attention. One other vineyard (and one that was to be much favoured by Americans) – Cheval Blanc – was described by a visitor in 1934 as 'a fine property – and well kept': it was thought to be on the market in 1934, although it still remains in the hands of the same family that has owned it since 1852.

Dillon was also told rightly or wrongly that another famous vineyard in the St-Émilion district, Château Ausone, was for sale. In name, at least, this vineyard was associated with the Roman beginnings of wine-making before the Middle Ages. Ausonius was a fourth-century Latin poet who lived in what is now Bordeaux when wine was already being produced and drunk there.

It has been suggested that what determined Dillon's choice of Haut-Brion rested on accident. According to a familiar story, often told – although with variations – it was a cold and foggy day when he arrived in Bordeaux, and the 35 kilometres between the city and Château Cheval Blanc seemed far to go. On the way he had stopped to buy a rug and his driver had become lost. The very real charms of the St-Émilion district were therefore kept from him. By contrast, Haut-Brion, 'at the very gates of Bordeaux', as it has often been described almost in Roman terms, seemed just right.

The story might have been invented by Maurice Healy, who would doubtless have gone on to speculate about the effects of that particular fog not only on the subsequent history of Haut-Brion but on that of Cheval Blanc – and Ausone.

Where facts merge into legend is never easy to place. A rug still exists, but it may not have been 'the rug itself', bought on that day, and the day of travel towards St-Émilion may have followed rather than preceded his decision to acquire Haut-Brion. Dillon was the kind of man who would never have moved by impulse alone, and he finally secured Haut-Brion only after months of negotiation – and advice. A man of great importance in the wine trade who advised him in 1934 was Daniel Lawton, one of the great wine brokers, the *courtiers en vin*, of Bordeaux. Lawton was a descendant of an Irish trader from Cork who had arrived in the city in 1740.

It may well be that in the long perspectives of time the story of our own century, particularly the recent decades since the Dillon purchase, will stand out as being of equal importance in the history of wine as the seventeenth and eighteenth centuries. It is during these decades that science has been applied to wine-making in a way that it was not and could not have been applied to eighteenth-century industry during the years when the *grands crus* were first recognized. It is during these decades also that there has been a revolution in marketing as striking as that of the late seventeenth century.

Successful marketing in the *'révolution des boissons'* of the late twentieth century has depended upon a combination of information and imagination comparable to that demanded in Enjalbert's first revolution which brought with it not only 'new clarets', port (at that time unfortified) and sherry, along with champagne, cognac and *eaux-de-vie*, but also tea, coffee and cocoa. The first coffee house was opened in London in 1652, eleven years before Pepys first tasted 'Ho Bryan'.

Holland played a key role in some of the most interesting episodes of the earlier story. Renowned for their beer as much as for their Calvinism, the Dutch employed their sea-power to search out new drinks. As Simon Schama has shown in his brilliant study *The Embarrassment of Riches* (1987), the wine-carrying trade subsequently became central to the fortunes of the Dutch economy. They did more, however, than carry wines for their own or other people's consumption. They significantly influenced the production of wine in the Bordeaux area and the area behind it, particularly that around Bergerac, by demanding sweet white wines which were not greatly favoured by the English then or during the Middle Ages.

Some of these they blended. They cared nothing for what was 'natural', and irritated traditional wine-growers by urging *vignerons* to keep grapes on the vines for as long as possible in order to squeeze out all the mature sweetness.

Not all white wines could be made sweet enough, so that the Dutch also encouraged the making of highly alcoholic *eaux-de-vie*, *aygordents*, spirits which they not only consumed themselves – along with gin – but sold to avid customers in Britain, Germany, Denmark and Sweden. That was the first revolution.

The second revolution – a twentieth-century one – had its origins in the United States and brought with it an array not of *eaux-de-vie* but of composite 'soft-drink' and 'semi-soft-drink' products, some of them completely synthetic. It has also introduced a far wider range of mineral waters and fruit juices than ever before, and an equally wide range of liqueurs and other alcoholic blends. There are far more flavours and colours than there ever have been. Yet there is also more wine. It is being drunk in increasing quantities. It now comes not only from France and other traditional sources, but from the United States, Australia, New Zealand, Chile and other places that did not figure at all on the eighteenth-century wine map. Wine from grapes (as well as from rice) is being produced and drunk in China.

There are organizational changes too, including national and international mergers in the drink and food trade, often dramatic. Sometimes vertical integration now links vineyard, wholesale depot and retail store. The acquisition of Château Latour by Allied Breweries in 1989 was one of the latest and most striking of these. Now is again in private hands. The Médoc is as much subject to change as it was in the eighteenth century. So, too, is the Graves.

As for retailing, the sale of wine in large multi-produce supermarkets – and I have seen Haut-Brion on sale in several of them – has taken it far from the grocer's shop, from the cellars of the specialized wine dealer, and from the shelves of the wine chains. It continues to figure prominently, of course, in restaurants, and these have changed as much as shops or factories since the time of François-Auguste de Pontac. Haut-Brion has figured for long in the wine lists of all the world's great restaurants from Paris to New Orleans and from New Orleans to Tokyo. 'We plumped for a bottle of Haut-Brion 1976,' a Swiss columnist wrote in 1988 after visiting the Beef Club restaurant, 'and were still enthusing about it long after the last drop had helped the beef on its way.'

On the demand side, fortified by large-scale advertising, there has been an impressive increase in wine consumption in many countries – at home as well as in restaurants. Travel has had its obvious impact. So, too, has 'prosperity'. The marketing of Haut-Brion, particularly in the United States, where it is greatly coveted, must be set within this frame. Quality is still greatly prized, and it has been a feature of the wine history of the late twentieth century that the consumption of wines of quality has increased in France itself.

Haut-Brion stands out as a product of exceptional quality within this second revolution, and is at the heart of the story just as it was during the first revolution. Its customers are now to be found not only in France, England, Ireland, the Netherlands and other European countries or in the United States – countries that were already buying it in the eighteenth century – but in the Far East. Its merits are acclaimed in video as well as in words. The marketing technology is as impressively up to date as the superb new *chai* at Haut-Brion. It is there that the wine is made.

Remarkably, the first quoted use of the word *chai* in the dictionaries takes us back once more to the seventeenth century. And the example is interesting in that it introduces yet another Anglo-French connection. In Robert's great *Dictionnaire de la langue française* the date is given as 1611, an obvious reference to the pioneering English/French dictionary compiled by an Englishman, Randle Cotgrave, secretary to William Cecil, later second Earl of Exeter. In some other parts of France the *chai* might have been a *cave* or *cellier*. Robert relates *chai* etymologically to *quai*, an appropriate historical cross-reference in Bordeaux. In the age of St Bernard there were references to *cella vinaria*. Everyone in Bordeaux knew the word *chai* long before the French Academy formally accepted it in 1878.

Now in the new *chai* at Haut-Brion science as well as history is introduced into the picture. The fermentation process, described in a later chapter, was felt even as late as the nineteenth century to have something 'miraculous' about it. The fact that fermentation is no longer thought of as a completely mysterious process that either worked or did not work – and that science has illuminated it – may have disposed of other legends, but it has not transformed wine-making from an art into a science.

Although information about what is happening in the wine vats is carefully charted at each stage at Haut-Brion, Jean-Bernard Delmas, who has for thirty-three years been in charge of the process, as was his father Georges before him, has refused to proceed by formula. He has always been aware both of the benefits of science and of its limitations. Born in the year that Clarence Dillon acquired the property, he has been called more than once since then 'the guru behind Haut-Brion'. 'Wine still retains its mystery,' he maintains, 'even though hundreds of its different chemical compounds have been discovered'. The reputation of Haut-Brion as a *grand cru* is assured because Delmas has devoted his exceptional knowledge to the art of wine-making in a château with a long history and a strong commitment to the future.

2

The Place

────────

This precious corner of the earth.

Bertall, *La Vigne, voyages
autour des vins de France*, 1878

'It is one of the delights of a great claret,' André Simon wrote, 'that
its exact place of origin is defined'; and the exact place in Pessac
and Talence where the château and estate of Haut-Brion are situated figures prominently in every account of 'the wines of Bordeaux', of 'the claret country', or of the *département* of the
Gironde, which was carved out of the huge pre-revolutionary province of Gascony.

There is no wine-producing region in the world outside the
Gironde where variations and combinations of soil, climate, art and
science produce so many varieties and qualities of wine; and visitors, some of them pilgrims seeking out vineyards, quickly discern
contrasts as clearly as similarities.

While Locke led the way in the late seventeenth century in point-
ing to the distinctiveness of Haut-Brion as a site, there have been
many accounts since then of Haut-Brion within its geographical
setting, some based on acute personal observations, as was Locke's,
some essentially travellers' guides. The accounts have covered soil
as well as landscape. For Maurice Healy it was small differences of
soil that made Médocs 'such silky, gracious wines, and red Graves
such noble warriors': the distinction for him was like that between
'glossy and matt photographs'.

Many accounts of the wines of the Médoc and of Graves have
been official or semi-official; and they set out details of acreage and
quantities of wine produced rather than evoke a vivid sense of

place. Yet statistics can be made both to live and to provide a living. Nineteenth-century editions of E. Féret et C. Cocks's *Bordeaux et ses vins*, an invaluable work of reference, the first edition of which appeared in 1850, sold out in six months. Earlier in the century, in 1832, another well-known nineteenth-century survey – Jullien's *Topographie de tous les vignobles connus* – had won the coveted statistics prize of the French Académie des Sciences.

'The essential ingredient in a book of information,' Édouard Féret wrote firmly in the preface to his *Statistique Générale de la Gironde*, 'should be accuracy'; and later editions of Cocks et Féret, some bearing only Féret's name, speak of the importance of precision, of '*documents certains*'. Yet Féret offered his readers far more than exactitude – or utility: his range of information was surprisingly comprehensive. His *Statistique Générale* (1874–89) was, in fact, a multi-volume work that ranged widely from archaeology to biography.

The Féret family directed a publishing house that produced other books on many local Bordeaux themes, like an *Essai sur la Ville de Bordeaux et ses Monuments* (1892) and *Nos Notabilités Bordelaises* (1896–1907), and, not surprisingly, Édouard was one of the founders of the *Revue Historique de Bordeaux et du Département de la Gironde*, which was to print many important articles on the history both of the city and of wine.

A strong sense of place runs through all that Féret wrote, and perceptive English visitors to the Gironde could catch the sense of place too. Thus, Angus Reach's widely read *Claret and Olives* (1852) had many memorable passages dealing with urban and rural contrasts in the Gironde. Writing, for example, of the sharp variations between land used for making the best and worst wines in the area, Reach remarked:

> You can almost jump from a spot unknown to fame to another clustered with the most precious vintage in Europe. Half-a-dozen furrows often make the difference between vines producing a beverage that will be drunk in the halls and palaces of England and Russia, and vines yielding a harvest that will be consumed in the cabarets and estaminets of the neighbourhood.

A gazetteer of places must go with a *répertoire des crus*, each with its own identity – and price – although over the years these can and do change in relation to one another. Yet *crus* and châteaux do not

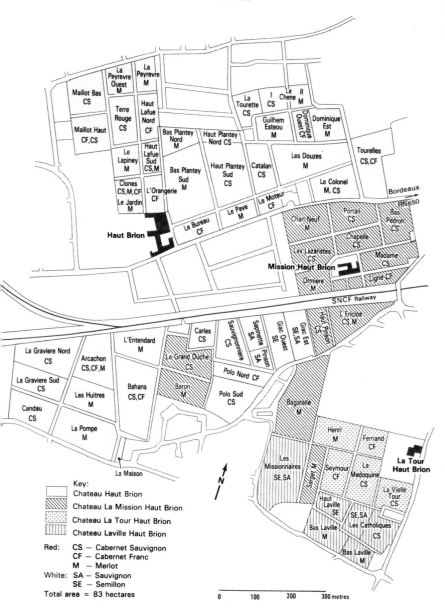

The Domaine of Haut-Brion

always go together. There are now, 4,000 châteaux of various ages and sizes in the Gironde, although only 200 of them produce *crus classés*. It was not until 1942 that a wartime decree linked the name 'château' to 'a particular *cru*, a specific vineyard that has been known for a very long time [scarcely a precise phrase] by the name in question, in accordance with its meaning, and with local, faithful and reliable usage'. The decree looked back to a law of 6 May 1919, setting up judicial procedures, 'and subsequent laws', including important laws of 1927, 1929 and 1935, which developed the concept of *appellations*, and culminated in 1935, when the Institut National des Appellations d'Origine des Vins et Eaux-de-Vie, a self-governing body endowed with public authority, was created. The system had more distant origins, however, and important initiatives had already been taken in Bordeaux in 1913. Long before then, Gironde producers and Gironde merchants alike had realized the importance of having the right basic information on the labels of wine bottles. The Institut was their creation.

Appellations are granted only after the most careful and the most precise questions have been asked and answered by the owners of vineyards, *inter alia* about the extent of acreage devoted to vines, about varieties of grapes and their yield and about the degrees of alcohol in the wines produced. There is also blind tasting. The more specific the *appellation*, the better the quality of the wine is likely to be. By comparison, the much used term 'château', carrying with it not so much a sense of place as a social aura, has no legal precision.

Such a system would have surprised Reach, although as a good Victorian he would have appreciated the importance of classification. Another lively nineteenth-century visitor to Bordeaux, the Frenchman 'Bertall', a *nom de plume*, had very little that was Victorian about him. He obviously preferred liberty to control and the town to the country. He was clearly completely at home in the cafés and estaminets of the city, and his well-illustrated book *La Vigne, voyages autour des vins de France* (1878) was designed not for the information but for the entertainment of his readers. His comprehensive subtitle 'a physiological, anecdotal, historical, humorous and even scientific study', spoke for itself.

Very soon on his journey round France Bertall found himself in Bordeaux, 'the capital of wines', and very soon after that in 'that precious corner of the earth, Pessac', the commune in which most of Haut-Brion was located. At first sight, there seemed to him to be nothing particularly 'precious' in the gravelly soil itself. Nor had there seemed to be anything precious to Locke. 'Graves' means 'gravel'. Yet Bertall recognized that it was precisely the nature of the soil of Pessac, so near to the city of Bordeaux, so unsuited to the growth of anything but vines, that was literally the foundation of the glory of Haut-Brion, the *goût de terroir*, the peculiar flavour of the wine that bore 'the stamp of the place'.

By the time that Bertall visited it, Haut-Brion had already been singled out as one of a small number of wines that headed any hierarchy. Yet the soils of the *terroir* of Haut-Brion – and their levels – are distinctive not only within the Bordeaux area, but within Pessac itself, and sharply distinctive from the sandy soil, '*les landes*', on the other side of the parish. Within the *terroir*, too, there are marked differences in soil between different patches of land, *parcelles*, each of which is known to and appreciated by the *régisseur*. Detailed knowledge of this kind is, and always has been, crucial to the making of the wines of Haut-Brion.

La Mission, on the other side of the great road that leads from Bordeaux to Arcachon, was a vineyard developed between 1682 and the French Revolution by the Lazarists, priests of the Congré-gation de la Mission, a group that looked back to St Vincent de Paul; and a Gothic chapel, dedicated to the Virgin, was opened there in 1698. Its architect was Étienne Buisset, and it was heavily 'restored' in the nineteenth century – and given imposing iron gates – by which time the management of the vineyard had passed into secular hands. The ceiling now bears the dates of the memorable vintages that had followed the coming not of the priests but of the railway: 1847, 1848, 1858, 1864, 1869, 1870, 1875, 1877, 1890, 1895, 1914, 1916 and 1918.

The funds for the vineyard and the mission had been provided first by Olive de Lestonnac and in 1666, the year when François-Auguste de Pontac opened Pontacks in London, by Cathérine de Muller, widow of another de Lestonnac. Their founder, Jean de Fonteneil, held lands, as did the de Lestonnacs, in the Haut-Brion area. The original benefaction described the land bequeathed in the deed as 'la paroisse de Talence'. Already there was a *grand chay cuvier* there.

Another place mentioned in the deed – six *journaux* of land at Arraguedix – had a significance greater than the size of the land would suggest, for the ancient name Arrequeduix had been associated with medieval vineyards. It was a difficult name that, not surprisingly, was spelt in almost every kind of way: Arregueduex, Arequeduix, Arqueduix, Arreguedhuis, Arreged'huys, Arecsdhuchs, even Le Ragedieux. The syllable 'Arcs' or 'Ars', however, was to be found in other local place names, and may have been derived originally not from the stream called the Ars but from an ancient aqueduct.

This small piece of land is easier to locate precisely than the 'Graves region' as a whole, a non-administrative unit within the Bordeaux area, the official boundaries of which were not confirmed until the 1930s. Yet it had an identity of its own even in the Middle Ages, when it served as 'the wine cradle of Bordeaux'. It now constitutes a thirty-five-mile strip of land, at most ten to fifteen miles wide, on the west bank of the River Garonne, beginning just above the city of Bordeaux and ending in the south below the commune of Langon. Blanquefort is just outside it in the north, and Bazas well outside it in the south. Pamela Vandyke Price has compared it vividly with a long glove flung down over the map of the Gironde.

The region is slightly larger in area than the Haut-Médoc, although in at least one would-be authoritative account of 1884, in the *Wine Trade Review*, it was said to be only sixteen miles by six. In appearance – and terrain – it contrasts with the east bank of the Garonne, where the vineyards called the Premières Côtes and Entre-deux-Mers are to be found. It is the only district in France to have a place name derived from the nature of the soil that has subsequently been applied to a category of wines, both red and white. Entre-deux-Mers is a very different kind of topographical designation when applied to wines. It has no geological dimension. It refers simply to wines produced between the Garonne and the Dordogne, 'between the two waters'.

In the nineteenth century the red wines of the Graves region were themselves divided quite simply into 'better wines' and '*petits vins rouges de Graves*', but in the late twentieth century 'the large and disparate district styled the Graves' has itself been divided at last into two. The northern district in which Haut-Brion is situated lies between Bordeaux and Saint-Morillon: the southern lies between Morillon and Langon. The great sweet white wine areas of Sauternes and Barsac belong to the south.

As long ago as the eighteenth century it was claimed that the finest red wines of the Graves came from the north and the finest white wines from the south, where the soils are more varied. None-theless, the geographical distinction between red and white wine districts can be overdrawn. Far more red wine is now being pro-duced in the south than ever before, and most of it can be and is being drunk young. Historically too, properties in the northern Graves have produced both red and white wines, as Haut-Brion itself does. It was not until 1989 that the total production of red Graves overtook that of white.

The Syndicat Viticole des Graves Pessac-Léognan, created in 1987, extends through the northern area which figures prominently in this book. Pessac is as old as Bordeaux: Léognan to the south-west incorporates many old vineyards. It has its legends too. The nineteenth-century proprietor of one of its most famous vineyards, Haut-Bailly, is said to have cleaned out his *cuves* before the vintage with a few litres of Grande Fine Champagne cognac.

The other communes include Cadaujac, Canéjan, Gradignan, Martillac, Mérignac, Talence and Villenave-d'Ornon, where large quantities of red Graves were produced in the mid-nineteenth century. No fewer than 500 hectares of old vineyard had been lost in this areas since the 1930s, but 450 hectares had been planted in the fifteen years before 1987. The Syndicat replaced the older Syn-dicat Viticole des Hautes Graves de Bordeaux, established at Pod-ensac, where there had been a Maison des Vins de Graves since 1799. The Syndicat had long requested formal recognition for an *appellation* called Haut-Graves.

Since 1987 the new *appellation*, Graves de Pessac-Léognan, granted after sustained pressure, covers all the classified growths produced by fifty-five estates in an area of around 900 hectares, a quarter of the surface area of the Graves district as a whole. The new distinction, not without its boundary problems, formally splits the district into two, with the boundary drawn north of La Brède, Montesquieu's eighteenth-century *domaine*. According to the Presi-dent of the Syndicat, Pessac-Léognan 'should have been identified as a separate *appellation* from the beginning because of the particu-lar geological structure of the soil'. 'We're not rejecting Graves,' another spokesman insisted. 'Our labels must include *cru classé de Graves* or *Grand Vin de Graves*. We just want to emphasize our unique heritage and character.'

In Pessac itself, eighteen proprietors had been listed in 1845, among them a Bahans, the name of today's second wine of Haut-

Brion, and a widow, 'la Veuve Giraudou', who produced 15 to 20 *tonneaux* a year. The Haut-Brion vineyard – 50 hectares in area within a *domaine* of 165 hectares – then produced between 100 and 120 *tonneaux* of wine, and La Mission, divided between Pessac and Talence, produced 55 to 62 *tonneaux*.

Taking both Pessac and Léognan together, the total area of wine-growing fell to a low point of 550 hectares in the late 1960s as compared with 1,500 hectares in 1937. Since then, as a result of a deliberate promotion drive, there has been an increase. There are now 900 hectares devoted to vines. Five growths are classified as 'Graves-Pessac', and two others, while not classified, can add Graves-Pessac to their names. The comparable figures for Léognan are thirty-four and thirteen. Three-quarters of the Pessac-Léognan wines are exported.

During the twentieth century the gravelly land of Pessac-Léognan has proved suitable for house building and for minor industries; and as the city of Bordeaux has spread, some have said 'anarchically', the reduction of vine-growing was inevitable. For a time Haut-Brion itself was under threat. In some places the whole geography has subsequently changed. Including its scattered outer suburbs, Bordeaux now has a population of 840,000, living within a radius of 37 miles: during the 1930s, only 125,000 people inhabited the urban district of the city as compared with 600,000 today.

In some communes land devoted to vine-growing has virtually disappeared. Thus, Mérignac, site of the Bordeaux airport, which had thirty vineyards before 1914, now has only one. There is also a further threat to surviving vineyards near to Bordeaux in a plan to develop a 'Technopole', a science and industrial park, on 320 hectares of precious land.

During earlier centuries, agriculture had posed no threat. 'Some of the most famous clarets come from stunted vines on land where a carrot would not grow,' wrote Raymond Postgate, who did much to popularize wine – and food – in Britain in the 1950s, when Pessac was already beginning its transformation. If left to itself, the land 'would support heather, thistles and a little clover'.

There are, of course, many other parts of the Gironde, the largest *département* in France, where that would have been equally or even more true, particularly the sandy Landes. The English visitor to Bordeaux, Charles Cocks – later of Cocks et Féret fame – was forced to note in 1846, when he was looking for romance in the south-west, that the *département* of the Gironde, which had been created, like the other eighty-two *départements* of France, in 1791, had 'the greatest quantity of sterile or uncultivated land' of all French *départements*: of 345,000 acres of agricultural land there were only 86,000 of rich earth. Indeed, according to Cocks, 'agriculture, generally speaking, was little understood in this part of France'.

To Cocks, the Landes was 'flat, cheerless, monotonous and inhospitable', 'a vast, wild uncultivated desert' seemingly 'disinherited by creation'. Nothing could be done with it. Yet this did not stop the *département* from becoming rich. Nor did it stop timber from pine trees in the Landes being exported across the seas. In the middle of the nineteenth century Féret described it as 'one of the richest *départements* in France'. And in the twentieth century even the Landes have begun to seem romantic. Pyla-sur-Mer, four miles from Arcachon, at the end of the road that leads past Haut-Brion, has a great sand dune, an extraordinary work of nature, which is now one of the Gironde's tourist attractions.

Cocks was a young schoolmaster who, on the title page of his beautifully illustrated *Bordeaux, its Wines and the Claret Country* (1846), published in English and in French, called himself grandly 'Professor of Living Languages in the Royal College of France'; and if he was disappointed by the Landes, he was excited by what he saw from a railway train between Bordeaux and Haut-Brion:

> On leaving the Bordeaux station, a fine substantial building, the traveller passes for some time through a country adorned with delightful villas and fruitful vineyards. One of the first interesting objects, on the right is an estate named La Mission Haut-Brion, the wines of which are much esteemed; the rest is the domain of Haut-Brion, so celebrated for its famous red wines of the first *cru* of Graves. The train then passes over a magnificent viaduct which spans the valley from Haut-Brion to the village of Pessac . . . and then [after] a grove of acacias a property which, as well as its wine, is still named after Pope Clement V.

By contrast, at least one twentieth-century English visitor to 'the claret country', Barrie Thorne, was disappointed by the approach to Haut-Brion along the route d'Arcachon when he arrived, a century after Cocks, not by train but by tram. 'As a typical (and how unromantic) approach to wine,' he asked in 1949, 'who would have thought of street cars running alongside Haut-Brion? . . . It might have been Headingley cricket ground in Leeds.' In 1928 another English visitor, P. Morton Shand, went so far as to call the street cars 'sacrilegious'. A more recent American traveller, Richard Reeves, has said of the château that it is 'as if the palace of Fontainebleau had been dropped into Elizabeth, New Jersey. Right across the street is a tobacco shop where people line up for lottery tickets.'

The streetcars themselves seem romantic now that they have been replaced by buses, and even when they were there they might have seemed romantic (as Headingley does) to travellers of a different disposition from Thorne or Shand. Indeed, some travellers have been fascinated by the simple fact that Haut-Brion comes from an urban rather than a rural vineyard. For example, only three years after Thorne, Alexis Lichine, who was devoted to Haut-Brion, wrote poetically of 'the highway with its clinking tramway line dividing the vineyards', while Reeves forgot New York and added still more poetically that 'behind the walls of Haut-Brion, fantasies of seventeenth-century France are fulfilled. Taking in the sweep of the vineyards, you suddenly encounter an honor ground of rose-bushes planted at the end of each row of grapevines.'

Why the roses are planted there has been a matter of debate, with some explanations (like the fact that roses show up invasions of fungi before vines do) sounding less poetical than others. Inside the château, however, nothing has ever seemed debatable since the changes of the 1930s. For Reeves, the wainscoted dining room was particularly impressive: 'it takes a great wine to fill such a room'.

A new railway station, three-quarters of a mile from Haut-Brion, was opened at La Médoquine after the First World War, and after the Second World War the highway became busier than ever before. The nearby airport at Mérignac, where the Pontacs once owned land, represents an even more recent revolution in communications. And there are suggestions that this is not the last phase in the conquest of distance: signposts there direct visitors to Aérospatiale.

Land transport mattered in the nineteenth century as much as sea transport had mattered in the Middle Ages and more than air transport matters now; and the opening of the railway from Bordeaux to La Teste, which passed by Haut-Brion and which was in the early stages of its operations when Cocks visited Bordeaux and Pessac for the first time, was an important historical event. It was built by the Compagnie de la Teste, which won the franchise in 1837. The fourth railway to be built in France, the line was opened with great ceremony in July 1841 in the presence of the Archbishop of Bordeaux. The railroad from Bordeaux to Paris was not opened until 1852 – after years of delay. There were later links, too, with La Rochelle, ancient rival of Bordeaux.

Cocks was by no means the first visitor to describe the railway. The novelist Stendhal had observed in 1838 how 'railway mania' had broken out in Bordeaux 'as elsewhere', but Cocks, like most other visitors, thought quite differently about it. What Stendhal considered 'madness' (*folie*) Cocks thought of as 'progress'. The railway was for him a testimony to the spirit of 'active enterprise', characteristic of the age. His book on Bordeaux and the claret country was dedicated to King Louis Philippe's Minister of the Interior, the Comte Duchâtel, a lover of decanted ancient wines, who owned Château Lagrange in Saint-Julien, one of the six districts of the Haut-Médoc and who welcomed all kinds of railway development in the opening up of the whole region.

People on the spot were less sure. The port of Bordeaux blocked railways on the *quais* until 1867; and in 1838 the then proprietor of Haut-Brion, like the proprietors of a number of other vineyards, had objected – to the Prefect – to the coming of the railway into the outskirts of Bordeaux: 'who in Bordeaux would dare to propose the devastation of our vineyards even for the sake of a railway?' The question had point at Haut-Brion, for the new railway entailed the destruction of one of the three tiny 'hills' on the historic Haut-Brion property, the Haut-de-Carle, and of four *parcelles* of precious land. La Mission, too, lost a share, an even bigger one.

Joseph-Eugène Larrieu, the then proprietor of Haut-Brion, was doubtless shocked also by the fact that one of the keenest supporters of the new railway had interests in the development (at the other end of the railway line) of La Teste as a spa. Water seemed more important than wine to such a man. We do not know, however, how Larrieu felt about the subsequent failure of the railway to make money or the near bankruptcy of one of its administrators, D. G. Mestrezet, a Bordeaux wine broker from Switzerland, who was also Swiss Consul. Geneva had had to come to the help of

Bordeaux. Later the railway was bought out by the national company linking Paris, Spain and Portugal.

In the late twentieth century, when European transport routes by road and rail are being radically reorganized – with European integration in mind – it is of strategic importance that the electric railway past Haut-Brion links France with Spain and Portugal. It is as characteristic of our own age as the old pioneering line from Bordeaux to La Teste was in the early nineteenth century – or the romantic railway in Portugal along the River Douro.

The arrival of the twentieth-century tramway had involved the demolition of part of the wall of Haut-Brion during the 1930s; and this time the proprietor was on the offensive rather than the defensive. A characteristic letter of November 1936 from André Gibert to the Director of the Compagnie Française des Tramways Électriques et Omnibus à Bordeaux has survived. It told him that while Gibert was willing to abandon, without charge, a small band of precious Haut-Brion territory for *la route nationale*, he would hold the Director personally responsible – 'and not your contractors' – if anything went wrong 'when work began'.

Bordeaux as 'the capital of wines' is in the position of being a trustee for lands outside its own urban area; and it is when it recognizes its trusteeship most authoritatively that it is living up to its traditions most effectively. It is impossible to separate cityscape and landscape, although individuals pursuing their own interests without thought of the whole inevitably do so.

Back in the nineteenth century, it could be as thrilling to arrive in Bordeaux by rail as it had been for seamen to arrive in Bordeaux by sea in the Middle Ages. Thus, for Cocks,

> When the traveller, drawing near his journey's end first obtains a view of Bordeaux as he descends the green hills of the Bastide, he is instantly struck with the imposing grandeur of the scene opening before him: the variegated place below, the noble river beyond, the city with its graceful spires and antique towers in the distance, the semi-circular port, bounded by the elegant crescent of the Chartrons, and crowded with many hundred ships, displaying flags of every nation.

Here, for Cocks, who was to write more about wine than about 'living languages', 'a panorama' opened up that was perhaps 'unrivalled in Europe'.

Most other visitors before and since have had the same feeling about the great city, Bordeaux, which is set on the last great curve of the River Garonne before it joins the Dordogne at Bec d'Ambès to become the estuary of the Gironde, after which the revolutionary *département* was named. More than a century before Cocks, the author of *A Trip to Languedoc*, written and published in the reign of Louis XIV, describes the River Garonne as being 'so large at the point of land where it forms a junction with the Dordogne that it is really like a sea'.

It was the ordered symmetry and elegance of the recently built eighteenth-century *quartiers* of Bordeaux – along with the commercial bustle of the waterfront – that appealed most to discerning visitors, like an English traveller of 1775 who observed that the city 'yields to very few cities in point of beauty; for it appears to have all that opulence which an extensive commerce can confer'. A generation later, after many further great 'improvements' had been made, another Englishman, Arthur Young, compared approvingly the Bordeaux of 1787, two years before the Revolution, with contemporary Liverpool, at the same time favourably comparing the Garonne with the Thames. In Young's opinion – and he was a great traveller who made his reputation through travel – few cities in the world equalled Bordeaux for either beauty or commerce.

The commerce of Bordeaux expanded greatly in the eighteenth century, when the share of wine in total exports fell. It was then, however, that the leaders of the wine trade, the merchants and brokers of Bordeaux, most of them foreigners, established their social as well as their economic position along two kilometres of quayside in the imposing Chartrons area, 60 hectares in size, where they lived and worked in style, forming dynasties related by marriage as well as by business.

The Chartrons district, outside the old city walls, was described by the Abbé Baurein as 'the most substantial suburb and perhaps the most commercial suburb in the whole of Europe'. A later visitor called it a 'European principality of wine merchants'. Certainly, many of the merchants who lived there were not French by origin. The Carthusian origin of the name Chartrons dated back to the Middle Ages, but some of the new merchants were Protestants. Several kept their links with 'home': others did not. The fine houses in the Pavé des Chartrons, some built in the seventeenth century by the Dutch architect Van der Hem, deeply impressed Young. And some of the greatest of the imposing warehouses there, built not in the eighteenth but in the nineteenth century, were equally to impress Victorian visitors, who were fascinated by what happened behind their brightly polished brass plates: one *chai*, where wine was made and stored, was said to hold wine stock worth £100,000 in 1863.

By the last decades of the eighteenth century, the power of the merchants, foreigners or not, princes or not, over the wine-growers, some of them titled, was already conspicuous, and it increased further in the nineteenth century, when new finance capital was injected into the vineyards both by Paris bankers and by Bordeaux *négociants*. With access to information, as precious a business commodity as wine, and with clients in expanding foreign markets who had different tastes in wine, *négociants* could sometimes buy out a whole wine crop. Thus, twelve merchants, eight of them 'English', bought out the whole Latour crop two years before Young visited Bordeaux.

By 1863 Bordeaux had long become familiar with one new imposing urban feature that had been missing when Young stayed there. The number of ships lying in Bordeaux had long given it what Young called 'the *richest* water-view that France has to boast', but surprisingly, perhaps, there was no city bridge over the Garonne – 'an immense, rapid-flowing river' – until the year 1822, long after Young had paid his visit. Napoleon saw the need for a bridge when he visited Bordeaux *en route* for Spain in 1808, but he was in exile by the time that it was built. It was 1,500 feet long and nearly 45 feet wide, and it had seventeen arches. For Cocks, the view of the town, river and shipping from the bridge was 'truly magnificent'.

In 1872 a writer in the *Wine Trade Review* dwelt on the 'affluence of Bordeaux', which was then a city of 200,000, with a million people directly associated with it in a bigger urban region. While the total value of French trade in French seaports had risen by 36 per cent between 1859 and 1869, the value of the trade of Bordeaux had risen by nearly 50 per cent; and about a half of the tonnage of the French merchant fleet was Bordelais. This was proof, the author concluded, that the port had great 'natural advantages'.

You did not have to be a Napoleon (or a Young) to appreciate why a port – or a city – had developed there. Any map proclaims the virtues of the site. 'There had to be a city there,' Camille Jullian wrote in his *Histoire de Bordeaux*. What kind of city, however, had depended, not on the site, but on the inhabitants, and today every building and every street tells its own story of the Bordelais of different generations. 'The spirit of a city,' Jacques Chaban-Delmas, great citizen and long-time Mayor of Bordeaux, has written recently, 'takes bodily shape, so to say, across time and across the history that defines, affirms and perpetuates both its identity and its *raison d'être*.'

There were Basques and Celts on the site of Bordeaux before there were Romans, and the River Garonne was a boundary of the flourishing Roman city of Burdigala long before the English turned the river into an artery of trade. There were Normans there before there were French and English, and Vikings before Normans: a terrifying Viking raid in 844 is well recorded.

Parts of the rich medieval city of Bordeaux survive, like the cathedral, dedicated to St-André, which reflects medieval as well as modern change. The nave was begun in the twelfth century, and contrasts with a fourteenth-century choir. Some of the finest parish churches were built before the English kings and their agents were evicted from Bordeaux. That of Ste-Eulalie, with Haut-Brion associations, is said to contain the relics of seven saints of the third century, presented to the church by Charlemagne in 811. The Porte de l'Hôtel de Ville was constructed by Henry III of England in 1246. The fifteenth-century bell tower of St-Michel, separated from the church, has the loftiest spire in the south of France.

The main parts of the prosperous eighteenth-century city, careful at the time about its appearance and determined in consequence to improve itself by urban planning, are also visible. Jacques Gabriel and his son, Jacques-Ange, were among the architects called in. So also was Victor Louis, fresh from Poland. Not all the local plans were implemented, however. For example, a canal was not built round the city, as some of the people of Bordeaux had hoped, nor was Louis's 'scenographic' urban planning scheme of 1785 fully realized.

It required the impetus of the Revolution before the fortifications of Bordeaux, including the Château Trompette, were finally demolished. The château, built after the expulsion of the English, had been 'modernized' by the great Vauban, and on the eve of the Revolution there were abortive plans to pull it down and create a huge new square on the site. Now after the revolutionary demolition only a few gateways remain. With the destruction of the château, (where one of the proprietors of Haut-Brion, a Fumel, had been in command at the time of the French Revolution), the Chartrons no longer seemed an isolated town within a city. The area was to lose heavily, however, from twentieth-century developments carried out after 1924 by a port authority that built concrete warehouses to block the old houses from the river.

Delight in eighteenth-century Bordeaux has long since been revived. Indeed, some of the many proud eighteenth-century features of the city that belonged to the *ancien régime* are now appreciated more fully than they were at the time. The *Intendant* Louis-Urbain-Aubert, Marquis de Tourny, in office from 1743 to 1757, was a man of far-seeing great designs, and the Allées de Tourny are happily named after him. He was identified by Angus Reach as 'the creator of modern Bordeaux, under whose auspices a whole tribe of dolphins and heathen gods and goddesses were invoked to decorate the city'.

Yet not everything new was heathen. A new archiepiscopal palace, built by the Prince de Rohan, Archbishop of Bordeaux until 1781, had replaced 'a large, old irregular structure', while the Grand Théâtre, constructed between 1775 and 1780, has been described by its twentieth-century historian as the 'cathedral of the century of the great *Encyclopédie*', a symbol of enlightenment. The architect was Louis, and the ceiling was dedicated to the Maréchal de Mouchy, an ancestor of the present Duc, who is now an administrator and director of the Domaine Clarence Dillon. After the Revolution, in 1793, the theatre became 'the great theatre of the Republic'.

During the nineteenth century, when several medieval and eighteenth-century buildings were 'restored' (for example, the archiepiscopal palace in 1862, and the theatre in 1864 and 1881), there were interesting new buildings. Some of them were singled out by Cocks in 1846 – among them the Palais de Justice, the prison and 'the gas establishment', the last of these directed, he was proud to write, by an English engineer. Cocks also noted with pride how the old tower of St-Michel had a 'double telegraph' on it 'to correspond with Paris and Burgonne'. In the same century the impressive Esplanade des Quinconces echoed older traditions when it was embellished with huge statues of Montesquieu and of Montaigne, who also gave his name to the Lycée Michel-Montaigne, once the Jesuit College. There were also new boulevards and squares, including a Cours Victor Hugo.

Bertall, who admired the great boulevards of eighteenth-century Bordeaux more than he admired the narrow streets behind them, observed that the city had had its Haussmann before Paris did. Not long before, Victor Hugo himself had written: 'Take Versailles, add Antwerp, and you get Bordeaux.'

In the last quarter of the nineteenth century and the first decade of the twentieth a number of wine merchants acquired premises around the Quai de Queyries, for the first time forsaking the increasingly congested Chartrons district; and further upstream, near the Gare St-Jean, the Eiffel Bridge carrying the railway over the river had been opened in 1860. The so-called 'Château Descas', built near the station in 1890, was an opulent business centre, a *maison de négoce* which proudly expressed the spirit of this phase in the history of the city, recently described by Robert Coustet as 'the heyday of the alliance between the wine of Bordeaux and its architecture'.

Modern war has fortunately spared – or almost spared – Bordeaux, which on two occasions before 1940 briefly housed the government of France: in 1870 and in 1914. Much from the rich past is still present, therefore, in the streets of Bordeaux, although names and functions have often changed. The Place Royale, begun in 1730, is now the Place de la Bourse. The Chamber of Commerce is on one side of it. The archiepiscopal palace, built near the cathedral, is now the Hôtel de Ville. There is still a Place du Parlement, but there is also in the Esplanade des Quinconces an imposing monument to the Girondists of Bordeaux that celebrates the revolutionaries of 1791, 1792 and 1793.

Since 1928 the old Pavé des Chartrons has been renamed the Cour Xavier-Arnozan, after a local doctor, and the old Chemin du Roi the Cours Portal. There is also a Cours Clemenceau. In the Basilique St-Michel the majestic naves survive, but there are new stained glass windows, installed in 1959 to replace medieval windows that were damaged in an air attack in 1940.

It is an easy journey, if rarely for a stranger an entirely straightforward one, to travel by car from the centre of Bordeaux to Haut-Brion. Parts of the journey, however, should always be made on foot. There are many surviving narrow medieval streets – some with names like the Rue de la Fusterie, reminding travellers of the makers of casks and barrels, almost as important in the history of the wine trade as the vines themselves; and there are grocer's shops where you can still buy the *vin de l'année*. Some of the fascinating individual buildings, with 'quaint carvings in blackened wood and mouldering stone', still look much as they did when Cocks described them. On many buildings there is intricate decoration of a later period that is neither in wood nor stone but in metal. 'Few cities can pride themselves in possessing even a part of the wealth in metal work to be found in Bordeaux,' wrote the nineteenth-century socialist Louis Blanc.

Along with the old and the restored, there is much that is new – in the centre as well as in the suburbs. In 1939 the city acquired its first municipal stadium, and there has been enough new building since the 1960s to create entirely new vistas and perspectives. A huge Exhibition Centre was opened in 1969 just outside the city: it overlooks a large artificial lake, 160 hectares in area. Exhibitions and festivals are an important part of the life of Bordeaux, but it has libraries, museums and galleries, including a Musée de la Marine and a Musée des Arts Décoratifs, located in an eighteenth-century town house, the Hôtel de Lalande. Along with precious objects, including a marble bust of Montesquieu, you can examine there an early drawing of the Grand Théâtre and a contemporary *View of the Port of Bordeaux and the Chartrons Embankment* by Pierre Lacous: it was presented to the Empress Josephine on the occasion of Napoleon's visit to Bordeaux in 1808. One of the most interesting items in the Museum is a silver wine-taster, a *tasse-à-vin*, based on a sixteenth-century design: its rim frames a wide raised boss which allowed the taster to '*mirer le vin*', that is to say to examine its colour in reflection.

For centuries wine was made from grapes grown within the city limits of Bordeaux, for example in what is now the Place Gambetta, once called the Place Dauphin; and Bertall told all visitors to Bordeaux that if they did not inspect one or two city *chais* it would be *lèse-majesté*: 'it would be like visiting Paris without seeing the Louvre, . . . Nôtre Dame . . . and the staircase at the Opéra'. It has never been easy to forget wine in Bordeaux, either in the Museum or in the streets.

It is entirely in keeping with tradition, therefore, that diagonally opposite the eighteenth-century Grand Théâtre with its imposing colonnades you can find a late-twentieth-century *maison du vin*, appropriately shaped like the bow of a ship. This is the centre of the several official bodies that now regulate the wine trade; and facing it there is now a *vinothèque*, a kind of wine supermarket, where the wines of Bordeaux – and those from elsewhere – are on sale. The Académie des Vins was established in 1948, and in the same year the Conseil Interprofessionel du Vin de Bordeaux. There are also thirteen brotherhoods of wine producers.

Old and new coexist in Bordeaux, and both can be appreciated. Many other places have lost their historical identity: Bordeaux has kept it. Yet according to one uneasy critic, the city is 'a place of amnesia, a culture unaware of its richness'. A Châteaux Bordeaux Exhibition held at the Pompidou Centre in Paris in 1987 and 1988 demonstrated great interest in the heritage – the *patrimoine* – and in the future, but its promoters also expressed concern about what they called a failure to respond imaginatively to changing circumstances.

The beautifully illustrated book published by the Pompidou Centre, *Châteaux Bordeaux*, edited by J. Dethier, has been translated into English and provides full details both of threat and of achievement. So, too, does the equally beautifully produced magazine *L'Amateur de Bordeaux*, the co-editor of which, Michel Guillard, played a prominent part in arranging the Exhibition. *L'Amateur de Bordeaux* is essential reading both for lovers of the city and for lovers of wine – it includes in each number articles on wine and reviews of wine books – and its advertisements alone are worth the price. Its approach should be compared with that of an official brochure which describes the conservation of the past – *Que Renaisse le Vieux Bordeaux* – and which includes alongside a section called 'a city contemplates its heritage' another called 'a new art of living'.

Whatever the balance of hope and fear, the art of wine is recognized everywhere in Bordeaux as a necessary part of any new art, as it has been at every stage in the transmission of the heritage. 'There are many ways of knowing Bordeaux,' wrote Gaston Marchou, winner of the Grand Prix de Littérature de Bordeaux in 1961,

> through its great writers . . . through its port and its monuments; through its history, thanks to which one discovers, not without surprise, that the grandeur of a city is not related to the number of sieges and massacres which it staged . . . If one admits that there exists a 'Civilisation de la Vigne', pure of all violence . . . it is in Bordeaux that this civilization has reached its peak of perfection.

Machou was no more satisfied, however, with general praise of the *civilisation de la vigne* than Cocks and Féret had been with general accounts of the 'wines of Bordeaux' or the authors of the various chapters in *Châteaux Bordeaux* were to be. He wanted to be specific:

> The city will not yield up its spirit nor deliver its secret unless one questions it with a glass in one's hand. And this glass should contain a red Graves wine. Far from me any unworthy desire to deny to Saint-Émilion or to the Médoc the right of representing Bordeaux which owes them a large part of its universal reputation. I am simply saying that *Graves*, . . . which was the dear child – and for long the sole child – of the *Privilège des Vins*, carries the most familiar and distinctive features of its father.

While there is great, if threatened, civic pride in Bordeaux, with which the history of Haut-Brion and its proprietors is entangled, there is local pride too in Pessac, the place where most of the Haut-Brion vineyard is situated. Yet that pride also is threatened. Indeed, in the late twentieth century Pessac, which has changed more than Bordeaux itself, has frequently been dismissed as a suburb of the city, with Haut-Brion as an 'oasis' within it. Pessac has also lost much of its dependence on wine. On the side of it furthest away from Bordeaux, where the streets bear the names neither of grapes nor of vintages but of music and composers, the word 'suburbs' was used two generations ago. A rue Rossini and an avenue Mozart stand on land which until the early 1920s belonged to the park of the Château of Haut-Brion itself.

In 1921 the promoters of the sale of parts of the estate, which then comprised 146 hectares, described it as 'an island in the suburbs of Bordeaux', albeit an island 'where we can find a wine which always does honour to the national *richesse*'. Fifty hectares were then devoted to vines, 20 to *prairies*, meadows, and 70 to woodland or dunes, *bois ou landes*. 'It is not rash to foresee the day', the promoters added in a quaint version of English, 'on which realization by shares will arrive, when the castle, its park and its growth will be like a jewel in the middle of an inhabited country.' In another section advertising lots for sale, *lotissements*, the promoters referred to 'smiling countryside' and 'perfect salubrity'. Haut-Brion was 'a Paradise'.

Such talk, with its deliberate stress on the consolations of 'suburbia', contrasts sharply with the talk of Raphaël Saint-Orens and Les Amis du Beau et du Vieux Pessac, who spurn suburbia and traverse centuries of excitement and conflict as freely and as happily as do the historians of Bordeaux itself. There has been learned discussion in Pessac, for example, as to whether the origins of the name of the commune are Celtic or Roman. There was certainly a Roman villa there, and there was equally certainly a medieval church, built in the twelfth century, when vines were planted. The formidable Pey Berland, Archbishop of Bordeaux after whom a *quartier* of Bordeaux is still named, had a mill there. Pines were planted too so that Pessac became a place of '*vins et pins*'.

As Saint-Orens states emphatically in capital letters, in his account of Pessac in the twelfth century, 'PESSAC N'EST PAS DANS LA BANLIEUE DE BORDEAUX'. Pessac was not just another suburb. Another striking heading in his account of the history of fourteenth-century Pessac, when an ox was used to plough the vineyards, reads '*A Pessac pas de bourgeois: à Bordeaux pas de serfs*' ('at Pessac no middle class, at Bordeaux no serfs'); and a later account of sixteenth-century Pessac (during a century of change) is introduced under the heading '*La Paroisse de Pessac vendue deux fois*' ('The Parish of Pessac sold twice over'). Saint-Orens is interested also in the English inheritance, as was the Abbé Baurein who two centuries ago described how land in Pessac and Villenave d'Ornon was held in the early fifteenth century by a future Archbishop of York who sold his titles in 1409.

In writing about the seventeenth century, Saint-Orens describes Pessac vividly as 'a gateway to the world', and directs attention to the story of one well-known Pessacais, François Saige, who began his career as a shipper in 1654 with a boat of 18 *tonneaux*. Ten years later, he acquired a frigate of ten times the size, and in 1670 he became the head of the Bourse in Bordeaux. Shipping families like his intermarried, forming a powerful presence in the burgeoning Bordeaux of the eighteenth century.

The Revolution of 1789 converted Pessac in 1790 from a parish (St-Martin) into a commune within the same boundaries. On the east were Bordeaux and Talence; on the south Gradignan, Canéjan and Cestas; on the west Saint-Jean-d'Illac; and on the north Mérignac. More important, however, than this constitutional change was demographic and social pressure over several generations, a pressure that had begun before the Revolution and that has been recently examined meticulously by Marie-Thérèse Lauer in a Bordeaux University thesis of 1985 supervised by Professor J.-P. Poussou. It is fitting that large parts of the modern university complex, where wine is a special subject of study, are located in Pessac itself and in neighbouring Talence, within easy walking distance of Haut-Brion.

It was this population pressure that converted a scattered collection of isolated dwellings and vineyards into a new kind of community, more compact and more aware of its own identity, while at the same time Haut-Brion was being converted into an even more compact vineyard. By 1692 Haut-Brion consisted of precisely 825 *journaux*, 29 *règes*, 63 *carreaux* (264 hectares in all). Most of the *vignerons pessacais* worked at Haut-Brion, and some family names (Dumeau, for instance) survive. Only lands situated in the *plantier de Haut-Brion* and in Cameyract paid their dues in kind. The rest paid in cash. This was obviously deliberate policy on the part of the landlord. At the end of the eighteenth century the *plantier de Haut-Brion*, always distinguished from the *maison noble* and from the *seigneurie*, had around 132 *journaux* under vines, rather more than in 1692, and was producing 100 *tonneaux* of wine; and when during the Revolution seigneurial rights were abolished, tenants of Haut-Brion held around 104 hectares, 30 hectares more than the *seigneurie*. Only one tenant in two grew vines and nothing else, however, and among the tenancies there was only one sizeable *vignoble*, of around eight hectares.

In neighbouring Talence, described by Franck in 1845 as 'furbished with beautiful *maisons de campagne* and situated in an agreeable position', three-quarters of the inhabitants listed in late eighteenth-century parish registers were described as *vignerons*. In the nineteenth century, however, the commune had been divided into two parts, Haut-Talence and Bas-Talence, the first renowned for its vines, the second for its meadows.

Among Pessac wine properties adjacent to Haut-Brion, Les Carmes-Haut-Brion, which in 1584 had benefited from a donation from Jean de Pontac, lay to the north. Others were Le Moulin (the mill) de Crespiac, which included a vineyard; Château-Verthamon, Fanning-Lafontaine, and La Passion Haut-Brion, once called Le Loup Blanc or Artiguemale. The last of these vineyards was still there in 1949, as was Château-Laburthe, which in 1868 had incorporated a substantial part of Château-Brivazac, a property on the highest slopes of Pessac, that once produced a wine called Château-Brivazac-Haut-Brion. That was before the slopes were built over. The quest for an explanation of old Pessac and Talence place names, many of which survive, has never been solely of antiquarian interest, for before the twentieth century the use of the name Haut-Brion on the labels of particular wines produced outside the Haut-Brion estate – there were once as many as twelve of them – troubled producers of Haut-Brion.

There was no local census in Pessac until 1820, but from parish registers before 1792 and from civil sources afterwards, there is evidence, if patchy and incomplete, of population growth. In 1700 there were fewer than 1,000 inhabitants, and by 1839 over 1,200, but between then and 1865 the population doubled. In the 1881 edition of Cocks et Féret it was stated that Pessac then had 2,799 inhabitants along with a further *population flottante* of 600. It was said to consist then of a *bourg*, '*important et bien bâti*', complete with a new *mairie*, near the old village of Le Poujeau, and 'a score' of other villages, among them Ladonne, Lartiguemale, Coudourne and the beautifully named Tocquetoucau. Cocks et Féret also stated that there was an omnibus travelling between the commune and Bordeaux, half-hourly in summer, hourly in winter.

In the 1886 edition, however, there was no longer any reference to the scatter of people, and the population was given more precisely, if somewhat unconvincingly, as 3,227. The local brook, Le Ruisseau du Serpent, was mentioned too: it joined another stream at Talence to form the Ruisseau d'Ars. Of the 3,873 hectares of the commune, 600 were said to be devoted to vines. Just as prominent a feature of the landscape, however, were pine forests, although these had been badly damaged by great fires in 1870, 1871 and 1872.

It is notable that Pessac exported to England not only wines but timber to make furniture, telegraph poles and paper. The commune was renowned too for its strawberries: Féret observed how acceptable they were in the Paris of the Second Empire. Other economic activities included 'coopering' and straw-making. Haut-Brion, however, was singled out in the *Dictionnaire des Postes et Télégraphes* for 1898: 'Haut-Brion, Gironde, 25 habitants, commune de Pessac'.

There was far greater population growth in Pessac after the 1890s than there had been in the nineteenth century, a significant part of it based on local immigration from other areas in Bordeaux and the Gironde. Its population increased from over 3,000 in 1900 to over 37,000 in 1970, and during the same period Talence grew likewise from 4,629 to over 31,000. There were new names also, reflecting new history: thus, one important road was renamed the Avenue Jean Jaurès after the socialist leader.

Some old landmarks have disappeared or changed in use. Thus, the Vieux Abattoirs, not far from La Mission, are no longer abattoirs: the then owner of La Mission, Henri Woltner, had complained about them in 1926 to the Mayor of Talence, who is said to have replied soothingly that on a visit there he had given 'specific instructions that the cries of the animals should be reduced to a strict minimum'.

A remarkable collection of local postcards, assembled by Christian Delord, a true *Pessacais*, although by birth a *Limousin*, depict scenes that in the words of Saint-Orens have 'disappeared, have been modernized, or have been massacred'. One postcard displays the image of a spa, a '*station climatique*' that was in operation from 1898 to 1905, complete with a casino. Another shows a health centre, with an *hôpital des convalescents* and a sanatorium. A third card depicts Bellegrave, the old hunting lodge of Haut-Brion, which had by then become public property, although Château Bellegrave was producing 10 *tonneaux* of wine in the 1870s.

During the early 1920s 22 hectares of the Haut-Brion domaine still consisted of paddocks. The wine-growing area was limited then to 31 hectares, compared with 50 at the end of the First World War. It remains the same today. Meanwhile, Pessac, like Bordeaux, has continued to change, not least in land use and in appearance, while retaining its sense of identity.

The fact that Pessac enjoyed a brief spell as a *station climatique* directs attention to the role of climate in influencing the wine of Bordeaux, the Graves and Haut-Brion in particular. The congenial adjective 'temperate' is usually applied to the weather of Bordeaux, the English writer Cyril Connolly describing it as being as 'near perfection as a temperate maritime climate can be'. Montesquieu, who believed in the influence of climate on everything, was doubtless of the same opinion. A climate that is ideal for the vine is a climate that is agreeable for man.

Nonetheless, 'temperate' does not mean 'Mediterranean', and Saint-Orens was right to point out in his history of Pessac that the first vines to be planted in Roman Burdigala had to be of a sturdy variety capable of surviving in an Atlantic climate. The same was true of medieval vines. They had to stay alive in what we know were often extremely cold winters with extremely strong winds. As Pijassou has observed in his detailed study of the Médoc, which begins not with history or geology but with meteorology, the vineyards of the Graves are on the very edge of the vine's natural habitat. It is interesting that when King John showed great interest in the wines of Bordeaux medieval temperatures seem to have reached their peak. During the French Revolution, in Year III, they fell to exceptionally low levels. In different centuries there have been different preoccupations concerning the weather.

A distinguished French historian, Emmanuel Le Roy Ladurie, in his fascinating book *Histoire du Climat depuis L'An Mil* (1967), has shown that while it is impossible to forecast – in Bordeaux or elsewhere – what next year's weather will be like, in retrospect there have been whole sequences of years that seem to have shared distinctive meteorological characteristics. There have been years of ice and of sun. Writing before there was any talk of 'the greenhouse effect', Le Roy Ladurie generalized boldly about such sequences after carefully studying the movement of glaciers and the height and rings of trees. He did not find it easy, however, to discover adequate explanations for them. Little of his data related to the Bordeaux area, and when we compare the record of that area with those of other wine-producing areas, we are usually left with far from bold generalizations such as 'the climate in Bordeaux is conditioned by

the Atlantic and is generally better than Burgundy'. Another possible generalization is more interesting: good summers and wet
springs seem to go together in Bordeaux and in England. The Atlantic rules both.

Pijassou's *Le Médoc*, which substitutes detail for generalization,
distinguishes carefully between regional, local and micro-climates.
He has had at his disposal three series of weather registers: one
from Château Margaux, a register which covers the long period
from 1795 to 1918; one from Château Mouton-Rothschild, which
covers the period from 1800 to 1973; and one from the Tastet and
Lawton archives, which covers the period from 1740 to the present.
It is possible, however, to go back further in time than these continuous records – even to the Middle Ages for detailed descriptions
of the weather, although in the absence of thermometers all statements are necessarily impressionistic.

Galileo invented the first of the new instruments of measurement
in 1612, with Fahrenheit following in 1714 and Celsius in 1742.
Barometers came later than thermometers: the first recorded use of
one – in 1643 – was by Torricelli, formerly one of Galileo's assist-
ants. Even after that, however, 'peasants and their families', as a
British historian, Richard Muir, has well put it, 'did not see climatic
change as a wiggly line on a graph'. Still less would they have
understood recent headlines such as 'Global changes will be long-
term'. What they would have understood was the first sentence of
the report of a conference on 'environmental damage and climatic
change', held near Oxford in 1989: 'Of the numerous themes running through this conference, the one that struck a layman most
forcibly was uncertainty.'

The distinction between the three kinds of climate in the Graves
and Médoc – regional, local and micro-climate – rests on the inter-
action of weather and *terroir*. There are particular places, we discover, which because of their topography have different *micro-
climats*, just as they have different degrees of drainage. A small hill,
for example, like the *croupes* of Haut-Brion, may offer protection
against frost: a gentle slope may catch more sun. It has been argued
also that the micro-climates of La Mission and Haut-Brion have
been partly man-made and that proximity to Bordeaux has had a
moderating effect on the temperature even at night.

What largely conditions the regional weather is the Atlantic
Ocean, and for this reason springs in Bordeaux can be as dangerous

as winters, for rain in spring can fall on the blossom on the vines and lead to *coulure* or the falling off of fruit. Later in the year, protracted rain at harvest time can ruin the prospects of the best of years. Between these two dates what happens to vines depends on degrees both of cold and of heat and of rainfall and humidity. Even psychology is relevant. Peter Sichel has shrewdly observed that a heavy rainfall continuing into May can have little effect on the year's wine but a bad effect on morale. The study of the effects of weather on vines cannot be compressed into one year. The growth processes of vines over several years have to be examined, and different years vary from one another sufficiently for the historian to have to relate one year to another. 'In the final analysis,' Pijassou concludes, 'we may say that the climate of Bordeaux is just unfavourable enough to the vine to make poor, pebbly soil bring forth vines not in great quantity, but of extremely high quality.'

In 1895 M. Rayat, Director of the Observatory in Bordeaux, published his *Recherches sur le climat de Bordeaux*, a study that brought science to a subject which Cocks, though armed with thermometers, had continued to deal with impressionistically. It was Cocks who wrote in 1846 that the Bordeaux climate was 'generally mild and temperate. The thermometer seldom descends below 0° in winter: in summer it rises to 20°; the winds are generally from the south-west and north-west quarters.' Only 'the miasma' exhaled from the marshes exposed to the burning heat of the sun – a characteristic nineteenth-century expression – 'interrupted the general salubrity of this country, which, after all, figures among those that are the most remarkable for longevity'.

Average temperatures in twentieth-century Bordeaux are clearly higher than those of Burgundy, France's other great wine-growing area, and higher than those given by Cocks. Moreover, there are fewer bouts of heavy rainfall than there are in Burgundy. Temperatures at Haut-Brion have ranged from $-7°$ to $-8°$, at their lowest, in January, to as much as 35° at their highest, in July and August, but there have been marked variations from year to year both in rainfall and in humidity, variations which are themselves localized. The misty day when Dillon never reached St-Émilion was not untypical. The skies of Bordeaux are often overcast. Pijassou was right, therefore, to use the qualifying words 'just unfavourable enough'. Fortunately, the spirits of the Bordelais usually are not. 'Bordeaux,' wrote Reach, is 'emphatically what the French call a "smiling" [*riant*] town, with plenty of air.' Cocks called its citizens 'lively, petulant, gay, jovial, witty, and taunting; easily incensed and as easily pacified'. Duijker, a century and a half later, observed how in Bordeaux 'life is enjoyed', and 'so is a well stocked table'.

In 1989, when I was preparing this book, the citizens of Bordeaux had exceptionally good reason to be cheerful, for this was the year of what *Sud Ouest*, the leading newspaper of Bordeaux, called 'the vintage of the century' ('*la vendange du siècle*'). 'Euphoria' ('*euphorie dans les vignobles*') was a heading in *Le Monde* on 4 September. For the first time in almost a hundred years the harvest at Haut-Brion had begun in August, well before the general opening (*l'ouverture générale*), set for 11 September: the last occasion when the harvest had begun in August had been in 1893. For England's *Daily Telegraph* this was 'the warmest year ever'. The favourite adjective employed in the French press was 'precocious'. 'The dry climate, characterized by daily and nocturnal heat,' one journalist observed, 'has been a positive factor for winegrowers.' The grapes had a high sugar content, and it was after the red Merlots had been gathered in just one day after the white grapes that there were signs of 'euphoria'. Knowledgeable journalists, nevertheless, drew distinctions. Thus, Didier Ters singled out '*les premiers blancs*' as the wines most likely to be outstanding, and added cautiously that it was 'important not to reach conclusions too hastily'. 'The great diversity that had been observed in the study of the balance of planting or the naming of the *appellations* had provoked a general mood of prudence.'

The influence of climate can now be checked. In 1893, a year when the vintage began in August, torrid weather at harvest time (35° to 40°) had made fermentation exceptionally difficult. In 1989 fermentation could be effectively controlled. Another simple innovation has affected the vines themselves: anti-rot sprays can be effective at the flowering stage, and they remain so until within a month of the harvest.

If the influence of climate can now be checked, can the influence of 'place' itself be overcome? Californian wine-makers have sometimes said yes, claiming that French wine-makers and French writers on wine have overstressed the significance of the soil. One Californian, Joe Heitz, told Simon Loftus, author of highly informative and highly readable articles collected in his *Anatomy of the Wine Trade* (1985), that French talk of *terroir* was 'hokum'.

Robert Mondavi, outstanding leader in the Californian trade, would once have agreed. Later he came to disagree, as any historian must. 'I can show you samples from different parcels of wine,' he claimed, 'with the only variable being the soil. There are huge differences.' The present proprietors of Haut-Brion would not disagree with this proposition. Nor, of course, would Locke or any of the past proprietors from Jean de Pontac onwards.

3

The Soil

Why did the flinty dust (if it be that) contained in
the meagre soil of the Bordeaux vineyards give to
all good Bordeaux wines an aroma which has been
compared to the perfume of the violet?

Wine Trade Review, 1875

The people of Pessac have always realized that, leaving on one side
questions of climate, their destinies have rested in the soil; and
among the legends is a local one, as charming as Healy's Irish
legend, that, in the words of a fanciful writer of 1878, it was Pope
Clement V who doubtless (*'sans doute'*, the right words to begin
the telling of a legend) 'had bestowed his blessings on the particular
soil of the vineyard, thereby guaranteeing it an exceptional future'.

During the 1870s 60 *tonneaux* of wine were being produced in
Château Pape-Clément (the figure for the 1940s was 50 *tonneaux*)
as against 100 in Haut-Brion and 25 in La Mission. There was
also a wine being produced *'au quartier Pape-Clément'* by Edward
Forestier, whose seven-hectare estate included four hectares of
fields and *jardins anglais* and a fountain named after the medieval
Pope. The property, which had been in the hands of the Church
until the French Revolution, was owned by an English family, the
Maxwells, between 1919 and 1937, when after a terrifying hail-
storm it was on the point of being sold for building lots. The poet
Paul Montagne, who saved it, lived to be ninety-four, although he
was blind for the last fifteen years of his life. The present vineyard,
29 hectares in area, produces 130,000 bottles of red Graves, rather
less than Haut-Brion's 150,000, and 1,200 of white as against
Haut-Brion's 9,600.

Another charming local legend that also has a geological dimension dates back appropriately to the formative eighteenth century. It relates equally appropriately not to a bishop but a courtier, a courtier in the English sense: either le Comte d'Hargicourt or the Marquis de Ségur, probably the former. Wearing gleaming buttons on his waistcoat, buttons that appealed to King Louis XVI, the courtier replied to the King's question as to what they were and where he had acquired them with the unforgettable words 'diamonds from my estate'. They were in fact quartz and quartzite stones from the gravel of the Gironde, constituents of the site at Haut-Brion that made even better wine than they did buttons. Indeed, in their account of the wines of the Graves, Cocks et Féret placed these stones first in their story: 'The soils which produce these wines consist of a mixture of pebbles, siliceous in colour and of different sizes . . . The thickness of the bed of gravel varies from 50 centimetres to 3 metres at the most.' Why such soil was so suitable for *grands vins* they did not say. Nor could the anonymous writer in the *Wine Trade Review* of 1875 who, having examined 'the flinty dust (if it be that)', was certain only of the fact of the coincidence of odd characteristics of soil with 'the best Bordeaux *crus*'. The simple statement still stands, although many eloquent words before and after have been used to describe the soils of the Graves and the precious crystals which they incorporate.

One of the most memorable descriptions is that of Jouannet in his *Statistique de la Gironde* (1843):

> The soil under the gravel is sometimes, but seldom of clay; in some places, rock, and more generally pure sand, or the ferruginous formation known in this country by the name of *alios*. These lands, so unfavourable for cultivation in general, seem created on purpose for the vine. One would think that every circumstance of formation, constitution, and situation, had united to exclude every other kind of produce, in order to fix imperiously there the cultivation of the vine, the produce of which is so extraordinary as to admit of no comparison in ancient or modern times.

Because soil is so important in the history of wine, in any attempt at explanation of the distinctive qualities of a particular wine or group of wines geology usually comes not only before history, ancient, medieval and modern, but before geography – and, *pace* Pijassou, even before meteorology.

At the end of the Tertiary Age, the Aquitaine basin had emerged from beneath the oceans, and the mountains of the Pyrenees rose above the waters, leaving debris spread out over the foothills stripped by erosion. At the same time, sand, gravel and clay were pushed north by the force of the waters. Left among the geological debris were the small pebbles of quartz that were to fascinate Louis XV. At a later date a layer of large stones was deposited in some places on top of this first stratum: it was the soil of the future. The topsoil also sometimes contains '*alios*', a type of hard iron-rich sandstone. Below is *arène*, a coagulated bed of marl. In many places there are fossils.

Most of the stones in the top stratum of the soil at Haut-Brion are six to eight millimetres in diameter: some, larger than those on most other *domaines*, measure ten to twelve millimetres. Their colours vary as the colours of jewels. The subsoil is deep – in places the gravel, a product of the Pleistocene Era which geologists call 'Gunzian', goes down sixty feet – and it allows the roots of the vines to penetrate deep. 'Allows' is an inadequate word. '*La vigne*,' it has been said, '*souffre à se nourrir*': 'The vine suffers in order to feed itself.'

The proportion of gravel varies from one part of the *domaine* to another. Indeed, three distinct soils can be found there. There are important differences too in land levels. Within the area that was transformed millions of years ago Haut-Brion has been described as '*une croupe graveleuse*', inadequately translated as 'a gravelly brow', with a 'hillock' ('*un mamelon*') below it. The words *croupe* and *mamelon* refer also to parts of the human body, and this gives them special associations. On the plateau, the clay and the fine soil have been washed away to produce a kind of sandy gravel. On the more or less exposed slopes, small though they are, erosion has turned the gravel into soil with more clay in it. Below the gentle slopes, themselves called *croupes*, where over the centuries soil has been washed down, there is an artificial rise in the level of the soil because of matter which has fallen from the slopes; and there the thicker layer of soil protects the vines from the influence of the wetter level of soil underneath.

The particular balance at Haut-Brion is unique. In more general terms, however, much of the soil in the Graves region as a whole is retentive: it reflects light, and in the evening it gives out heat that it has absorbed during the day. In this way the growing day is lengthened. There is also protection from frost. Crops other than vines would require greater humidity.

All this is understood and explained convincingly at the prestigious Institut National de la Recherche Agronomique, INRA, consecrated to the vine, as Florence Mothe, a French writer on the wines of the Graves, puts it. Appropriately it has its headquarters at Villenave d'Ornan in the midst of the region of 'terres graveleuses', where there is a Norman castle which reminded nineteenth-century visitors of the novels of Sir Walter Scott. Neither science nor history is needed to describe how the appearance of the soil at Haut-Brion changes in different lights. Sometimes it looks like shot silk: sometimes it seems 'a dusty yellow'.

The lie of the land at Haut-Brion, what in England would once have been called 'the aspect', demands detailed attention, since another consequence of the huge disturbances of the earth at the end of the Tertiary Age was the creation of terraces (terrasses) of slightly raised land on the left bank of the River Garonne. Being higher, these provided better drainage and additional nourishment for the vines planted there. Even when the land in the Graves seems at first sight flat, there are undulations. Yet the so-called croupes de Graves are the product not of the huge initial disturbances, but of erosion of sand and pebbles over the centuries.

There are large parts of Pessac where the soil is not gravelly but entirely sandy; and it is these other soils, carried by great winds from the west, that set geological as well as historical limits to Haut-Brion. They are worth careful study. On one side of a wall there are flowers and vegetables: on the other side grapes. Also worth study are the small streams on each side of the property, the Peuge in the north and the Ars in the south. Over the centuries these streams have washed much of the sand away, leaving the gravels behind.

Differences in the level of land – of 12 to 15 metres between the highest land and the nearby beds of the streams – are particularly significant. In the seventeenth and eighteenth centuries, when the property was being actively developed for the first time, there were three small hills of more or less equal height, the highest points in the domaine, looking out over roughly equal areas of land some 27 metres above sea level. It was one of those hillocks, the Haut-de-

Carles, that was demolished when the railway was built, leaving behind the hill of the Chai-Neuf and of the hill of Bahans. From the brow of these there are very different views. Slopes that are not visible at a distance stand out clearly from them.

Some of the names of numbered *parcelles* of land at Haut-Brion, each with distinctive soil characteristics, are strictly topographical, like Terre Rouge, Bas Plante, Haut Plantey, Sapinette, Grand Bois de la Lande, du Haut de Carle and Le Pavé. Others, however, are historical, like Catalan, the name of a former part proprietor, Le Colonel, La Pièce du Bureau and Moteur. Every *parcelle*, therefore, has its own historical pedigree as well as its geological features. In an early twentieth-century map the first thirty-five numbered pieces were in Pessac, the next ten in Talence, the next fifty in Pessac and the last thirteen in Mérignac.

Some mystery attaches to the name Haut-Brion itself, a point emphasized by the twentieth-century proprietor before Dillon, André Gibert, when, like his nineteenth-century predecessors, he was contemplating taking steps against vineyards other than Haut-Brion that used the words Haut-Brion as part of the name on their labels. One of them, La Passion-Haut-Brion, produced only four *tonneaux* a year. This did not spare it from Gibert's attack, however. What was at stake for him was the fact that vineyards which used Haut-Brion in the names on their labels were being sold not because of their own reputation but because of the reputation of Haut-Brion itself. '*Y-at-il un lieu dit Haut-Brion?*' Gibert asked, by which he meant was there a place called Haut-Brion independent of the château and of the *domaine* which he had purchased. It is a question which has been asked by lawyers – and judges – more frequently than by historians, and it is they who have perused the most ancient texts and maps. Gibert's own answer was an emphatic no: 'the name of Haut-Brion has never been given to any *parcelle* of land except those belonging to the Château itself'. The historian's answer must be yes. Since the fifteenth century – and the earliest relevant text seems to be a legal document of 1425 – there appears to have been a '*lieu appelé au brion*' or '*aubrion*' – and the two parts of the name (or other variants of it) have subsequently often been joined together. The tribunal that examined Gibert's case concluded that there really was a place called Haut-Brion 'situated between the Beck du Peuge and that of the Serpent, a place comprising a vast plateau to which the name of Haut-Brion had been given'.

In one fifteenth-century register (*terrier*) of the neighbouring parish of Ste-Eulalie in Bordeaux there is a reference in 1435 – before the departure of the English – to vines at Haut Brion (*au brion*), '*trens de vinha qui es en las Gravas de Bordeu au loc aparat au puch boquey et aux monts en en autre maneyre au brion ayssi cume es*'. And after the departure of the English, another parish document of 1478 refers to '*un trenz de vigne sciz au lieu a haut mont atrement aubrion*'. The name '*puch boquey*', transformed into '*pey bou quey*', survived earlier this century to designate a path which crossed two vineyards.

The Abbé Planchard, who studied the question of names in the twentieth century on behalf of Les Carmes Haut-Brion, a vineyard which had belonged to the Carmelites between 1584 and the French Revolution, did not go deeply into the meaning of the name. He suggested, however, that the '*brion*' in '*au brion*' referred to a rise in the level of the land – a *croupe* or a *monticule*: '*brion*', '*monts*' and '*puch*' might have meant the same thing. Planchard admitted, however, that this was hypothesis. It may have been of the same order as Healy's more captivating story of O'Brien. Other writers have suggested that '*brion*' is a local word for gravel. Planchard's is an appealing hypothesis, nonetheless, in that he takes the 'high' out of *haut* and transfers it to *brion*; and in this respect it it interesting to note that *la fite* means a height, that Mouton is derived from *motte de terre*, an eminence, and that Margaux was known as La Mothe in the middle ages. Heights, however low, have always counted in the cartography of claret country.

It is interesting to note also that there was no place called 'bas-brion' in the locality of Pessac until the nineteenth century, although there are fifteenth- and sixteenth-century references to 'petit haut-brion' and to 'grand aubrion' before capital letters came into use for Haut-Brion. It was only in the eighteenth century that the term 'petit brion' appears to have been used. An eighteenth-century plan produced by the Abbé Baurein shows that the traveller leaving Bordeaux for the château by the route de Pessac would pass by 'Petit-Brion' and 'Petit Haut-Brion' before arriving at Haut-Brion about a hundred feet above the level of the sea. A better-known map by Belleyme, which showed Haut-Brion as a place name in large letters, gives interesting detail, and this is complemented by later maps kept at Haut-Brion itself. The tribunal that examined Gibert's complaints was particularly impressed by 'the sincerity and precision' of Belleyme.

As far as maps are concerned – and they were of considerable importance in the law cases brought by Gibert – we have the same need to pass from the general to the detailed as we have in focusing on the different districts of the Gironde. Gibert was asking for a new and more detailed cartography in a period of transition that was reflected in the scale of the maps available to him. France had to wait until the 1940s, however, for Louis Larmat's *Atlas de la France Vinicole*, and England until 1971 for Hugh Johnson's *The World Atlas of Wine*.

4

The Vines

─────────

Fine wine comes only from *cépages nobles*.

Steven Spurrier

The vine was described in English – somewhat roughly – in the middle years of the nineteenth century as 'a shrub with a tortuous trunk, of a hard wood, and covered with a peeling bark . . . Its branches are long, slender, knotty, striated, and furnished with alternate leaves, often opposed to tendrils, by which they fasten on surrounding bodies; the leaves are large, gracefully scalloped, often dentated, and held by a long firm stalk.' The writer had the grace to add that 'cultivation and the diversity of climates' had produced 'an infinite variety'. He added, too, that 'grapes ripen faster or slower, according to the species, the climate and the position'.

It is impossible to dispose of the *cépages nobles* grown at Haut-Brion in such summary fashion. Soil and vines are in perfect harmony with each other. This guarantees quality. Effort too is required, however, as are imagination and the will to experiment. It is J.-B. Delmas at Haut-Brion who is responsible for ensuring that at every stage in the production of wine – and the first stage begins in the vineyard – quality comes first.

The mix of vines (*l'encépagement*) used to produce the red Haut-Brion of the late twentieth century varies from year to year. In 1988, for example, the proportion of Cabernet Sauvignon was as high as 59 per cent; in 1992 as low as 42 per cent. The proportion of Cabernet Franc in 1990 was as high as 15 per cent; but in 1987 no Cabernet Franc grapes were used at all. The Merlot has varied from around 25 per cent in 1992 to around 55 per cent in 1990. The 'arounds' matter: within the proportions there has to be flexibility, not least at the margin. There is a lower proportion of Cabernet Sauvignon in the present Haut-Brion wines than there was in the time of Georges Delmas. Ten years ago, the proportions were given as Cabernet Sauvignon, 55 per cent; Cabernet Franc, 22 per cent; and Merlot, 23 per cent. Then – and now – we find a smaller proportion of Cabernet Sauvignon than there would be in Lafite or Mouton. By contrast, most wines of Saint-Émilion have a higher proportion of Merlot (more than 60 per cent), and Pomerol has almost 100 per cent. On the eve of its acqustion La Mission had a far higher proportion of Merlot (35 per cent) and a far smaller proportion of Cabernet Franc (5 per cent) than Haut-Brion. A few years earlier the proportions had been Cabernet Sauvignon 65 per cent, Merlot 25 per cent and Cabernet Franc 10 per cent.

The first of the three Haut-Brion black grapes, the Cabernet Sauvignon, described by Cocks et Féret in 1949 as the 'king of grapes' ('le roi des cépages de vins rouges'), is by now well known throughout the world. Cabernet Sauvignon grapes are grown, for example, in California, Australia, New Zealand and Chile – and produce a well-structured wine of 'richness and complexity' that has an average level of alcohol and contains much tannin. In consequence, outside as well as inside Europe, Cabernet Sauvignon has been described as a cépage classique, the basis of many fine, though very different wines, and it has become interesting to compare different Cabernets at 'generic wine tastings'. They are regularly compared, too, like Chardonnays, in wine magazines and in articles in newspapers.

In the Gironde, however, it has seldom been believed that Cabernet Sauvignon by itself can give to the different wines of the region their characteristic properties: they require a mix of grapes, and that is why 'from times past other cépages have been added to it in different proportions according to the regions'. The second of the Haut-Brion grapes associated with the region, Cabernet Franc, produces a wine that is lighter in colour and has less 'structure' and less tannin than that produced from Cabernet Sauvignon, sometimes called its cousin: it is an aromatic fresh wine of extraordinary 'finesse' and 'elegance'.

The third black grape constituent, Merlot, produces a wine that is particularly rich both in colour and in alcohol: it can be full-flavoured and supple. The quality of the soil on which it is planted – and it thrives in clay – has a great influence on the character of the wine produced, perhaps greater than that of any other important Bordeaux variety. Merlot is always the first grape to ripen and to be picked. In general grapes can be allowed to ripen longer than they used to be. Testing of sugar content makes this possible.

The present constituents of white Haut-Brion are 55 per cent Sauvignon white grapes, known in other parts of the Gironde as Douce Blanche or Blanc Doux, and 45 per cent Sémillon. Sauvignon is said to be the heir of wild vines grown in France centuries ago; Sémillon, which ripens eight to ten days later, is a *cépage aimable*, easy to grow and resistant to diseases. The white wine, produced at best in small quantities, comes from grapes on 3.5 hectares of land on each side of the route d'Arcachon, an area which was slightly increased in 1950. The Sémillons are treated differently from the Sémillons of the Sauternes-producing area, known as Sémillons Verts. There the grapes are picked when they are over-ripe or nobly rotting. At Haut-Brion they are picked when ripe but not over-ripe. The Sauvignons require very careful attention although they grow with vigour: the small 'cylindrical' grapes easily rot. They are the first grapes to be ready for the harvest, which always starts with Haut-Brion *blanc*.

Wine samples produced at Haut-Brion solely from the Sémillons – and there are now many such saleable wines from New Zealand and Australia – are by themselves '*limpide, fin, onctueux et séveux*', difficult words to translate but words that speak for themselves. Wine from the Sauvignons is '*corsé, tres bouqueté, facilement liquoreux*'. These adjectives, too, scarcely require translation. Sauvignon carries with it natural aromas which blend well with more refined Sémillon.

The conditions of growth of each of the grapes grown at Haut-Brion can be related to the final product, and to anyone wishing to know how the different wines can be 'harmonized' to produce a great wine, red or white, Delmas recommends a walk round the vineyard as well as a tasting of the separate wines based on each of the constituents. It is possible to grasp during the walk not only how much of each variety of grapes is being produced but *why* particular grapes are planted in particular places. Slopes, sunshine, soil, drainage all count. The Cabernet Sauvignons, for example, prefer well-drained, well-exposed and well-ventilated gravelly land.

In Delmas's office and in the laboratory there are detailed maps of the '*parcelles*' of land, showing what is planted on each of them.

It is interesting, too, to walk around the vineyard at different times in the same year. The sights of late winter and spring, when vines are cut back and replaced and the land is ploughed and fertilized, are as revealing as the sights of summer, when the grapes are near maturity. A hundred days – or, less romantically, 110 or 90 – are often taken as the interval between first flowering and picking. Weeds are removed and chemicals are used with care to prevent disease. There is much to see. And even the sights of autumn after the vintage, when many healthy grapes are still left on the vines, are revealing too. The discarded grapes had not been deemed ripe enough or attractive enough to use at the time of the vintage. It is surprising how many of them there are. Controls on the quantity of the *grands crus* to be produced from each hectare of land are meticulous and stringent, although they vary from year to year.

Cabernet Sauvignon grapes, blue-black in colour and in other respects 'visually different from the two other varieties of grape', develop slowly and later in the spring than the rest, and thus they are less affected by frost: the grapes are small, '*plus longes que larges*', grow in close-set clusters and have thick skins. They ripen late and resist rot. Cabernet Franc vines grow faster and ripen earlier. They can support dryness, but they are more susceptible to frost and disease, particularly *coulure*, lack of pollination due to wet or cold weather – *couler* means to fall off – and they take longer to mature. The grapes are bigger than the Cabernet Sauvignons, and the shoots are a greyer brown. The Merlots, faster growing and more prolific than either of the Cabernets, are particularly susceptible to *coulure*, and their annual yield fluctuates more than that of the Cabernets: the vines bud early, the leaves are more round, and the grapes are small and subject to spring frosts. They mature quickly.

Soil and climate have to be related to each other in determining planting policy; as Delmas puts it, 'decisions relating to the planting of different proportions of *cépages* in a vineyard are essentially an empirical matter'. He knows through experience which *parcelle* of land is more appropriate for Cabernet or for Merlot. The latter resists dryness less well than Cabernet: hence Merlot is planted in '*les parcelles les plus fraîches*'. The root depth of the vines is in every case important, since the vines have to find moisture deep down when the ground is very dry. The Cabernet Franc does not like water: the best wines produced from it have been made in dry summers and autumns.

Recently, considerable attention has been paid to the role of water as a factor determining the quality of Haut-Brion and other *grands crus*. Given the soil, water can never accumulate around the roots of the vines. However heavy a rainstorm, they can never get sodden. Nor can the distinctive *goût de terroir* ever be lost. Gérard Seguin, a professor of agronomy at the Institute of Oenology in Bordeaux, an authority on the effects of water on the growth of vines, has discerned a permanence in the role of water in the *très grands terroirs* from generation to generation.

Delmas knows that the grapes that he blends at Haut-Brion for either the red wine or the white would not necessarily produce the same wine in a different place – even if the proportions were exactly the same. Soil and vine have to be in harmony with each other. The *terroir* 'imposes' on the vine its *structure* and its *régime*. It dominates the vine. Micro-climate goes with soil. Delmas insists, therefore, that Cabernet Sauvignon, treated in some circles as 'a universal panacea' in wine-making, is a 'mastodon of a vine': in hot climates it oxidizes quickly. 'To make a *grand vin*, Cabernet Sauvignon should ripen perfectly.'

The proportions of the different varieties of grapes grown in previous periods of history in the Graves, all varieties of *vitis vinifera*, have seldom been noted. Indeed, no grape names at all have been recorded in the Bordeaux area in the period before the sixteenth century, when La Bidure, in the patois of the Graves 'Vidure', was identified as such. It has been suggested that this vine is the same as the Latin *Biturica*, the common vine, mentioned by Pliny. Montesquieu explained the name *vidure* in terms of *vigne dure*. Cocks et Féret call it Cabernet Sauvignon. Thudichum referred to Vidure Sauvignon. Other names of vines grown in the Graves were Balouzat, Massoutet, Carmenère (or Cabernelle), a vigorous plant with grapes that were similar to Cabernet Sauvignon, and Malbec (Melbeck or Le Cot), which produces a soft, well-coloured wine, and which is still favoured and widely grown in the Médoc as well as in Bourg and Blaye. There were – and are – many local variations of naming and spelling. In places as near to Haut-Brion as Brède and Podensac, the Vidure of the Graves was called Carbonet. In Saint-Émilion, Cabernet Sauvignon is still called 'Gros Bouchet'. Merlot, sometimes called Bigney in the Graves, is of recent origin, although Alexis Lichine had a Merlot (Murelau) vine which he claimed was pre-1800.

It is surprising to note how few English writers on claret in the nineteenth century – through into the twentieth – ever bothered to relate the qualities of wine in the glass to 'the mix' of grapes in the vineyard. Cyrus Redding, for example, listed a few grapes without talking about how they were grown or blended; and unlike most Victorians, who loved lists, he was unhappy even about his own attempt at limited listing: 'to record the names and descriptions of all the varieties of the vine, many of which appear and disappear every considerable term of years,' he wrote, 'would be superfluous besides occupying space that should be spared.' Redding gave a better reason, however, when he noted that 'the denominations given' were often 'capricious and uncertain': 'the distinctions of the different varieties of the vine will be found obscure even in the descriptions given on the spot where they grew'. At that time, little effort had been made in the botanical gardens at the Luxembourg and at Montpellier to clear up the nomenclature, although Olivier de Serres had published his *description des cépages* in his *Théâtre d'Agriculture* (1610), and the *Intendant* Dupré de Saint-Maur had produced another *description des cépages de France* in Bordeaux on the eve of the Revolution, in 1783–6.

The detailed history remains difficult to clear up even now. Cabernet Sauvignon, which was to move from Bordeaux round the world, gained in importance in the Bordeaux area itself only in the eighteenth century. Merlot was widely used only in the second half of the nineteenth century, while Malbec (or Le Cot), once among the most widespread of vines in the Bordelais, declined in importance, as did Petit Verdot, which is said to have given 'backbone' to Malbec in the eighteenth century and which still does so in the Médoc. Wine-makers then and later had to make adjustments in their annual mix of grapes in their wines in the light of how the different grapes had fared that year while they were still on the vine. One reason that the production of both Malbec and Petit Verdot fell was disease. Petit Verdot was vulnerable to oidium: Malbec, which resisted oidium, was ravaged by phylloxera.

These two diseases of the vine had quite different origins and manifestations, although both came from the United States. Oidium, a fungus disease first observed in 1845, affected the surface wood and leaves of the vine as well as the grapes: the leaves curled up and the grapes split and dropped off. The result was powder. The disease was first discovered not in France, but in England, by a gardener called Tucker – in a greenhouse in Margate in 1845. Phylloxera, spread by the *phylloxera vastatrix*, the *puceron*, a minute if stout yellow plant aphid one millimetre in size, attacked the roots of the vine. It too was first identified in an English greenhouse – this time in Hammersmith, in 1863 – and the diseased vine leaf covered with minute gall-like excrescences that was found there was diligently studied far from the scene of its terrifying French ravages by an Oxford professor, I. O. Westwood.

Called at first 'an unknown disease', when it struck two slopes of the Bas-Rhône in 1863, it had already hit the Midi before it reached the Bordeaux area in 1869, and by the end of the following decade it had affected vineyards almost everywhere, including Haut-Brion, where Larrieu, who used skilled grafters and sustained his young vines with iron wires, had already replaced many vines affected by oidium. It must have been a tragedy for him when a third disease of the vine, the mildew fungus, *peronospora viticola*, described by one proprietor as 'a disaster more terrible than phylloxera', affected the replanted vines during the 1880s. Nonetheless, 'dewy mildew' was a disease that could be treated by chemistry – spraying the vines with copper sulphate (*bouillie bordelaise*). The success of this treatment – and it was treatment, not cure – had other useful consequences for vinification: it enabled grapes to ripen earlier.

The regrafting of vines on American vine stock, *vitis riparia* and *vitis rupestris*, after the phylloxera outbreak of the late nineteenth century, obviously changed the pattern in the Bordeaux region, and several older vine varieties were totally eliminated as a result – but as late as 1951 Warner Allen had little to say on the subject of vines in his *Natural Red Wines*. He was content to generalize on one page – and it was a sensible generalization – that 'if the great vineyards of the Médoc were deprived of Cabernet Sauvignon and planted with inferior vines, the glory of their wines would have departed'. Similarly, he went on, if the Cabernet Sauvignon grapes were torn away from 'the soil that they love' and 'Pauillac, Pessac and the other communes of the Gironde' – and here he was to be proved wrong in the long run – they would 'offer nothing better than an average beverage wine'. Given the subsequent history of Cabernet Sauvignon grapes outside France, it is interesting – if not surprising – to note that there was a far fuller reference to grapes in the one chapter of Warner Allen's book that was written not by him, but by an American, the very perceptive critic Frank Schoonmaker. In an informative, but inevitably dated, chapter devoted to 'the Red Wines of America' Schoonmaker observed that 'a California Cabernet is a Médoc in another octave, played if you like to different instruments, and less well played, but the basic theme is there'.

French writers had more to say than English writers on the subject of grape varieties in the nineteenth century. Thus, in 1855 the Marquis Armand d'Armailhacq in his survey *De la Culture des Vignes, la vinification et les vins dans le Médoc*, published in the same year as the quasi-official classification of Bordeaux wines, noted that of the main varieties of grape then being cultivated in the area, which for him included the Graves, were 'Cabernet Sauvignon, already much esteemed by *régisseurs*', the cultivation of which was increasing, and Merlau (*sic*), described as a very recent arrival. D'Armailhacq himself was one of the pioneer growers of Cabernet Sauvignon grapes at Mouton d'Armailhacq, which in 1933 was to become Mouton-Baronne-Philippe but is now Château Armailhacq again. Armailhacq won a medal of honour for his book from the Agricultural Society of the Gironde.

What Armailhacq then called Gros Cabernet (or Carmenet or Carminière) was the ancestor of Cabernet Franc; and other grapes that Armailhacq mentioned include Malbec, which he called 'a prolific grape, but one not likely to add to the quality of the wine', and Verdot, then a common grape, also 'much esteemed by *régisseurs*', particularly in the *palus* area. It was said to blend well with Cabernet. There were three varieties: the Petit Verdot, the Gros Verdot and the Verdot Colon.

In the year when Armailhacq was writing, a year spotlit by Penning-Rowsell, the Latour vineyard consisted of 56.8 per cent Cabernet Sauvignon, 22.7 per cent Cabernet Sauvignon and Cabernet Franc, 5 per cent Merlot, 13.9 per cent Malbec, 'a tiny amount of Verdot', and 'a relic of Syrah', a *vigne de soleil* that it was claimed took its name from the ancient city of Shiraz in Persia. It was planted on the banks of the Rhône in Roman times.

In 1883, when phylloxera had already struck the Bordeaux vineyards, Cocks et Féret listed in what was called 'order of merit' eight grapes then used in making the wines of the Graves: Cabernet Sauvignon, also called Vidure Sauvignon; Petite Vidure or Petit Cabernet, Cabernet Franc; Grosse Vidure (or Gros Verdot); Petit Verdot; Carmenère or Carbouet; Merlot; Malbec; and, last in the list, Petit Sirrah, which thrived, they said, in 'the dried and well exposed Graves'. It is interesting to note that Malbec had by then slipped almost to the bottom and that the notion of combining Cabernets and Syrah had been virtually dropped. (It has now been revived successfully in Australia.) The most extensively used of the grapes for making white wine were the Sauvignons, Sémillon, Muscadelle and Blanc Verdot, and the first two still are. Sémillon had a higher yield. Muscadelle is still widely grown also.

In 1947 Germain Lafforgue noted that in recent years there had been a marked decline in the production of grapes that needed ideal weather conditions and matured slowly, and this, he claimed, was the cause of the virtual disappearance of Petit Verdot and Gros Verdot wines. There do not seem to have been any *parcelles* of Petit Verdot either at Haut-Brion or La Mission in the nineteenth century. In Delmas's opinion Gros Verdot produces in abundant quantities a mediocre wine; Petit Verdot, however, is grown at Margaux, Lafite and Latour.

In 1989 Delmas produced a beautifully illustrated booklet, *La Collection Ampélographique du Château Haut-Brion*, which describes carefully a fascinating collection of old vines now grown at Haut-Brion in a long garden at the back of the château and beside the vineyard devoted to Cabernet Sauvignon, Cabernet Franc and Merlot. It was a *jardin potager* with fruit trees at the side separated from the vineyard by a high stone wall. The purpose behind the collection, which is the oenological equivalent of a well-stocked library, is to throw light on the past history of particular vines and why they either disappeared or were grown only outside Haut-Brion. There is an element of conservation also as well as of recall. There are eight square plots, each growing ten *cépages*, some of which were once constituents of Haut-Brion in the seventeenth, eighteenth and nineteenth centuries. One vigorous vine which has almost disappeared, La Carmenère or Cabernalle, finds its place alongside Cabernet Sauvignon, Merlot and Malbec or Cot, which under one of its many names, Noir de Pessac, was a constituent of

Haut-Brion when it first established its reputation. There is also a Cabernet Malbec, the product of late nineteenth-century crossing.

Some vines in the collection have never been employed at Haut-Brion or, indeed, in the Bordelais. They include the Riesling, the Pinot Noir, Gewurztraminer, Le Tannat, which is the *cépage traditionnel* of Madiran, and Le Duras, first mentioned in 1484 and named after the hardness of its wood as was Le Durif. One famous vine, Le Chenin Blanc, was also grown in the Middle Ages, and in the twentieth century it has made its way around the world. The geography of migration springs to life in the *Collection Ampélographique*, which finds a place for Petit Verdot, which made its way from the Médoc to Chile, Zinfandel, which made its way from Italy to California, and Le Jurançon Noir which made its way to Uruguay under the name of the man who imported it, Vidiella. The most romantic names include La Folle Blanche and Le Colombard.

Delmas deals frankly with the merits and demerits of each vine, appreciating fully how vines which flourish elsewhere can find there the same harmony with the soil that Cabernet Sauvignon, Cabernet Franc and Merlot find at Haut-Brion. There is even a vine, Le Sensit, that likes the sandy soil of the Landes. Yet the merits of the three constituents of Haut-Brion become fully apparent only when grapes produced from different *parcelles* in the vineyard are vinified in turn. Each proto-wine thus produced has its own particular characteristics which are taken into account when the different varieties are subsequently blended together. I have tasted them separately myself at Haut-Brion in different years, comparing one year with another as Delmas does professionally. Of the different constituents of the 1988s, for example, he wrote that the Merlots surprised by their '*intensité phénolique*': 'the perfumes are sharp and fruity and develop quickly'. The tannin in the Cabernets was '*un peu agressif*', but the aggression, he believed, would soon go. Left to themselves, Cabernet Sauvignon grapes usually produce a brilliantly coloured wine, often concentrated, which is strong in tannin, and the wine takes time to assert itself. It can reveal both *finesse* and *souplesse*, and as part of a blend it gives depth to the final product. The grapes of Cabernet Franc produce a softer and more aromatic wine that is less brilliantly coloured. The Merlot grapes produce a velvety wine that is less tannic but higher in alcohol content than the two Cabernets. It matures fast but it can last.

The wines that are blended with great art at Haut-Brion have become 'varietals' in many wine-producing countries in the late twentieth century, sold simply as Cabernet Sauvignon or Merlot; in January 1990 *Gourmet's Wine Journal* described a Californian party where a panel, presented with single varietals that included Cabernet Sauvignon, Merlot, Cabernet Franc and Petit Verdot, all produced in a local vineyard, set about blending them. As at Haut-Brion, the Cabernet Franc was found to be aromatic enough to provide 'a bite to perk up the palate'. The Merlot was more 'fruity and compact' than it is in France. The Petit Verdot, not now used in Haut-Brion, proved 'the heavy of the team'.

The panel was reassured to be told by experts that there is no 'right' formula to follow in blending the varieties. In 1988 Delmas proportions were 33 per cent Merlot, 8 per cent Cabernet Franc and 59 per cent Cabernet Sauvignon. The comparable proportions for 1989 were 40, 9 and 51.

Changing the balance is an annual event, but changing the balance of a vineyard is a long-term venture. In recent years there have been changes which are as important in long-term perspective as the changes of the nineteenth century induced by phylloxera. What was once 'the laborious cultivation of the vine', as Warner Allen called it in 1951, has now become a meticulously researched activity. Paradoxically it was in large measure due to the ravages of phylloxera that science, in the first instance chemical science, and later biological science, has been applied to the vineyard. For the first change, a change in attitudes as well as techniques, Louis Pasteur, born in 1822, was largely responsible, although long before him Chaptal with his sense of mission had pointed the way. A great chemist, who studied bacteria and fermentation, Pasteur was interested in all forms of life and he was an obvious choice for membership of a Paris Commission, set up to examine phylloxera (he was later to become its chairman), which in 1873 offered a large prize of 300,000 francs for a remedy, and which received no fewer than 696 suggested remedies other than replanting, some ingenious, some fatuous, some stupid.

In his inaugural professorial lecture at Lille in 1854 Pasteur had taken the potato as his example – in the knowledge that potato diseases had changed the course of history – but in 1866 he had published his *Études sur le vin; ses maladies; les causes qui les provoquent*, which was printed at the expense of the state. A year before that he had introduced 'pasteurization', the process which has transmitted his own name into history. (Another process, chaptalization, the adding of sugar to wine, was named after Chaptal.) The results of Pasteur's studies of wine were significant even outside the wine industry, as René Dubois has shown in his book *Pasteur and Modern Science* (1963). Thus, tartaric acid was the first chemical associated with wine to be manufactured commercially. In Bordeaux Pasteur is known as one of the founders of *oenologie*, which after 1880 was developed as a science inside the university by his pupil, Ulysse Gayon. In viticulture, however, as distinct from wine-making, the application of science came later, with Haut-Brion acting as a pioneer. It was through the systematic planting of new vines that Haut-Brion triumphed over phylloxera and moved into the twentieth century, but it is through new techniques, developed through the biological sciences, that Haut-Brion under Jean-Bernard Delmas is moving into the twenty-first century. His father, Georges Delmas, who is said to have had a green thumb, had improved all the traditional practices of viticulture without radically transforming them. Vines were carefully selected; old vines were removed (forty years was then their limit); soil was allowed to rest; young vines were planted out separately before being placed in *règes* (rows) in favoured spots with roses at the end of each row; pruning 'in the two-armed double *guyot* way' was carefully supervised; the vines were allowed to grow rather taller than the vines in the Médoc; and the white grapes, like the red grapes, were picked when they were deemed just right. Their picking came first, as it still does.

Decisions relating to all these aspects of viticulture required a long-term perspective and a willingness to forgo short-term advantages. It was only after soil used for Sauvignon and Sémillon grapes had been allowed to rest for six years before planting started again that in 1945 a superlative white Haut-Brion was produced. Quantity of grapes was never itself an objective. Quality was crucial. According to Alexis Lichine, Georges Delmas told him that the quality of the 1945 and 'an even more sensational wine' of 1948 was 'decisive proof that the soil is what makes the wine'.

Georges Delmas knew well – with little scientific apparatus to assist him – how to judge when the grapes were ready. There was nothing experimental at that time about his approach. It was thoroughly practical. He appreciated that if immature grapes are added to the press, the wine that is produced will not hold up, and that if over-ripe grapes are added the wine will be too sweet. These were among the essentials of the old arts of wine-making. Delmas had to determine for himself when there was a relative stability in the grapes – no increase in sugar, no diminution in acidity – almost as precisely as though he had had instruments at his disposal. Skill in the art was described by the Abbé Dubaquié as 'an extra sense, purely animal'. Refractometers, however, which enabled the ripeness of grapes to be measured, qualified this judgement.

The exact point of maturity is now determined with the help of science – by testing regular samples of grapes that are sent to the laboratory in the days before the harvest. Jean-Bernard Delmas, therefore, is less at the mercy of nature than his father, and he can order grapes to be picked much riper than they had been in his father's time. The period of time after flowering has risen by as much as ten days during the last twenty years, and the resultant wines are less 'acidic' than they used to be. Both men have profited, however, as their predecessors had done, from the fact that at Haut-Brion, with no human intervention, grapes are said to mature rather earlier than at other vineyards, providing an extra measure of strength and 'body'.

The radical scientific change, cloning of vines, began at Haut-Brion in 1974, when ten clones of Cabernet Sauvignon and eleven of Cabernet Franc, acquired from INRA, the National Institute of Agricultural Research, were planted in a plot of two hectares on the *parcelle* called Bahans. The object was to discover which individual clones within the different varieties had the greatest potential in wine-making in terms of alcoholic strength and colour intensity and 'phenolic content'. Later, the range of criteria was widened. Delmas and INRA communicated regularly about the results. Careful notes were taken at each stage.

The word 'clone' first figured as a noun only in the 1972 Supplement to the great *Oxford Dictionary*, although apparently it had been used as early as 1905. As a verb, meaning 'to propagate or cause to reproduce so as to form a clone', it goes back only to 1959, by a coincidence a great year in the vineyards. Clones are genetically identical to the original vine that has served to produce them, a point well known to readers of science fiction novels and viewers of science fiction films. Human clones are controversial, but human beings have already benefited from the application of genetics to agriculture and horticulture. In the late twentieth century the advantages of cloning selected plants that are not grown from seeds, as plants like sunflowers or radishes are, but from cuttings, have been seized upon in many different branches of botany. The subjects range from tea to roses. Where, as in the case of vines – or roses – there are different varieties, there are obvious advantages in moving from random selection. Different plants of the same variety – Cabernet Sauvignon or Merlot for example – have different potential, potential that can be realized through improvement. Some plants are far more productive than others even though they may look the same. There are variations in their patterns of growth too: some push out in a vertical rather than a horizontal direction.

The idea of selecting 'the best' vines and seeking to clone them is logical. Indeed, before 'clonal selection' became possible, *viticulteurs*, like Georges Delmas, already practised selection by observation in the vineyards, marking the best of their vines and, after watching them for four or five years, using them as stock. If the plants had been of a kind that would have been planted from seed, this stock would have been thought of as 'seed corn'. *Sélection clonale*, a sophisticated process, made possible by remarkable advances in the life sciences, demands time to be carried through. It is only after years that the progress of cloned vines can be fully assessed. They then began to talk for themselves. The purpose of clonal selection goes much further than protection against viral or other diseases. The object is to promote the health of the vine, to develop its full potential.

Some people who thought themselves knowledgeable smiled, Delmas recalls, when he began his researches into cloning, but as these proceeded, they smiled less. It was exciting for him when the first grapes from certified INRA clones were picked in 1976 and 1977, and it was then that he reached his first conclusions about which vines were 'specially linked to the personality of our vineyard'. Delmas also ordered clones from other sources, private enterprises, *pépiniéristes*, and in 1976, a nursery of 'mother vines' from a variety of sources was established, and the offspring – note the family analogy – were planted elsewhere at Haut-Brion in different, carefully chosen *parcelles*, one of which was called Seymour.

Details were tagged of clonal development, and two years later sixty carefully selected Cabernets and five Merlots were planted in a 'reference plot', an area of just over one acre, called Le Jardin. Later, five or ten vines of each clone were established, usually on 420A rootstock; and at the time of the harvest five vines of each clone were picked, weighed and assessed for sugar, acidity and quality. Now there are no fewer than 360 clones.

Analysis of results has led inexorably to the laboratory. Individual macerations and micro-vinifications are the main part of the testing process, with micro-vinification providing an experimental link at Haut-Brion between viticulture and vinification. There is a link, too, between the life sciences and chemistry, for in maceration the skins of grapes from the clones that have been selected are separated from the pulp, before being cleaned, dried and macerated in a solution of alcohol for three weeks so that the tannins and anthocyanes in the skins can be measured. Meanwhile, in parallel, juice from a number of different clones is vinified separately. The wine is then prepared in micro-vinifications from grapes stalked and crushed by hand and is analysed and tested after being racked twice. The testing involves the search for clonal correlations between clone stock and 'phenolic potentiality' ('*potentialité phénolique*'), the likely power of tannin in the wine. Other criteria include the 'aromatic richness, complexity and particularity' of the micro-wines produced. Inexorably the computer has come into play as a precise agent of experiment.

Delmas recognizes that testing processes will necessarily be protracted and that hasty conclusions should not be drawn. Cloning is no more a 'miraculous' process than fermentation. There remains an art in both. It is just as essential to avoid standardization of vines and to preserve their 'individuality' and 'variability' as it is to avoid standardization of the wines of Haut-Brion. The purpose is always to guard carefully 'the personality of the wine'. Evidence collected so far suggests that a mixture of wines derived from several clones is superior to any wine derived from a single clone contributing to the mixture.

Within the vineyard some clones which at first sight seem to be less good than others cannot be immediately ignored or dismissed. Nor is anything done to iron out differences in ripening time for, as Delmas puts it, 'we do not necessarily want all our vines to ripen at the same time'. Indeed, varieties ripening at different times reduce the risks of the effects of bad weather on wine production. There are other risks to guard against. A 'universal clone' would be susceptible to 'new diseases', however resistant it might be to old ones.

There is a further compelling consideration. As far as Haut-Brion is concerned, the quantity of grapes on a vine is – and always has been – far less important than the quality of the wine that can be produced from it. As it has turned out, the best clones in respect of final quality have proved to be those which give, if not the greatest production, at least a satisfactory level of medium production.

While much in clone research is measurable, Delmas clearly realizes that there is much that is not. The multiple criteria that can be applied in judging clones – range of alcohol content, for example, or within the vineyard susceptibility to rot – do not always lend themselves to precise results. There remains a part even of the theory of cloning that is 'subjective'. It is interesting, Delmas believes, to keep some clones that do not seem to be the best. There is also doubt about which really are the best.

Fortunately there is no set period for experiment on clones, and work goes on continuously – and enthusiastically. By the year 2000, however, all the property at Haut-Brion will be planted with selected clones.

5
From Vines to Wines

Is there not something fanciful and poetic in the
notion of this change [from vines to wine] taking
place mysteriously in the darkness, when the doors
are locked and barred?

Angus Reach, 1852

The making of Haut-Brion follows the same steps year by year,
whatever the arts and techniques applied in the process (and these
are still changing): assembling the grapes; pressing; malolactic fermentation; blending together; racking; fixing and bottling. Initially
the grapes are taken as quickly as possible to the vat room, the
cuverie – the Merlots come first – and all the leaves inadvertently
gathered with the fruit are eliminated on large stainless steel trays,
mounted on sorting tables (*tables de tri*). So also are any grapes that
have split or any grapes that have stayed green. Only the ripe intact
fruit remains. The process of sorting is called *triage*. It is important
not to damage the grapes in this process or to leave them too long
in contact with the air. Initial *triage* in the vineyard itself has
become increasingly common as new machinery has been introduced and transport improved.

Once in the *chai*, an *égrappoir*, a finely regulated machine, gentle
in its mode of operation, removes the stalks (*la rafle*) and leaves
only the pulp of the fruit along with skin and seeds. These then
are pumped into the stainless steel vats (*cuves*), the grapes being
submerged in their own juice, known as the must. In the slow
maceration 'all the feel of the summer' is translated into wine. In
the past, maceration and fermentation did not necessarily begin
immediately after the grapes had been gathered. Now they do.

Fermentation, the transformation of the fruit of the vine into wine, can be described in chemical terms. Through the action of natural yeasts, grape sugar is converted into alcohol; and must, the fermenting juice, which remains for a crucial time in contact with skins and pips, is converted into wine, wine with colour and body. In the process carbon dioxide gas is given off: '*le vin bout*'. In Warner Allen's language, not dissimilar to that of Angus Reach, 'a countless host of microscopic organisms, the yeasts or ferments of alcoholic fermentation', preside over 'the conversion of the sugar contained in the grape juice, into alcohol, carbonic acid, gas and infinitesimal quantities of glycerine and other substances, imponderables of vital importance in their influence on the wine's bouquet and aroma'. Allen added that 'perhaps the strangest part of the miracle is that the mysterious agents responsible for this transmutation are not to be found inside the grape. They are as it were visitors, who come we know not whence or how to the ripened grapes and settle on the outside of their skins lurking in invisible millions amidst the bloom of the fruit.' There was as much religion as science – or alchemy – in such talk, although Warner Allen clearly understood the basic science as it was then presented. Oak for him was 'the wood divinely appointed for wine', and the oak vat was not a 'mere neutral receptacle'. Delmas's approach by contrast is genuinely scientific. Fermentation is no longer thought of as a completely mysterious process which either worked or did not work. Yet the role of the natural yeasts is of fundamental importance.

Once grapes have been transferred to the vat, the processes of fermentation are regulated by thermostatic control of temperature. That was one reason for introducing stainless steel. If temperature rises too high – the danger point is variable – the fermentation may 'stick' and the wine become volatile, even vinegary. If too low, fermentation may cease and have to be restarted. Steel vats can be controlled more easily than wooden vats. Latour realized this – after Haut-Brion – in 1964. Stainless steel has other advantages. It is not only possible to cool steel vats more easily. Like tiled vats set in concrete, they can be washed more easily than vats made out of oak. Labour too is saved. The metal itself, however, is important. Its use facilitates the introduction of necessary accessories, particularly a cooling system which runs cold water over the outside of the vats.

Bordeaux possesses an almost ideal climate for natural fermentation – neither too hot nor too cold – but there are and have been years, already noted, when the climate was no more propitious than the soil. Nor were there accurate weather forecasts. Experiment started, therefore, in difficult years before thermostats (or weather charts) were brought into use. As long ago as 1926, following a relatively poor harvest at Haut-Brion when the summer had been 'too hot', Georges Delmas introduced rapid fermentation in order to retain the freshness of the grapes. At a time when some châteaux were leaving grapes to ferment in the vats for up to three weeks, Haut-Brion was the first to seek to complete the process in five to fifteen days. Other châteaux followed the example of Delmas, as many of them were to follow that of his son in employing stainless steel vats.

In some years the shortness of the fermentation period at Haut-Brion broke records. Thus, in 1953, a very good year with a 'fabulous August', when the grapes seemed to begin fermenting in the pickers' baskets, the juice and the skin and pulp were left in contact for only seven days. The result was an outstanding vintage in a year when the heat had been so intense that some critics were fearing 'scalded wines'. Delmas favours automatically controlled high temperatures in the fermentation process: in his opinion, it assists the extraction both of flavour and of colour from the grape pulp.

Neither Delmas father nor Delmas son has ever worked according to formula. Yet each has been assisted by increasingly reliable scientific information at each stage of wine-making. The information covers the treatment of the solid matter, consisting largely of remnants of grapes and skins,'*le chapeau de marc*', 'murk' which rises to the top of the vat during the course of fermentation. This gets hotter than the liquid below. Thermostatic control and automatic cooling of the stainless steel vats prevent it from getting too hard and dry. There are electric pumps on each vat that at the turn of a switch pump the wine up, over and through the *chapeau*.

Information about what is happening in the vats is carefully charted at each stage, and as soon as the new wine is deemed to have extracted sufficient flavour and colour the vat is 'run off'. The new word 'informatics' is particularly relevant to control of the wine-making process. The first computer installed at Haut-Brion in 1981 did not deal in the relevant data: an IBM 36, installed in 1988, does. There is now a system. Analysis is as sophisticated as tasting. There is no formula, however, for determining the answers to a number of crucial questions, for example how much *vin de presse* drawn out of the *chapeau* should be added after the first fermentation. *Vin de presse* is a concentrated extract, heavy in tannin, sometimes produced from as many as three pressings. Delmas, who compares it to a perfume, decides by *tâtonnement*, 'feeling his way', if any or how much of it to add to the new wine. This is a delicate task in which his main concern is not the state of the wine as it is but the prospect of the wine as he believes it will – or might – become.

Peynaud has written that 'wine-making, which is an operation designed to transform grapes into wine is a simple thing to discuss, but is infinitely more difficult to realize'. If the miracle may have gone, the art remains. The chemistry too has itself become more complex as the processes of fermentation have been carefully scrutinized. Larger and larger numbers of chemical ingredients have been identified as being present. In that sense Allen was right.

One other chemical aspect of fermentation has been spotlit since 1955 by chromatography: not the changing of grape sugars into alcohol, but the changing of malic acid in the fermented wine into lactic acid. This malolactic fermentation leads to a reduction in tartness and is usually described as a 'second fermentation'. In some respects this continuing process, the timing and duration of which once were difficult to determine, remains mysterious to the layman, but complex as it undoubtedly is, it has been studied systematically at Haut-Brion since 1964. The consistency and 'stability' of wine can be guaranteed. 'Second fermentation' begins in the stainless steel vats, thereby overlapping with the period of 'first fermentation', and for this reason it may be desirable to keep the fermented wine in the vat for a longer period than otherwise would be deemed necessary. Haut-Brion did this: La Mission did not. The process takes place mainly, however, not in the vats but in the casks of new oak into which the blended wine is transferred before the *assemblage*.

The blending together (*assemblage*) of the different constituent wines already produced in the different casks, some of which may taste better than others, remains unequivocally an art, as the California experiment demonstrated. Samples are tasted, and retasted, and no quick decisions are taken. The objective is to discover the right blend of wines for that particular year, and it is a blend that has to be not only harmonious but consistent. There is no standardization. Given this approach, the final proportions of the different constituents obviously do not necessarily reflect the percentage of the grapes planted in the vineyard. Nor do they determine future percentages. The wine from one *cuve* of, say, Cabernet Sauvignon will not necessarily be exactly like wine from another *cuve*: as has been explained, wine from different *parcelles* or different clones will have different qualities. It is necessary, therefore, in the cause of harmony to complement the products of different *cuves* as well as to reject some of them.

It is in the casks, 225-litre *barriques bordelaises*, that a 'slow interchange' begins between wood and wine, an interchange which has always fascinated wine-makers and wine-lovers alike. The use of new oak – and only new oak is used for maturing wine at Haut-Brion – adds tannin to the wine, but leads to a greater loss of wine through evaporation. It might be more hazardous if the wine were less powerful than Haut-Brion. No fewer than 400 new *barriques* are now bought each year.

The term *élevage*, upbringing, applied to the development of the wine in the *chai* is appropriate, for *élevage* is a long process lasting two years or more, with the wine growing up as it grows older in new oak casks that not only diffuse tannin, but dispel impurities and develop fragrance. The casks have become extremely expensive, but quality is of major importance. During the first year the casks remain open: they have a bung-hole topped by a loose-fitting glass stopper from which gas can be released. At the beginning of the second year, the cask is hermetically sealed: it is given a corked bung and turned on its side. Since absorption of the wine by the wood is constant, a partial vacuum is produced which eases the transfer of oxygen through the pores of the wood. Gentle and very slight oxidation helps in the ageing and improvement of the wine. Words like *élevage* point to care; and care in upbringing is what is needed as the wine develops in the *barrique*.

Tradition still holds, and in an operation known as *collage* beaten whites of egg – four or five per cask – are still employed, as they were in the past, to 'fine' the wine before it is bottled. Meanwhile, any solid or suspended particles that remain or appear in the wine are removed three or four times a year by racking (*soutirage*), drawing off wine from one *fût* to another. These ensure the clarity of the final product. *Ouillage*, regular topping up of the casks as often as two or three times a week in the initial stages, ensures that there will be no harmful contact of immature wine with air. It helps to compensate for expensive losses of wine through evaporation and absorption, losses that can amount to around 15 per cent in two years.

There is less improvisation now – and more system – in all stages of wine-making than there was in the past, but, again as at other points in the process, there is still no formula which determines how long wine should be stored in *barriques* or when the wine has to be transferred from *barriques* to bottle. Some vintages require longer in wood than others: some gain by early bottling. There has been a tendency at Haut-Brion, as elsewhere, to keep wine for a shorter time *en barriques*.

Bottling and corking are carried out at the château in processes that have since 1962 been increasingly automated. A conveyor-belt system was introduced in 1982, and no fewer than 2,500 bottles pass over it in an hour. It now seems strange that in 1923 when château bottling began to be developed as a regular process by Gibert, as it was by Baron Philippe de Rothschild at Mouton, there were many sceptics in Bordeaux. There were also active enemies among the *courtiers*. Now such bottling is taken for granted. The shape of the Haut-Brion bottle is distinctive, as is the label. It carries with it an image of its own.

Before 1900 château-bottled Haut-Brion was sold without any château label on the bottle, although the corks were branded with the name of the château and the date of the vintage. There was also a seal. The first vintage to be clearly labelled as well as bottled at the château was the 1900, picked out as 'an exceptional year' ('*une année exceptionnelle*') in the guides to wine. Yet not until 1904 was the name of the proprietor, Héritier Larrieu Propriétaires, printed on the front of the label. A sketch of the château now figures prominently on the label itself. The traditional shape of the bottle was restored by Clarence Dillon. The word 'traditional' is of course somewhat misleading. Wine began to be bottled only in the eighteenth century. Glass played the key role. In 1723 Peter Mitchell of Dublin founded a glass works in Bordeaux, and by 1790 there were five such works producing 400,000 bottles a year. The factories were powered by English coal, evidence that the *révolution des boissons* and the industrial revolution had converged.

There had been a stone age in bottles before glass came into use, and an age of seals and glass globes before corks – and the cork-screw. Bottles began to take on their modern shapes only in the late eighteenth century. Just after the century ended, one London patent-holder sold as many as 10,000 corkscrews in a year. Such by-products of wine-making and drinking are now collectors' items, as indeed are wine labels; and as the 'culture of wine' continues to change they will survive as representatives of the past even when most of the great wines have disappeared. Fortunately, the new *chai* at Haut-Brion enables these to be stored in larger quantities than was possible in the past. Very few old Haut-Brions have survived at Haut-Brion itself.

6

The Wine

With a glass of Haut-Brion before him, whoever does not tremble with happiness will never understand anything of the wines of Bordeaux.

Florence Mothe, *Graves de Bordeaux*, 1985

Maurice Healy was so attached to Haut-Brion that he wrote that he suspected that London learned to judge all claret by the standard of Haut-Brion. This, he explained, was why English claret was esteemed the best in the world. It was a bold assertion, which sidetracked all references to France and to the United States, where Haut-Brion was placed officially and unofficially in the top group of all listings of the wines of Bordeaux, a phrase more often used there than 'claret'. Yet it reflected correctly the special place of Britain in the history of the reputation of Haut-Brion, and it rightly directed attention to comparison between Haut-Brion and other wines of Bordeaux, including the *grands crus* of the Médoc.

The wines of the Graves were well known, as has been explained, before the wines of the Médoc were produced in significant quantities. In a list of 1645, set out in a *Mémoire des pratiques de commerce des étrangers dans la ville de Bordeaux*, Graves and Médoc were at the head; and a half-century later, when the *révolution des boissons* was already through its first phases, the *intendant* at Bordeaux picked out Graves in 1698 for their quality and high price. They were picked out again in the years before and after the social and political revolution in France at the end of the eighteenth century, when there was a new emphasis not only on the differences between the different wines of the Graves – and there were many of them, red and white – and the wines of the Médoc, but on the differences between the various Graves themselves. It was on the eve of the Revolution that the Abbé Baurein, in his book *Variétés bordelaises*, turned one by one to the differences between the wines of different parishes and of different vineyards in the Bordeaux region.

Fifteen years later, Jean-André Chaptal, the Abbé Rosier and 'Citizens Parmentier and Dussieux' in their impressive *Traité Théorique et Pratique sur la Culture de la Vigne* re-emphasized how the same climate, the same categories of grapes, even the same kind of soil, often furnished wines with very different characteristics. Chaptal was a chemist who became Minister of the Interior under Napoleon. There is an encyclopaedic quality in his work. Chaptal and his collaborators described the Haut-Brion of that period as '*vif, brillant et léger*' ('lively, brilliant and light'). For them it did not then possess the '*bouquet*' of the wines of the Médoc, but – and to them it was the greatest of compliments – it was 'of all the wines of Bordeaux that which was nearest to the best of the wines of Burgundy'. In similar vein too, André Jullien, writing a generation after Chaptal, claimed in his survey of the wines of the Gironde that Haut-Brion had 'more substance' ('*étoffe de corps*') and more spirit than the smoother Lafite, Latour and Margaux. It also possessed '*une sève*', a key word in the wine vocabulary that can mean 'stamina' or 'pith'. It was 'richer in aromas'. A writer in the ninth volume of the fifteen-volume *Grand Dictionnaire Universel* of 1868 agreed. None of these works had much to say about alcoholic content. Burgundy, Napoleon's favourite, was deemed to be stronger. The *Dictionnaire* noted, however, that Haut-Brion needed to be kept in the barrel for six or seven years.

In the nineteenth century an already knowledgeable English wine merchant, T. G. Shaw, sensitive to differences in price between clarets, set out to discover more about the differences in constitution between Graves and the wines of the Médoc, not only by drinking them – or by consulting maps – but by looking back into remote history. In his quest he consulted Professor Francisque Michel, an authority on books as well as on wines, who proved to be a learned *magister* rather than a casual informant; and in the stately Victorian correspondence that ensued Michel explained to Shaw just how young the Médoc district was when compared with the district of the Graves and just how distinctive were its wines. Shaw himself was still a learner, for the differences had not been fully explained by Henderson in his pioneering *History of Ancient and Modern Wines* published in 1825.

Although Henderson had ranged widely in time and place from the ancient Greeks to the modern Dutch at the Cape of Good Hope and from France to Persia and to Chile, it was left to one of his reviewers, writing in the *Quarterly Review*, to tell his readers that they should be discriminating in what they drank even if it was in a Bordeaux bottle:

> Let no man in England, while he sips his CLARET dream that he is drinking Château Margaux or Haut-Brion. The real quantity of the finer growths is so inconsiderable that they could not by any possibility supply a tenth part of that which usurps their name . . . A bottle of the best wine is a rarity, for which even at Bourdeaux [*sic*] the best *vivant* is content to pay six or seven francs.

Back to price, therefore, but through price to quality, always a necessary move in discussing a *grand cru*. During the early stages of the *révolution des boissons* the quest had been for quality. In its later stages, between then and the time of Chaptal, proprietors and *régisseurs* had taken care to establish a particular set of qualities which would be associated with a particular wine and which would define its 'character'. Shaw, Henderson and other reviewers confronted the results.

From 1855 onwards, however, reviewers had at their disposal a semi-official classification of 'the wines of Bordeaux' in which Haut-Brion was singled out. The date, the year of a great *exposition universelle* in Paris, was not coincidental. In the nineteenth century there was a passion for classifying everything, and it was given full scope at each of a remarkable sequence of great exhibitions, many of them international exhibitions of things of every kind, including wine. On the occasion of the Paris Exhibition the commissioners who planned it, spurred by the Emperor Napoleon III, insisted that if French wines were to be exhibited the names of the different *crus* and of their proprietors should be indicated in an up-to-date table of merit. The Bordeaux Chamber of Commerce, nervous about local reactions, including those of its own members, was at first reluctant to comply, arguing that there was already an unofficial classification, a traditional hierarchy, established by *courtiers*, largely on the basis of recorded prices, that it would be unwise to disturb.

Three decades earlier, in 1823, the *régisseur* of Latour had written that it was 'the trade itself which fixed the prices and formed the different classes of wines of the Médoc a very long time ago', and in the same decade a Bordeaux *courtier*, Paguierre, produced his own *Classification et description des vins de Bordeaux*, published not in French but in English and not in Bordeaux but in Edinburgh. At that time Haut-Brion commanded around the same price as the *grands crus* of the Médoc – 1,500 to 2,400 francs per *tonneau* – as against the 700 to 1,200 francs for *bons bourgeois* clarets.

The Bordeaux Chamber knew, too, that for as long as could be remembered – before and after the abolition of feudal privileges – landlords themselves had been anxious to supervise cultivation and to safeguard quality on the properties that they rented. It was in their interests to do so. As Henri Binand was to write in the twentieth century after visiting Haut-Brion, the only things that really mattered in classification of wines were the jockey on the one hand and the owner on the other. Nonetheless, and recognizing that the export market remained of prime importance to the economy of Bordeaux, the Chamber collected reports, including newspaper reports, from London and from the United States and went on to test local opinion. It noted too that Burgundy had already agreed to present a selection of wines in Paris; and this must have provided a strong inducement for it to circularize wine producers about the exhibition and their possible role in it.

It was inevitable that when, in 1855, the Bordeaux Chamber of Commerce was finally driven to comply with the commissioners' request – by a majority – it called on the services of the 'Chambre Syndicale des Courtiers près de la Bourse de Bordeaux' to order and to classify names. 'The Chamber', it was added, was thereby 'sheltered from all criticism . . . With us . . . all tasting is carried out by specialists with long experience of the art, and only after ensuring that they had taken the most minute precautions.' Perhaps it was going too far to say that all criticism would be avoided. There were some proprietors and *régisseurs* who still felt that the *négociants* and *courtiers* had too much influence on the market. Indeed, some of the proprietors dreamed of cutting out middlemen and of dealing direct with their customers.

Along with Lafite, Haut-Brion decided not to exhibit through the

Chamber of Commerce but, rather, by itself, *à part de l'envoi de la Chambre*. In consequence, there was considerable friction, and wrangling, behind the scenes, particularly after the *régisseur* of Lafite had had a private audience with Napoleon III. The really great proprietors did not wish to leave the Chamber of Commerce free to act on their behalf. Moreover, when the Chamber did so act and produced the first quasi-official order of listing of the *grands crus* – Lafite, Margaux, Latour and Haut-Brion – the listing was interpreted in different ways by the different proprietors and *régisseurs*. In its published list the Chamber did not include the wines of St Émilion or of Pomerol, many of which at that time passed through Libourne, not through Bordeaux, or, with the exception of Haut-Brion, any wines from the Graves district. The so-called *crus bourgeois* were left out too, although they were marketed in large quantities in France, Germany and other countries later in the century and were to be classified nearly a century later on the initiative of the Syndicat des crus bourgeois.

There were classifications like that of Wilhelm Franck or of Paguierre that preceded the 1855 classification which, for all its omissions, was proclaimed as 'a complete and satisfactory representation of the wines of the Department'. There were also writers on wine after 1855 who left out all reference to the deliberations and conclusions of the Chamber. Thus, Armailhacq in his influential study *De la culture des vignes dans le Médoc* (1866) did not mention its classification, although he presented his own, along with a list of prices from 1855 to 1865. Nor was there any mention of the classification in the sixth edition of Jullien's *Topographie de tous les vignobles connus* (1866), although a scheme of classification of Jullien's own had been presented in his 1811 edition. Nonetheless, in the second edition of their great and authoritative work, published in 1868, Cocks et Féret did refer to 1855, stating that they were now following the listed classification, which 'serves as a basis for most of the buying done in the large communes of Médoc'. 'It is not the result of the personal appreciation of the brokers who met in 1855,' they added, 'but the fruit of lengthy observations and calculations of the average of prices paid for the principal *crus* over a period of many years.'

In the twentieth century, when many attempts have been made to reclassify (all of them placing Haut-Brion in the top group), Charles

Walter Berry, familiar with this and other lists and with far more history at his disposal than had mid-Victorian wine merchants, decided not to concentrate on books but to travel and see for himself. He had a long business history behind him, for Berry Brothers was founded in the last decade of the seventeenth century, when Haut-Brion was undergoing its first transformation.

In Search of Wine, a book he published in 1935 after he had completed his travels, remains the most readable of the autobiographical introductions to an inexhaustible subject that always needs to be treated in personal terms. Each new generation has to discover it for itself. Classification is only a starting point. Berry Brothers has always realized this, as its magazine *Number Three* regularly reveals. In his narrative, often exuberant in style, Berry describes 5,600 miles of travel through France in 1934, a very different France from that of the *ancien régime*, the Revolution, the Second Empire – or the 1990s. His journey began auspiciously. As he crossed the Channel, he caught sight of a heading in that day's *Morning Post*, a great newspaper that has long since disappeared: 'WINE 3300 YEARS OLD'. 'Here we are in search of the wines of 1934, yet barely made,' he told his chauffeur, 'and the first thing that is brought to our notice is a wine ... which his Majesty Pharaoh Akhenaten himself must have enjoyed with his friends, or maybe by himself.' Clearly his journey, like ours, was a journey through time as well as through space.

A visit to the vineyards of Bordeaux is still a testing, if delightful, experience even when there are innumerable twentieth-century maps and guidebooks, 'wine courses', television programmes and carefully organized visits. The last of these are sometimes thought of as pilgrimages, not least by wine merchants. There are far more visitors than Berry would ever have dreamed of during the 1930s.

While on his own journey, Berry tasted the last pre-Dillon Haut-Brion, when new, in the château at Gibert's invitation – and some of his other ventures with Haut-Brion are described elsewhere. At a memorable dinner in Paris a generous host offered him an Haut-Brion 1911 with his turkey and an Haut-Brion 1899 with his fresh *pâté de truffes*. Of the latter he wrote 'a dream – I would like to be Rip Van Winkle and take a bottle of this to bed with me'.

There are three footnotes to this story, all concerned with royalty, but only the second and third concerned with wine. First, it took Berry forty minutes in a taxi to travel to the dinner from the

Madeleine to the Arc de Triomphe on his day in Paris because of security arrangements surrounding a memorial service for the recently assassinated King Alexander of Yugoslavia. Second, Berry persuaded his Paris host to send two bottles of the Haut-Brion 1899 to Buckingham Palace – offering two of his own 'good bottles' in return – and those who drank it there (and they seldom speak for themselves) were reported as being 'unanimous in their praise and gratitude'. The third footnote relates to a later date. Haut-Brion was served to Queen Elizabeth II at a dinner in her honour in the Élysée in 1957 – as it was for President Eisenhower in 1959, President Nixon in 1969 and Chou En-lai (Haut-Brion 1964) in 1973.

The reputation of Haut-Brion has survived all the contrasting decades since the 1930s, and when Alexis Lichine, always a welcome visitor at Haut-Brion – his first job was working for Seymour Weller – identified a new category of *crus hors classe* after the Second World War, Haut-Brion, so often *hors concours*, was among them. He had been one of the figures responsible for the successful publicizing of the wines of Bordeaux in the United States during the immediate post-war years when, with the Prohibition years relegated to history, there were many increased signs of American interest between 1950 and 1970. A burst of active involvement came between 1978 and 1983, when the value of the dollar increased dramatically against that of the franc, a novel situation which inspired R. M. Parker, founder of the influential periodical *The Wine Advocate* and author of *Bordeaux, a Definitive Guide*, to write of a 'new-found Franco-American love affair'. Later still, a weakened dollar, which improved the prospects of wine exports from California, did not stop Americans from buying the *grands crus* of Bordeaux. Indeed, in 1988 one Chicago retailer declared that whatever happened to other wines in a period of relative dollar weakness he had no trouble selling the top wines of Bordeaux, with Haut-Brion prominent among them.

The author of one of the books on claret written during the early period after the Second World War, *Wines with Long Noses*, was George Bijur, an American ex-serviceman with whom (by coincidence) I worked at Bletchley in the Ultra-breaking team during the war. 'Château Haut-Brion,' Bijur wrote with enthusiasm, but considerable exaggeration, 'presides over a small army of skilled

labourers, among whom the most punctual, talented and indispensable is an unpaid, overtime worker, the sun.'

Although there have been later American writers who, like Bijur,
have preferred to look at the sky rather than at the soil, most
guides to wine have eschewed with most of the exaggeration and
generalities of earlier writing about wine. This is more because
more wines of greater variety are being drunk than ever before and
highly knowledgeable writers on wine in the American press, men
like Frank Prial, for many years wine editor of the *New York
Times*, have got down to the detail while at the same time encour-
aging knowledgeable 'wine-talk'. Wine became a favourite topic of
conversation, and there were connoisseurs of wine-talk as well as
connoisseurs of wine.

Every week in the *New York Times* and many other newspapers
Haut-Brion figures regularly in advertisements. 'This is being com-
pared with the legendary 1961,' I read of the Haut-Brion 1986 in a
spring advertisement in 1988: 'these wines are extraordinary value.
This is the best time to buy.' The Haut-Brion on sale by retailers at
that time cost $585 a case compared with $480 for La Mission,
$630 for Lafite, $625 for Margaux and $595 for Latour and
Mouton. At the same time, 'Standard Sales' were advertising 1983
Haut-Brion at $39.95 a bottle and white Haut-Brion at $42.95.
These were highly competitive prices of the kind that interest many
American customers, even the richest among them.

There is no similar listed advertising on this scale in London:
indeed, in more than one elegant wine catalogue it is stated firmly
that prices of Haut-Brion are supplied only 'on request'. Nor are
there many British lovers of wine comparable with Malcolm
Forbes, owner and editor-in-chief of *Forbes Magazine* and friend of
the Dillon family, who died while I was carrying out research for
this book. He had ten bottles of Lafite 1890 in his cellar and
secured for his fascinating museum what was reputed to be one of
Jefferson's bottles of wine, which cost him $156,000, only to be
broken soon after purchase. He placed it on his mantelpiece, where
the heat of the fire broke it. In his delight in wine Forbes may be
compared with George Saintsbury, totally different though their
backgrounds, experience and philosophies were. Forbes described
himself as an appreciator of wine rather than as a collector. He was
also a man who liked a bargain. He once bought several hundred
bottles of Haut-Brion 1965, described in a recent Haut-Brion

brochure as a poor year, at a bargain basement price of $5 a bottle, and concluded every time he drank it that the wine was getting better and better. 'You were quite right,' Douglas Dillon told him, 'the sixty-five did turn into a perfectly good wine.'

It should be added that an Haut-Brion brochure of the late 1980s itself chose these words:

> The '65 Haut-Brion only now is beginning to develop: it already had character: the bouquet of an old wine appears with hints of mushroom, wood. The tannin needs to age a little longer. Astonishing for the vintage.

Six thousand cases of Haut-Brion were produced in 1965. The comparative figures for 1964 and 1966 were 17,500 and 19,500. Forbes obviously knew what rarity meant. So too did Pepys.

R. M. Parker, a lawyer by profession, first launched *The Wine Advocate* in 1978, and he makes use of a numerical scoring system which he has devised to compare the wines of Bordeaux. Like Berry, however, he had started by touring the vineyards and sampling the wines, and he has toured regularly ever since. 'By dint of talent and a formidable capacity for thoroughness,' Frank Prial has written, 'Parker has become one of the most respected American wine authorities'; *Business Week* has gone further and described him as 'the world's most influential wine taster'. As was the case with Saintsbury, who was supremely influential in Britain in the years when claret was a cult, his descriptions of particular Haut-Brions can be rhapsodic. Saintsbury described an Haut-Brion 1884 as 'at least the equal of any claret I ever drank'. Parker called the 1982 an 'unctuous wine' with 'layers and layers of fruit . . . Anticipated maturity 1995–2015.'

For all American connoisseurs – and they included, two generations before Forbes and before Prohibition, J. Pierpont Morgan – Haut-Brion has long been a special buy. Morgan kept in his cellar magnums and double magnums of Haut-Brion 1878. He was in a position to compare pre-phylloxera clarets with post-phylloxeras and to compare Haut-Brion with Margaux, Lafite and Latour. The latter remains the most challenging of comparisons, and at dinner at Haut-Brion guests are invited to name unidentified glasses of the *grands crus*. It is a difficult experiment except, perhaps, for *régisseurs* and *courtiers*, but it is always a fascinating one.

It is customary also to serve wines from other châteaux at dinners when guests are present. At Latour I have drunk Haut-Brion as well as Latour with Alan Hare, knowing that André Simon drank Haut-Brion 1940 at a remarkable lunch at Lafite in 1948 and that Edward Penning-Rowsell drank the 1908 Haut-Brion at Mouton. Château d'Yquem can, of course, conclude a meal at any of the great châteaux. The beautifully illustrated book about it by Richard Olney, *Yquem* (1985), is itself a celebration.

There was always a sense of competition between Haut-Brion and La Mission. As one of André Gibert's lawyers, de Rocquette-Buisson, put it:

Haut-Brion is not only the product of the land on which the grapes that make it grow, but of old modes of vinification and arduous and persisting efforts on the part of its proprietors and management . . . to gain an unchallengeable superiority over their neighbours.

The later chapters of this book tell the story in detail. Whatever co-operation there has been in the history of the *grands crus*, competition has never been absent.

La Mission did not figure in the 1855 classification. Yet in its older and its newer versions it has always had its admirers, and with its small *récolte* it has usually commanded a price higher than any other non-first growth of the Gironde – up to two-thirds the price of Haut-Brion itself. There has long been a case for including it in an extended or revised classification. Of the distant La Mission 1899, Maurice Healy – lover of Haut-Brion though he was – wrote that 'it attained first-class excellence, a not unusual occurrence in this vineyard'. I drank La Mission myself with great pleasure before I ever drank Haut-Brion – or could afford to buy it – picking out the 1953, and I was never in doubt about its quality. It is immediately accessible, and that, I think, is a difference. I would love to have been present at a great Christie's sale of La Mission wines in 1978 when sixty-two vintages were on offer, the oldest wines going back to 1878, the youngest to 1976. As many as forty separate dozens of the 1970 to 1976 vintages were available. That would certainly have made for comparison.

Haut-Brion and La Mission were rivals for so long that their characteristics tended to be sharply contrasted with each other both in the guidebooks and before that by their *régisseurs*. When compared with other wines, they shared a not dissimilar *goût de terroir*, but there was a deliberately contrived contrast in style, dear to the respective proprietors: more 'earthiness' in La Mission, a quality prized by its then proprietor, Henri Woltner, who liked 'big wines'; and more 'sophistication', subtly sought after by its proprietors and *régisseurs*, in Haut-Brion. The 'lightness' of the latter increased during the 1970s, although the superb 1971 has rightly had adjectives like 'rich' and 'full-bodied' applied to it.

There are years when Haut-Brion can carry with it, doubtless from the *terroir*, a feel of austerity, a term used in relation to some other wines of the Graves: the vines from which it is produced, one feels, have had to prove themselves exceptionally. Yet the 'balance' achieved – and in this sense we can speak legitimately of balance – is the work of men, not of nature. Nor can all, or most, Haut-Brions be called 'austere'. The sumptuous 1961, which brings out all the great qualities of Haut-Brion, conveys a sense of luxury rather than of austerity: it seems 'full of flower and fruit at the same time'.

Cyrus Redding, writing before the classification of 1855, claimed that the flavour of Haut-Brion resembled 'burning sealing wax' and that the bouquet savoured 'of the violet and the raspberry'. No other wine from the Graves district compared with it, he added, although he praised Graves wines as a group, describing them as 'fuller in body and more coloured and vinous than the wines of Médoc', noting that they were best kept six or eight years in the cask 'according to the temperature of the year in which they are made: they keep a long while and in twenty years lose nothing of their good quality'. The judgement has often been quoted. Few commentators have noted, however, that Redding seems to have had a particular affection for the adjectives 'violet or raspberry' throughout his writings: in a very different connection, he referred in general to the 'violet or raspberry' perfume of wine must.

It is the reference to 'burning sealing wax', therefore, that stands out as distinctive in his description of Haut-Brion – only Haut-Brion had this quality – and since the perfume of burning sealing wax was more familiar to the men of the 1840s than it is to us, the imagery has lost most of its point. It has also doubtless lost much of its relevance as the mix of grapes used to produce Haut-Brion has changed. So, too, has the once familiar imagery of tobacco. Perhaps 'brick dust', a more recent phrase of Penning-Rowsell, now means more. Meanwhile, Clive Coates, very familiar with all the recent Haut-Brion vintages, talks of 'blackcurrant', 'truffles' and – once again – 'violets'.

A favourite Victorian adjective, still familiar today in the language of wine, is 'big'. In the case of the wines of the Graves it is an adjective that wine writers have applied not only to La Mission but to Pape Clément. In an obvious sense, however, it is an adjective that can be applied to all the present *premiers grands crus* of the Médoc. Fortunately, one of Britain's outstanding judges of claret, Harry Waugh, was bold enough once to make the kind of comprehensive comparison that is called for when dining at Haut-Brion. He directly related Haut-Brion to the *grands crus* of the Médoc.

> One might possibly compare the style and quality of Haut-Brion with, say Lafite, feminine, graceful and superbly bred, while La Mission resembles more Latour, the latter masculine, dark, sturdy and slow to develop. After that, it is merely a question of taste.

The word 'merely' stands out in this comment, not as a taste but as an after-taste.

Terms which at different times have entered the wine vocabulary to 'describe' tastes in wine derive from psychology and physiology. Some claim to be 'scientific'. Yet there are problems there also. Physiologists, concerned with the 'senses', recognize only four fundamental tastes – bitter, sweet, acid and salty – and although they are aware that the nose is more versatile than the mouth and can linger over the countless scents and fragrances that go with a great wine, they are also aware that no scientific instrument can measure adequately delicacies or subtleties either of 'bouquet' or of 'aroma', words which in common language are usually treated as synonymous but which have been distinguished from each other in different ways by different tasters. Time always comes into the reckoning, and Émile Peynaud, who has written much on the subject, settled in 1983 for definitions of 'aroma' as the sum of odour elements in young wines and 'bouquet' as the odours acquired through ageing which develop over a period of time. Three types of 'aroma' have been identified: a primary aroma, intrinsic to the grape; a secondary aroma, evolved during the course of fermentation; and a tertiary aroma, although this last is present only in age.

Any science that there may be in pursuing such descriptions is unlikely to be objective. Indeed, in describing the experience of tasting psychologists have always pointed to associations, while Delmas himself, at Haut-Brion, has drawn attention to the power of early memories in shaping the developed sense of taste – and of colour. He has also used the term 'codification' to describe one aspect of the professional wine taster's skills. 'Tasters are rare,' he concludes, 'who can without great risk identify a region, a *cru* and a vintage, and their skills are acquired only "progressively" after a large number of careful tastings.'

'The visual aspect of wine', as Peynaud calls it, is an aspect that must be taken account of by all wine tasters. There are now instruments that can measure colour. Indeed, as long ago as 1861 a French chemist, Chevreul, wrote a 900-page thesis on 'a technique for defining and naming colours, based on a precise scientific method'. He went on to classify colours in the best Victorian fashion in seventy-two groups, each divided into twenty shades. Fortunately, there are simpler propositions. Wines that look dull usually are dull. Different years of Haut-Brions have different colours. So, too, does the Haut-Brion of the same year as it ages. When it comes to tasting – and tasting is different from drinking – the sense of sight is engaged as well as the sense of colour, and as far as the sense of smell is concerned there are parallel and related changes to those associated with sight.

There remains, therefore, an art of tasting just as there is an art of wine-making, for as Warner Allen recognized, 'there can be no hard and fast classifications of the qualities of a great wine. One quality ranges into another through a series of almost imperceptible variations.' For that reason, Haut-Brion, like other great vineyards, draws upon the services of more than one experienced taster to 'interpret' a vintage, and there are sequences of tastings by the same taster at different stages. Comparisons are always essential.

As a non-expert who made my first notes before I read Peynaud on taste, I favour, when I describe a wine, a deliberately more restricted style than the lush language favoured by many popular writers on the subject. For me Haut-Brion as it now is – and it has changed – is in general 'drier' when compared with the *premiers grands crus* of the Médoc, which are produced in significantly greater quantities. It also carries with it unmistakably the *goût de terroir*, although the *terroir* by itself does not dictate the flavour, as it does with some other red Graves with which Haut-Brion can always be compared. Such general judgements constitute only the prelude to a sequence of personal assessments. Some particular red Haut-Brion vintages can be described as 'simple', others as 'complex', and it is not difficult to tell why. The taste need not be immediately certain, however, and different associations are recalled. Some Haut-Brions have rightly been called 'elegant', others 'aromatic', a few 'flinty'; and again these adjectives have their point when a vintage is being tasted for the first time. Clearly the weather and the timing of the harvest have exerted their influence. The word that is perhaps most generally used of Haut-Brion, red or white, is 'balanced', but that by itself says little. Without hesitation, I would employ another favourite Victorian word directly derived from music: 'harmony'. The different grapes in Haut-Brion work together 'harmoniously': the effect is derived from their blending, not a once-and-for-all blending but one that continues to transform. Again, comparing Haut-Brion with a musical composition, it is a wine that takes time to introduce itself.

All this, of course, is metaphor, and since all metaphor is as hazardous as talking about raspberries, cherries or sealing wax, it is tempting to move to a different one. Haut-Brion is meant to be savoured, not relished. Its distinctive flavour builds up as it is tasted just as the wine itself builds up over the years until it acquires 'fullness of character'. Knowing when it is best to drink and not just to taste is itself an art. So, of course, is where to drink it.

It is the final product which is always kept in mind by Delmas and his colleagues, the best wine that can be produced in that particular year, and that is a wine that will have a full life. 'You make good wines for tasting,' Delmas once told the Californian wine-maker Robert Mondavi, 'I make wines to drink.'

Far more has been written of red Haut-Brion than of white, not surprisingly given that the latter is produced in small quantities from grapes grown on land restricted to less than three hectares – and that few people, even people who love red Haut-Brion and have sung its praises, have tasted it. The amount of land devoted to white wine grapes was slightly increased in 1950, but in 1977 two-thirds of the vines used for making white Haut-Brion were uprooted for replanting. Only around 800 cases were produced in 1992. Since so little of the wine can be exported, it was deliberately excluded from the white wines mentioned in the 1949 and 1969 editions of Cocks et Féret, while Château Laville-Haut-Brion produced across the road at La Mission was not. The two white wines are as different to the palate – and in appearance – as the La Mission and Haut-Brion reds. Laville-Haut-Brion – the name stuck in Gibert's throat – was, and is, more golden in colour, the white Haut-Brion more delicate in taste. In an average year rather more cases of white Haut-Brion than of Laville-Haut-Brion are produced, although both wines command high prices because of their 'rarity', particularly in the United States. White Haut-Brion is much in demand, and orders often have to be refused.

For me, drinking white Haut-Brion is very much of a special experience, and one to be treasured. In my view, it is as much the best of the white Graves as Haut-Brion is of the red. It is dry on the palate and best drunk when matured. It remains fresh, but it acquires depth. I envy Michel Dovaz, who on one happy occasion was able to compare nine white Haut-Brions. He praised them one by one for their unique qualities, but acclaimed them all for what he called their 'rectitude'. I myself have greatly enjoyed the 1982s and the 1985s.

The second wine of Haut-Brion also deserves attention. Bahans is named after a particular *parcelle* of land and a residence that has disappeared. From the top of it you could have seen the belfries of Bordeaux. Bahans was once made from young vines or vattings which for whatever reason were not used in the making of the *grand vin*. Yet the vines were always very carefully selected, and the wine, relatively soft and immediately fragrant – it also had a delightful colour – could be as good, or better, than most other Graves.

From 1982 onwards – and 1982 was *une année exceptionnelle* – Bahans-Haut-Brion, as it is now called, has carried the name and year on the bottle, so that it has become a reasonably priced vintage wine that can be bought in New York or Dallas as easily as in Bordeaux. The merits of particular vintages are as carefully described in wine guides – after tasting – as the merits of Haut-Brion itself. In December 1990 *L'Amateur de Bordeaux*, for example, included a detailed article by Tamara Thorgevsky on the merits of particular vintages. She described Bahans not as a second wine but as a 'super-second *cru classé*'. In 1990 the 1982 was fetching 188 francs a bottle and the 1983 135 francs. The 1989 *en primeur* cost 85 francs. Once exclusively marketed by Nathaniel Johnson, a firm that has played a big part in the history of Haut-Brion, it is now distributed through a variety of *négoces*.

For some people on both sides of the Atlantic Bahans-Haut-Brion is easier to drink than to pronounce. There is a nasal touch to the sound: 'Baa' is pronounced like the sound a sheep makes, and the rest of the word approximates to 'onsse', with the final 's' sounded.

Bahans is drunk happily at Haut-Brion itself, where the pronun-ciation is authoritatively settled, and it is there, of course, that Haut-Brion itself is drunk in ideal surroundings. It can be tasted in the *chai*, where the quality of one vintage can be compared with another, and it can be drunk at the table along with the delicious foods of the Bordeaux region. 'Wine and dine.' The dinner table comes into the picture, therefore, as well as the laboratory and the *courtier*'s office. On my very first visit to Haut-Brion, in April 1986, an occasion never to forget, we started with the favourite white Burgundy of the household, Puligny Montrachet (1982), and as we ate *côte de bœuf charolaise* we compared red Haut-Brion 1964 with the Lafite, Margaux and Mouton-Rothschild of the same year. In the autumn of 1987, as we dined on *baron d'agneau* I enjoyed comparing (perhaps this time more knowledgeably) Haut-Brion 1966 with the Latour, Lafite and Margaux of the same year and Mouton-Rothschild 1955. Later on the same visit I compared Haut-Brion 1971 with the 1953.

It has not always been the case that care has been taken to associate the right wine with the right food. Indeed, it was only in the nine-teenth century that a separate wine for each course came into fashion, after the habit of dining *à la russe* (dining through a sequence of different courses) was taken up. Even then it took time for *grands vins* to establish themselves.

At the beginning of the nineteenth century, Talleyrand's great chef Marie-Antonin Carême had had little to say of wine and nothing to say of its role as a companion to the lavish dishes that he prepared; and it was not until 1825 that the lawyer Jean-Anthelme Brillat-Savarin, who (unlike Carême) was a great gourmet and ate often at Talleyrand's table, brought wine – and music – into the picture. In his highly acclaimed book *La Physiologie du Goût* he argued that not to change wines with dishes was 'a heresy'. Whatever their differences, Carême and Brillat-Savarin approached their subject historically, as did other writers on 'the table'. Meanwhile, antiquarians noted that in the ancient world Ausonius had said more about oysters than about wine. In what was said to be the first printed cookbook, *Le Viandier*, published in 1490 after the fall of Bordeaux to the French, nothing at all was included about wine. Brillat-Savarin was an innovator when he entitled one of his '*méditations*' – a name he preferred to 'chapter' – 'Beverages'. It was only one meditation, however, out of thirty.

In England it was not until 1846 that C. E. Francatelli's *Modern Cook*, treating cookery as an art – 'they manage things better in France' – gave clear advice to the English on how to relate wine to food. While unwilling to give 'elaborate or detailed instruction respecting the service of wines at dinner', he generalized that 'the palate is as capable and nearly as worthy of education as the eye and the ear', and described the 'English habit' of introducing sweet champagne in the first course as 'injudicious'. Instead, he recommended 'Madeira, Sherry and Burgundy' as 'better suited'. Francatelli did not mention claret, but C. D. Pierce, a *maître d'hôtel*, did, albeit briefly and inconclusively, when he gave a full account of a dinner *à la russe* in his book *The Household Manager* (1857). He recommended that after *hors d'œuvres*, soup and fish, *relèves* of meat should be served with 'such wines as Chambertin, Bourdeaux [*sic*] or if more suitable, others, to the host's taste'. Across the Atlantic, in the same year Chablis was drunk with oysters and Margaux with saddle of lamb at a Shakespere (*sic*) Annual Commemoration dinner in Philadelphia, and champagne came at the end. The dinner began, however, with 'Brandenburg Brandy, 1820'. The 'liqueurs' included the same brandy and 'Oxford Punch'. A copy of the complete menu was sent to the actor Henry Irving in England, and was subsequently reprinted in Fin Bec, Grant and Company's *Book of Menus* in 1876.

In the literature of wine, however, more continued to be written by Englishmen about drinking claret after dinner, about the custom of 'taking wine' with host and fellow guests at the dinner table and about 'the aesthetics of the table' than about the choice of wines to serve. Not until 1911 did F. W. Hackwood devote the last chapter of his pioneering book, *Good Cheer: the Romance of Food and*

Feasting, to both wine and food. Meanwhile, there had been no references to food in the successive editions of Cocks et Féret. The 'rituals of the table' were left to writers of another genre of reference books.

There had been only a few references to wine in Charles Sayles's expanded version (1899) of two articles in *The Quarterly Review* by the lawyer and essayist Abraham Hayward in 1835 and 1836, which he converted into book form in 1852 with the title *The Art of Dining*. The first article was a review of Brillat-Savarin and of Louis Vole's *The French Cook*, and the second a review of a book by Thomas Walker, who invented the word 'aristology' to describe 'the art of dining'.

Hayward, who lived on into his eighty-third year (in 1884), quoted Brillat-Savarin at length, observing that no Englishman had ever produced a book like his. In fact, the Scots doctor William Kitchiner's *The Cook's Oracle* had appeared in 1817, eight years before Brillat-Savarin's *Physiologie du Goût*, and was followed in 1822 by his book *The Art of Invigorating and Prolonging Life by Food, Clothes, Air, Exercise, Wine, Sleep etc.*, a formidable list complete with an 'etc.' that put wine in its place. In one of his recipes Kitchiner recommended that roast mutton should be basted with a mixture of herbs, butter and claret.

Choosing which wine to go with which dish – we now call it 'matching' – was touched on briefly by Hackwood in 1911 in a chapter called 'Aristology', in which he recommended 'a glass of good Bordeaux with a joint of mutton' and 'the best of red wines, Bordeaux or Burgundy, with the roast game'. And although he went on to quote a 'host of the old school' who still drank punch with the turtle and champagne, well iced, and claret afterwards, he added that the same host held 'variety of wines to be a great mistake'. Hackwood himself matched Chablis with oysters, sherry with soup, good Rhine wine with the fish, a choice of claret or Burgundy with the roast, and port, 'the king of wines', with the dessert. 'It must not be forgotten', he added as his own inconsistent postscript, that 'both prudence and digestion dictate the wisdom of not mixing red and white wines, or indeed, any wines at a meal. White wine should certainly never be taken after red. Whatever is drunk, however, should be of the choicest possible.'

As Charles Cooper observed in his book *The English Table* (1929), throughout the nineteenth century 'dining was dining and wine drinking was wine drinking'. The wine clubs of late nineteenth-century London always drank their best clarets after dinner, and it is interesting to note that the last words on the 'Shakespere' menu of 1857 read 'We adjourn'. They came from Shakespeare's *Henry VIII*. Drinking at, not after, dinner could pose problems, and Britain's Prime Minister, W. E. Gladstone, lover of claret as he was, recalled a host who asked a bishop who was dining with him whether he would like any more wine and received the reply, 'Thank you, not until we have drunk what we have set before us.'

André Simon, who did so much to relate wine and food to each other through the Wine and Food Society, founded in 1933, would have appreciated the story. His *Tables of Content*, which appeared in 1933 in the aftermath of his *The Art of Good Living* (not just the art of self-indulgence), was a kind of footnote which presented details (and critiques), 'gastronomic reminiscences' he called them, of particular menus and wines that had accompanied them in 1928, 1929 and 1930. It was more than a penned statement, however: it was 'designed to assist friends who have asked me to give a practical lead, how to avoid gastronomic heresies, how to order wines to fit in with different dishes'.

The word 'heresies' stands out. There were more subtle shades of spiritual interpretation, however, when discussion turned to the order in which to drink old wines – should one move from the least good to the better and the best? – and it was suggested that if chronology was followed care would have to be taken not to allow a wine of 'extreme violence', like the Haut-Brion 1906, to be drunk before less violent Haut-Brions of a later date. Likewise, if a reverse chronology was applied, an Haut-Brion 1895 would kill an Haut-Brion 1875. The conclusion that was drawn was that between two wines of such contrasting qualities, a *vin de transition* should be drunk as an intermediary.

The oldest wine drunk at an early lunch in the Wine Trade Club of 1913, when the Club had moved to new premises and when Ian Campbell was President, was an Haut-Brion 1869. And it was drunk last. Delving deep into the past provided ample scope for discussion in the 1920s too. Campbell, Francis Berry and, of course, Maurice Healy were present at an office lunch in January 1929 when Haut-Brion 1874 was served with the cheeses. The colour was said to be 'still beautiful' and 'there was just the faint suspicion of a squeeze of lemon' which made all the difference between the 1874 and 1875. At a later lunch, at which Healy was also present, the 1874 was again drunk with the cheese, and this time Simon found it 'superlative, the best bottle of this particular bin that I can remember'. He gave it 'full marks'. And he praised it again when it was served with cheese at the lunch to celebrate the publication of *The Art of Good Living*, where one of the guests was the French Ambassador.

Simon was impressed with an Haut-Brion 1920 which he drank at a lavish dinner for visiting American journalists at a West End hotel in March 1929, although he was unimpressed by the combination of food and wine at the dinner, which began with oysters and Montrachet. The Haut-Brion certainly spoilt the Forster Jesuitengarten Auslese which was served after it. A contrasting lunch which was just right was given in a City hall soon afterwards. On this occasion, Haut-Brion 1905 was drunk with a roast saddle of mutton, followed by Latour 1899. The Haut-Brion seemed to be at its best, with 'no sign of decay, but with no sign of reserves either'. Of an Haut-Brion 1910, the first he had ever tasted – it was served with *selle d'agneau* – Simon wrote that it was 'the only decent wine made in that sodden, rotten year'. It was not – and never would be – a fine wine, but it was an enjoyable wine, 'on the light side, a little sharp at the finish – but with a very cheering bouquet'. And he continued in characteristic Simon prose 'that it had the nose of an aristocrat, of an aristocrat in shabby clothes'. 'The clothes,' he concluded, 'do not make the man nearly to the same extent as does the nose.' Unfortunately, when later in the meal asparagus was served with Burgundy, both the asparagus and the Burgundy suffered from the Haut-Brion.

Since Simon's time, choosing wines to drink with dinners has become an art in itself, although in the books and articles of the mid-twentieth century it was still thought necessary to issue solemn warnings like: 'Whisky is not good to drink with oysters, because it hardens the mollusc and makes it difficult to digest.' 'Cocktails [by then they had been invented] should be drunk as long as possible before the repast as, owing to the many ingredients they contain, they spoil the palate for fine wines.' 'With the first whiff of smoke the palate ceases to demand either food or wine.' A generation earlier, it had been suggested that 'the introduction of a cigarette after dinner' had actually replaced after-dinner claret just as whisky had replaced light claret as 'an aid to recovery after an illness'.

The advice about smoking had been taken seriously in an age when food and wine had not yet been associated after Simon's fashion. There has since been even greater change in smoking than in drinking habits. Yet as early as the 1890s it had been written that 'the greatest enemy to traditional rites after-dinner,' was 'the barbarous plebeian custom of smoking when Vintage Port, Madeira and after-dinner Burgundies and Clarets are handed round the table.' It was 'fatal to the knowledge and appreciation of the different qualities and vintages'. And in one book there had been a postscript: 'Château Lafite, Château Margaux, Château Haut-Brion and Château Latour ought to be drunk in uncontaminated silence.'

Butlers were always in the background then, and many books were written telling them how they ought to behave. They had to know their cellars as well as their under-servants. There are now similar books for *sommeliers*, who are today thought of less as wine waiters than as a profession demanding knowledge both of wine and of food which can be presented to people who have never seen a cellar. It is not surprising therefore to find that *L'Amateur de Bordeaux* (No. 18, 1988) includes alongside an article called *Les humeurs du négoce*, which deals with trade practices in the wine industry, another article called *Cousins d'Amérique*, which describes how American *sommeliers* – in their case, at least, wine waiters is an inadequate translation – 'are in the course of structuring and developing their profession'.

It is not surprising either that among customers there have been signs of a reaction against 'rules' matching food and drink. 'Discard the rules and just enjoy' was David Rosengarten's advice in *Newsday* in January 1990, where he mentioned 'demon *sommeliers* looking over customers' shoulders'. 'Somewhere along the line' people had 'got the notion' that there are 'rules' in matching wine with food. In the second part of his article Rosengarten turned sensibly, however, to 'principles', which he considered more important than rules, and these were sound enough. Even when rules had been faithfully observed, there had been occasional problems when the principles behind them were forgotten. At the wine tasting at Lockets Restaurant in London in November 1972 the Haut-Brion 1962, which was drunk with the main course, was felt not 'to taste to its best advantage after the fish pie'. 'The fish pie had been very good but had had a stray herbs taste.'

Before the rules had been formulated, there could be problems too. Thus, in 1849 Sir Morgan O'Doherty was reported as saying 'some people tell you you should not drink claret after strawberries. They are wrong.' Delmas is less unequivocal when he advises that Haut-Brion is better with meat than with cheese.

Cocks et Féret seem to put all this into perspective. *Plats* began to appear as well as vintages as the twentieth-century editions were published and attention began to be paid to 'the taste of wines and their *accord* with dishes'. The tenth edition (1929) raised the question of the right order of drinking wines. The fourteenth edition (1991) directly asked the question whether wines should be chosen to fit in with the *plats* or the other way round. Wisely the answer was that there are no rigorous rules. *Chacun à son goût.*

7

Distant Origins

The taste that the English have for wines of the
Graves has distant origins.

P. J. Lacoste, 1947

The propensity of the British – and later of the Americans – to
drink claret has distant origins, though what they drank in the past
has little in common with what they drink today. For this reason
the first historians of the wines of Bordeaux were right to begin
their histories not with the *révolution des boissons* in the seventeenth century – they did not identify that – but to look back to the
beginnings in the Middle Ages and even earlier. A great historian of
wine of an earlier generation, Roger Dion, looked back happily to
the silver age of the ancient world and to the writings of Ausonius,
and although there is more legend than fact in claiming continuity
between the wines produced in Roman Burdigala and in modern
Bordeaux, there are important historical links in a long chain, particularly as far as Haut-Brion is concerned.

The innovating Pontacs, who introduced Haut-Brion to the
world, emerged out of the society of late medieval and early
modern Bordeaux, not out of seventeenth-century society. Moreover, and more generally, because for centuries Bordeaux was
associated – above all in England – with Gascon wines, including
the wines of the Graves, long before it was associated with named
wines, Haut-Brion was well placed to play a leading part in the
seventeenth-century *révolution des boissons*.

In English social history the inn or tavern was an older institution
than the restaurant, and from the time that trade records began to
be kept, particularly from the early thirteenth century onwards,

96

wine was certainly being drunk in inns along with local ale. In 1309 there were 354 taverns in London, a few of them dealing only in 'sweet wines'. Wine was sold by the gallon, pottle, quart or pint. How much, if any, food was eaten there – and what form it took – is not definitely known.

During the late Middle Ages London vintners, who in the early thirteenth century were electing two wardens each year to supervise the Gascon wine trade, were divided into two categories: *vinotarii*, or merchant importers, and *tabernarii*, or retailers, who kept cellars or taverns. The *vinotarii* frequently visited Bordeaux: the *tabernarii* had the monopoly of the retail trade. The Vintners' Company, which survives in strength today as one of London's twelve great City livery companies, had its origins in the early decades of the thirteenth century, when the vintners had the sole right of sale of Gascon wines in England. St Martin's in the Vintry, south of Guildhall and close to the River Thames, was their parish. 'The Company and Mistery of Vintners' was not incorporated by charter, however, until 1437.

Four out of ten vintner aldermen held important posts in the royal household in the long reign of Henry III, and no fewer than four vintners were mayors of London during the shorter reign of Richard II. One thirteenth-century vintner, Henry de Waleys, who sold large quantities of wine to the royal household, was at one time Mayor of Bordeaux, while in the fourteenth century the great poet Geoffrey Chaucer was the son of a vintner.

It was not until 1671, however, five years after the Great Fire of London, when named Pontac wine was now making its way to London, that the Vintners – after many vicissitudes – acquired a handsome new hall, largely built not in wood and plaster, like the old hall, but in fashionable brick. They were renowned at that time for their pageants as much as for their hall, and their great pageant in 1702 had as its central figure St Martin, the fourth-century Bishop of Tours and founder of monasticism in France, armed and mounted on a white horse, a symbol of continuity in the wine trade, a direct link between the Middle Ages and the birth of the *grands crus*.

Medieval historians, among them Y. Renouard, the author of *Bordeaux sous les rois d'Angleterre* (1965), who dealt authoritatively with '*le Grand Commerce du Vin au Moyen Age*' in his *Études d'Histoire Médiévale* (1968), and before him the great

Belgian economic historian, Henri Pirenne, have shown how from the early thirteenth century onwards wine as a commodity – along with wool – contributed considerably to the growth of Europe's trading markets. There were obvious links between agriculture and marketing, marketing and transport and, essential to the pattern, the rise of population. Since the sea routes from the west of France to Britain were more open and more accessible than the land routes across France, the Bordeaux wine trade crossed ocean frontiers, with both England and Ireland benefiting exceptionally because they were 'at the ocean edge'.

The price of wine, which fluctuated sharply during the Middle Ages, did not vary according to the *terroir* from which the wine came, but prices were always higher for new wine than for old wine. In 1342, for example, there is a note describing new wine selling at 21 livres a *tonneau* while old wine was selling at 12 livres. New wine meant wine of the most recent vintage, in the language of Gascony, wine of the '*primeyra culhida*'. It was the only wine that was drinkable, and it was low in alcohol content. Most of it had been drunk by the end of the year, some as early as September; and, as a direct consequence, it was a crime – albeit a crime regularly indulged in – to mix old wine with new wine to 'conserve' or to 'strengthen' it or to increase the quantities of wine available.

It is plain from ecclesiastical records that wines were mixed for a variety of non-criminal reasons also – for instance, to improve colour and to give the appearance of a strong wine ('*fort*') rather than one that was weak ('*faible*'). The habit did not die out. Darker wines not only looked better: they seemed to be rounder and fuller in flavour. What the French called *remontage* or *coupage*, blending 'natural wines' with something stronger, came to be known in the nineteenth century as '*travail à l'anglaise*'.

Whether or not 'blending' was conceived of as an art or treated as a scandal, there was no doubt in the Middle Ages, as there has been no doubt since, about what constituted really 'bad wine'. In 1356, for example, the wine of the year was either destroyed in the vineyards or given to the poor. More often the wine that for this reason was not consumed was turned into vinegar, *vin aigre*, a necessary preservative for food in medieval times. 'Bad wine' might be made: it did not always 'go bad', for in the preparation of new wine there were always dangers of contamination. For example, when demand was great there was always a temptation to use grapes that were not yet ready. The best years were those like 1341 or 1376, when the grapes ripened quickly – and there were plenty of them. The worst were years like 1343, when 'the sea froze'. Another source of contamination was dirty vessels. In the Middle Ages the best way of ensuring that you had good wine was to acquire a vineyard for yourself: '*Chacun veut être vigneron / Pour boire, comme il dit, du bon.*' ('Everyone wishes to be a *vigneron* in order to drink wine that he thinks good.')

Discriminating English drinkers who did not own vineyards chose to test barrels of wine when they arrived by sea and to pick out the ones that they deemed the best. By 1302 there were six official tasters in London, throwing away any wines that they considered bad. Merchants too might haggle about the quality of wine as well as about its price. There is no evidence, however, that the decisions reached were related in any way to the specific place of origin of the wine. Particular vineyards were not named as sources of supply.

In any given year there might be sharp competition in London, where retailing was strictly regulated and where there were some arguments about impurities and 'blending'. These related not only to the blending of one claret and another, but the blending of wines from different parts of the wine-growing areas of Europe. Customers had a choice. Thus, in William Langland's famous poem *Piers Plowman*, written at the end of the fourteenth century, the poet describes the London street scene – at the receiving end of the wine trade – where

> Cooks to their knaves cried 'Hot pies hot' . . .
> Taverners unto them told the same tale;
> White wine of Oseye and red wine of Gascoyne,
> Of the Rhine, and of Rochelle, the roast meat to digest.

London obviously had far more choice than most cities.

The men of Bordeaux would not have liked either the late reference to La Rochelle in the poem, for La Rochelle was the city which Bordeaux had supplanted in the English trade, or the mention in it of the wines of the Oseye and the Rhine. The poet reveals to us, however, that even at the time when he was writing there were Englishmen who could discriminate between new wines which arrived from different regions, if not from different places within the same region. There were, of course, Frenchmen too. One remarkable French medieval poem, *La Bataille des Vins*, written in the early thirteenth century, lists the merits of different wines. White wines come first. Significantly, the wine-taster in the poem is an English priest.

Of equal significance, perhaps, it was laid down in London in 1342 that innkeepers should not be allowed to keep Gascon wine in the same cellar as wines from the Rhine. There were rules also that 'new wines' should not be 'exposed for sale' until stocks of old wines had been removed. There was certainly no shortage of rules. These related to matters as different as offering 'full and true measures' and the form inn signs should take. The latter were often bigger than the seventeenth-century sign over Pontack's. London's mayor and aldermen once received a petition that inn signs should not be more than seven feet high.

Customers, whether or not protected by rules, mattered in the Middle Ages – bishops and kings were always well ahead of inn drinkers – although those medieval bishops and kings who were fortunate enough to hold land with the right soil and the right climate to enable them to produce wine for themselves usually did so. Bishops were as influential as kings, not only because wine was sacramental, but because the demand for wine as a secular delight could provide a lucrative source of ecclesiastical income.

The Archbishop of Bordeaux had vineyards at Pessac, near to the modern Haut-Brion, and Mérignac, and others further away at Lormont and Queyries that produced substantial quantities of wine of different types. His *chais* were the most important in Bordeaux, although his estate in Pessac was the least important of his scattered wine-producing centres. Not surprisingly, ecclesiastics were particularly knowledgeable both about the arts or techniques of wine-making and about the wine trade. The word *cleret* appears in the very first archiepiscopal accounts of Bordeaux to be written in French (not in Latin) in 1459.

Of great interest to the modern historian of Haut-Brion is the work of Jean-Bernard Marquette, who has gone back in time as far as he possibly can – to the years from 1332 to 1459. His evidence is sufficiently well documented to establish a number of points of importance relating to vinification in Pessac and other estates of the Archbishop of Bordeaux before the Pontacs became wine producers. His evidence covers a period, therefore, before and after the English left Bordeaux. What he says about the detail of medieval wine-making is important in longer-term perspective also, since there was very little change in the vinification of the *vin de l'année* between then and the late seventeenth century. What is recorded in the Archbishop's accounts presumably applied in the case of the first Pontac vineyards before the evolution of the *grand cru*.

There was one difference in structure, however, that clearly affected the management of wine production. Although the Archbishop's and the Pontac vineyards both drew some of their grapes from lands cultivated by their feudal vassals – and within the feudal framework land might be offered to tenants specifically to plant vines – the estates of the Archbishop were scattered. Their disposition was the result of gifts to the Church. By contrast, the lands that the Pontacs were to assemble were compact, and their disposition owed nothing either to chance or to charity. The Pontacs were in a position, therefore, to supervise the planting and care of their vines closely and directly and to check on the quality of their grapes.

Marquette does not deal in detail with viticulture – the evidence is limited – although some of the hardest work in medieval wine-making must have been concerned with the opening up of new vineyards (*terres neuves*) on what was often, as we have seen, unpropitious soil. During the Middle Ages wine-making (*facienda vina, faire du vin*) was deemed to begin only after the grapes – and they may not all have been of one kind or colour – had been collected from the vineyards and trodden or pressed and only after the must that had been produced in the process had run into troughs (*maies*). The pressing, dependent on physical force, was a very different process from that followed in the crushing presses of the twentieth century. After the wine had been transferred into barrels, the vats were cleaned, an arduous occupation in itself. This was the conclusion of the annual *vendange*: it was spoken of as 'bringing the harvest to its head'. There might be racking, however, of surplus wine that was not immediately exported or consumed, wine that was cheaper in price.

According to Marquette, the quantity of wine produced in the Archbishop's *chais* exceeded 100 *tonneaux* in a good year, such as 1361. The average for the whole fourteenth century was 76 *ton-*

neaux, each tonneau around 900 litres. Of this figure, less than half came directly from the Archbishop's own properties.

We know little of the early wine presses in use – there is no archaeological evidence – and it is curious that in the medieval accounts for Pessac there are no references to the costs of their maintenance or repair. We do know, however, that much of the work in the Archbishop's *treuils* was carried out by candlelight since there was great pressure at harvest time after the grapes had been brought in from the vineyards. We also know that Pessac often led the way in the timing of the harvest.

After the *vendage*, wine from Pessac for export was taken to Bordeaux and placed aboard ships. The main fleet arrived in autumn and there was a second fleet to carry what racked wine still remained in spring. The wine was, of course, undifferentiated, and the most important point was to get it to the customer as quickly as possible.

As fond as Victorians were to be of classification, it was churchmen who first drew learned but necessary distinctions between different kinds of 'red' wine being produced in Bordeaux: *vinum clarum* and *vinum rubeum purum*. The first, in French *vin clair* or in Gascon *bin clar*, the wine described in 1459 as *vin cleret*, was prepared by rapid fermentation from a mixture of red and white grapes: it was weak in colour, for maceration had not yet been introduced, but it had no floating particles in it. It would now be called rosé, a term not then used. The second wine, *vin vermel* (later *vermeil*), *bin vermelh* or *vin rouge*, drawn later, was thicker and contained more tannin. The residual *vin de presse*, obtained after pressing the remaining grapes, was called in Gascon *pin pin* and it accounted for around one-fifth of the total wine output. A fourth type of local wine was noted also – *vinum rubeum lymphatum*, in Gascon *regrevin*, a term which can be traced back to 1354. This was watered wine, also described as *prima aqua*. This was the 'wine' that the grape pickers drank. It was made from pouring water over the lees, residual solids left over when the wine had been fermented.

The parallel use of the Latin and Gascon languages brings out some points about the nature of the wines themselves and about the differences between them that otherwise might be less clear. So, too, does the later substitution of the French for the Gascon language. Otherwise the use of two languages imposes exceptional scholarly demands on the historian of wine. It was not until 1520 that the *Jurade* of Bordeaux, a local representative body, regularly recorded its proceedings in the more accessible French language. This was seventeen years before an important ordinance decreed that French should be the sole language of the courts.

Given the medieval links between Latin, wine and the Church, it seems appropriate that a medieval Gascon Archbishop of Bordeaux, Bertrand de Goth, who in 1305 became Pope Clement V, has had a later wine of the Graves named after him. When he heard the news of his election as pope, he travelled first of all not to Rome but to Bordeaux. Indeed, throughout the whole period of his papacy he never went to Rome. He was the first of the Avignon popes, inaugurating the so-called 'Babylonian exile' that was to last for seventy years. He was also a scholar who founded chairs of oriental languages – one of them in Oxford – and in 1306 we find him convalescing on his Pessac estate, not far from the present Château Pape-Clément, which is very near to Haut-Brion. Until the French Revolution the vineyard remained the property of the Church.

Whoever served as Archbishop of Bordeaux, the staff under his control paid as much attention to the marketing of their wines as to their production. Many of the arts of vine growing and of wine-making which are now deemed basic were then unknown, but there is evidence of the Archbishop's staff taking customers or would-be customers and their agents to visit the local vineyards and to taste the wines. Marketing already mattered. The Bordeaux clergy were realists in other ways also. One of Bertrand de Goth's successors as Archbishop of Bordeaux, Pey Berland, son of a peasant, is still commemorated, as has been noted, in the place names of Bordeaux. He was the very active leader in the defence of Bordeaux against the kings of France during the last stages of the Hundred Years War.

During the Middle Ages there were a few scattered ecclesiastical vineyards even in the Médoc, although the only wines from the Bordeaux area that were then identified as such were *palus*, wines from the alluvial marshy land situated between the rivers Garonne and Dordogne, where there were vineyards owned by English kings, and Graves, wine from the gravelly areas around Pessac, Talence, Mérignac, Gradignan and Ceran. In both cases the generic designations related to the characteristics of the soil. A remarkable expansion of vineyards in the immediate area of Bordeaux had begun in the eleventh century; and by the end of the fifteenth century all available land inside as well as outside the city limits seems to have been taken over for the production of vines.

Not all the wines exported from Bordeaux were produced exclusively in the area very near to the city. Some of them came from a wide-ranging hinterland, an *haut-pays* or *arrière-pays*, linked to Bordeaux by river. It included relatively distant centres, like Cahors and Agen, which during the Hundred Years War passed into French hands. In the record year 1308/9, when over 100,000 *tonneaux* of wine were exported from Bordeaux, only 13 per cent of the total exports consisted of 'Bordeaux wines'. Around this time, there were no fewer than eighty-eight proprietors in Agen dealing in exported wines; and in Bazas, which was to figure later in the Pontac story, there were eight proprietors, one of them operating on so small a scale, however, that he exported only one *tonneau*.

Difficult though it sometimes is to distinguish clearly between *vignerons* (growers) and *marchands* (merchants) in the fourteenth-century wine-growing areas outside Bordeaux, there was less ambiguity about the role of the citizens of Bordeaux in the active and lucrative wine trade. Following the grant of a charter by the English King Henry III in 1235, they enjoyed remarkable privileges, not always exercised, of a protectionist kind that were confirmed or extended by later English kings and which outlasted the English kings themselves. First, they had an almost complete monopoly of the whole of the local trade. Second, they were exempt from paying both the major export tax, known as the *grande coutume*, a tax that was levied on outgoing ships, and the *petite coutume*, a local sales or excise tax that otherwise would have been levied on the retailed wines that they drank in Bordeaux itself. Third, they were in a position to control much of the trade with the *haut-pays*. The *haut-pays* merchants had to pay the *grande coutume*, and the merchants of Bordeaux could control the timing and movement of their wares. The wines of the *haut-pays* could not be exported before St Martin's Day (11 November) and, from 1373 onwards, before Christmas Day. Distinctions for tax purposes between wines from English dominions and wines from territories controlled by the king of France were also drawn and redrawn at various times.

All histories of wine are histories of taxation, and we learn almost as much about wine from tax returns as we do from ecclesiastical records. Along with taxes – and the *grande coutume*, which was to survive the passing of the kings of England, was the most important of them – went tax exemptions. The medieval kings of England themselves enjoyed substantial tax favours both through the receipt of royal revenue from taxes and through their own exemption from paying any. On all ships reaching London Bridge that carried more than 21 *tonneaux* of wine they had rights of *prisage* which entitled them to a *tonneau* of wine from before the mast and a *tonneau* from after the mast. In addition, they received a single *tonneau* for each ship carrying less than 21 *tonneaux*.

The City Charter of 1235, granted to the citizens of Bordeaux by Henry III, was a sign not only of royal favour but of mutual recognition that Bordeaux was a *ville de vin*. The events leading up to it were momentous. Seventy years after Henry II's strategic marriage to Eleanor of Aquitaine at Poitiers, the city of La Rochelle (Rupella) further north, which was then the main outlet for the wine trade, opened its gates in 1224 to the French King Louis VIII, 'the Lionheart', and closed its harbour to English ships. Poitou, east of La Rochelle, was then the principal area for the English market. 'What a race of traitors these Poitevins are,' commented the lively thirteenth-century Benedictine chronicler, Matthew Paris. Yet the 'treachery' led to Bordeaux wresting the wine trade from its rivals and this was to prove the greatest of prizes.

There was even a sense of 'justice' in the outcome, for Eleanor, one of the most remarkable women of the Middle Ages, whose life was long and stormy, had been a 'girl of the Graves' and lived long enough to see her son Richard I, also called the 'the Lionheart', set off from Bordeaux on his famous crusade in 1190. His younger brother John, under whom Normandy was lost to the English Crown in 1203, knew Bordeaux well. He also loved wine. In 1212 he bought 267 *tonneaux* of wine from Gascony and only 54 *tonneaux* from the Orléanais and the Île-de-France, and after a visit to Bordeaux in 1215, the year of Magna Carta, we find him ordering from a Bristol merchant a further consignment of 120 *tonneaux* of Gascony wines. John asked key questions about the transport of wine, as Jefferson was to do centuries later, such as just how many ships there were in Bristol capable of carrying 24 *tonneaux*. A *tonneau* of wine was only one unit of measurement: it amounted to around two pipes, and was the equivalent of four casks (*barriques*). It was not only Bristol that figured in the thirteenth-century scenario. The Mayor of London, who represented his city at the sealing of the Magna Carta, was himself a member of a dynasty of vintners. In Bordeaux itself John made grants to local citizens of marshy or woody land in the Bordeaux area on condition that vines were planted there, an incentive that seems to have been scarcely necessary then and that would have been sharply criticized centuries later. More momentously, in 1214 he released Bordeaux nobles and merchants from paying any taxes on the wines coming from their own vineyards.

Nor surprisingly, after La Rochelle had fallen and the citizens of Bordeaux were offered a city charter, they swore that they would remain eternally loyal to the kings of England: 'In the defence of Bordeaux, the city of the King of England,' they proclaimed, 'we will be faithful to our lord, and we will serve him as long as we shall live.' The point was made again two centuries later to the French King Charles VII: 'if the city of Bordeaux is one of the biggest and most populous cities of this realm, it owes its prosperity to the island of England . . . a great realm, and rich . . . The said English bring in to our city gold and silver, which they convert into Gascon wines.'

At first, the fifty *jurats* of Bordeaux elected the Mayor, and together through the *Jurade*, which was subsequently reduced in size, they governed the city as an oligarchy, drafting and enforcing regulations and determining the tone of its social life. They were to remain an important body (with shifting composition and powers) until the eighteenth century, even after the rise of the *Parlement*, one of a group of French provincial *parlements*; and they enjoyed rights not only in Bordeaux but in Pessac, before the Pontac estate was to be located there.

Factional conflicts in the city, notably fierce in the thirteenth century, had little to do with pro- or anti-English alignments: indeed, in relation to a feudal society, where dependences and loyalties crossed what became national boundaries, the use of such terms is anachronistic. Wine always mattered, and it was in difficult times in 1416 that the *Jurade* declared simply but remarkably that wine is 'our substance': '*le vin de nos vignes est notre substance*'. It was to refer back to this basic declaration many times later.

Power was based on wealth, and wealth was derived in large part from wine. The city was able to furnish three-quarters of the medieval wines consumed in England's royal palaces – the *vinum regis*, ordered by the royal butler – and much of the wine drunk elsewhere in the kingdom, not all of it produced in vineyards in or near Bordeaux itself. Henry III, who spent the winter of 1242/3 in Bordeaux, bought large quantities of what was said to be a fine 1242 vintage, and under his son Edward I, who had married a princess from Castile, another Eleanor, a new *Tour du Roi* was built in the city, where Edward and future English kings lived when they stayed in the city. The connection of England and Gascony was closer than ever before. Edward favoured Gascon merchants and granted them special privileges in London in 1280. They were not tied to one quarter of the city or compelled to stay for limited periods only; and by a controversial new charter of 1302 they were given new tax advantages. Edward's son, Edward II, who became king in 1307, redressed the balance, however, and English traders came back into their own, soon regaining half the import trade. For his wedding feast in 1307 Edward II, who chose a French princess as his wife, ordered 1,000 *tonneaux* of wine from Bordeaux, the equivalent of over one million modern bottles.

The Anglo-Gascon wine trade was for the most part prosperous during the first third of the fourteenth century, and all records were broken in the year 1308/9 when the amazing figure for wine exports of 104,895 *tonneaux* (around 850,000 hectolitres) was attained, with most of the wine coming from the *haut-pays* above the city. In that year, no fewer than 747 ships carrying wine left Bordeaux (as compared with 603 in 1306/7). Unfortunately, the records do not give details of their destinations: we know, however, that at least one of them was Irish, the *St Jacques* from Waterford. We know also that large quantities of Gascon wines were consumed in Bordeaux itself, a true *ville de vin* in that sense. The wines of Bordeaux were making their way, too, to ports on the French side of the Channel, like the Normandy port of Honfleur – the first mention of a shipment there relates to 1227 – and modest quantities of Graves and *palus* were being drunk in Paris. They even reached Damme, the now long-abandoned port for the great medieval city of Bruges. There they were in competition with wines from the Île-de-France and the Rhine.

In her scholarly collection of *Studies of the Medieval Wine Trade* (1971) Margery Kirkbride James has examined in rich detail the pattern of fluctuations in the fourteenth- and fifteenth-century wine trade between Bordeaux and Britain, for which Bristol and Southampton, along with London, were the leading ports. When at their peak – as in 1308/9 and again in 1376 – wine imports constituted as much as 31 per cent of all English imports. Retail wine prices for the public were fixed at assizes: the royal butler, however, had direct access, at fluctuating prices, to the wines of best quality. Particulars of his accounts survive in an almost complete series between 1327 and 1350.

The scale of fourteenth-century enterprise looks striking when compared with that of the twentieth century. Indeed, the figure of 'average' wine imports over a period at the beginning of the fourteenth century was greater than it was in the year that Britain joined the European Community. Absolutely as well as relatively this was an outstanding period in the history of wine. It was not until the 1980s that imports into Britain of the red wines of Bordeaux reached figures which were comparable with – if still significantly smaller than – the medieval figures when the population of the country was small. Loads were up to 200 to 300 *tonneaux* – always sent in barrels – and the barrels were often unracked. The journey could be stormy and dangerous, and did not help the quality of the wine on arrival.

Fluctuations in the medieval wine trade were even more striking than fluctuations in modern times. Thus, the export figure for 1308/9 was halved the next year to 51,351 *tonneaux*. The fluctuations were influenced not only by the state of the weather, but by politics and by the outbreak in 1337 of what came to be called the Hundred Years War, a protracted war that was bound to have substantial consequences for wine producers, for shippers and for customers. Its effects were felt almost at once as French armies ravaged the *haut-pays* in the years between the outbreak of the war and 1340. In 1337 total exports were less than a quarter of the volume of the previous year. Wine ships were harassed so severely that a convoy system was introduced. There were particular years during the later stages of the war when most wines commanded very high prices, as they had done immediately after the outbreak of war when a scarcity of wine in London led to costly transporting of wine from Southampton and Bristol. Prices fell again, however, after a five-year truce was agreed upon in 1340.

After 1348 came a new problem, when the Black Death struck Bordeaux. Only 6,800 *tonneaux* of wine were exported in that year, when only twenty-one ships sailed. By 1350 prices were more than double what they had been at the beginning of the century, and they were still as high at the end of the century when the English market accounted for three-quarters of Bordeaux's exports of wine. By then most of the wine was coming from Bordeaux vineyards. The *haut-pays* had been cut off by French soldiers.

It was because the Hundred Years War was so prolonged – and at times so savage – that it posed exceptional threats to the trade on which Bordeaux depended. The great warrior, the Black Prince, victor of the Battle of Poitiers in 1356 and the greatest feudal lord of his time, played an important part in the history of Bordeaux; and men from Bordeaux fought in his armies. During the years that he spent in Bordeaux, more Gascon wine must have been drunk than ever before, for his entertainments were especially lavish: he is said to have entertained 400 people daily at his tables. His son Richard II, who was to be deposed in 1399, had been born on Twelfth Night in or near Bordeaux and was baptized in the cathedral there when he was three days old.

In bad years, when the demand for wine of quality outran supply, business could be highly lucrative for the merchants, but other sections of the population suffered. It was not easy to grow sufficient grain in Gascony to meet local needs, particularly when population was increasing; and the balance between wine and food – imported or exported – was a matter of strong local concern in Gascony, as it was to be in the eighteenth century. Significantly, in 1401 Richard II's successor Henry IV ordered that merchants living in areas controlled by the king of France – and these were by then very close to Bordeaux – should send one *tonneau* of corn to Bordeaux along with every two of wine.

It is of importance that after Richard II's dethronement neither of his successors, Henry IV and Henry V (1413–21), the latter the much-vaunted English hero of the Hundred Years War, visited Bordeaux. On the eve of the Battle of Agincourt in 1415, however, Henry V ordered wine – and guns – from Bordeaux. During the fifteenth century imports of Gascon wines into England fell to an average of 13,000 *tonneaux*, and there were particularly bad years, like 1425/6, when the volume of imports collapsed to 7,000 *tonneaux*, and 1446/7 when there were severe frosts throughout the wine-growing area. During the years of 'peace' from 1444 to 1449, followed by the fall of Bordeaux to the King of France, the average was still 13,000 *tonneaux*.

Such figures were difficult to maintain, and during the last stages of the Hundred Years War, when the *haut-pays* was completely in the hands of the French and when the men and women of Bordeaux were often left to fend for themselves, the citizens of Bordeaux did not want the English to leave. When the city fell to the French for the first time in 1451, coincidentally the year of a prolific vintage, its citizens stressed the importance of their English connections and secured good terms from the French king. A year later, however, the city was prepared to open its gates again to an Englishman, *le vieux Talbot*, eighty-year-old John Talbot, Earl of Shrewsbury, and it was not finally taken again by armies of the King of France, Charles VII, until 19 October 1453. Talbot, his son, and many of the English nobles serving with him had been killed at Castillon in the last battle of the Hundred Years War. A long period of history, sometimes prosperous, often turbulent, had come to its end.

The dramatic flight of the remnants of the English army, who left Gascony for the last time in 1453, did not destroy the wine trade of Bordeaux. This was a point emphasized by the romantic historian, Jules Michelet, writing in the nineteenth century, a historian of a very different kind from most contemporary social and economic historians, who rely heavily on statistics as their main evidence. He was more concerned too with psychology than with physical warfare. 'As regards its commerce,' Michelet maintained, 'Bordeaux did not long lose over it. The commercial spirit, stronger in the English even than their pride, would not suffer them to give up their trade in the wines of Gascony.' It was not a coincidence that one of the first Victorian visitors to Bordeaux, Charles Cocks, later of Cocks et Féret fame, was a translator of Michelet.

The retreating English went with the vintage and were allowed to take their cargoes of 1453 away with them: 6,000 *tonneaux* were exported that year. Meanwhile, some English traders, who had become increasingly important in the late medieval wine trade, continued to operate in the city, along with Bretons, Scotsmen and Irishmen. They were subject to restrictions, however, and were made to feel and even to look as conspicuous as possible in the streets of Bordeaux. They wore a red cross and had to be indoors by seven o'clock. Meanwhile, a considerable number of the Bordelais went into forced or voluntary exile.

Trade fell off sharply between 1453 and 1463, but it did not cease – the 1455 figure was 3,000 *tonneaux* – and it rose again after 1463. By then, those citizens of Bordeaux who had fled to England after the fall of the city – there were as many as 2,000 of them – were gradually returning and providing a new link between London and Bordeaux. Many of them had settled in the parish of St Martin's in the Vintry in London, where they were in the company of people with whom they had long had dealings. Those who returned to Bordeaux, now irrevocably in the hands of the kings of France, were anxious to maintain trade. Equally important, the kings of France themselves soon realized the importance of maintaining commercial links. As early as 1454, the *Jurade* was re-established; and although Charles VII built the huge Château Trompette in Bordeaux in an attempt to cow its citizens, his successor, Louis XI, quickly accepted the proposition, enunciated earlier, that 'the whole basis of Bordeaux's wealth was the isle of England'. Louis conceded that no other country could take England's place as purchaser of Bordeaux's wines and that the English should therefore be allowed to trade once more 'as freely as they would'.

After 1475, when the English King Edward IV signed a treaty with France, English traders did not need safe conducts – although their ships were now granted them. Nor did they need to pay the whole of the *grande coutume*, the proceeds of which had now passed into the hands of the kings of France. Moreover, from 1482 onwards all restrictions on their movements were abolished, and a year later, the trade of Bordeaux with England had reached its pre-1453 level.

Although wine soon faced increased competition in England from beer – the use of hops in beer was to be introduced from the Low Countries, some said with the Reformation – by the end of the fifteenth century total imports of wine had risen again from 20,000 to 25,000 *tonneaux* and over the years 1509 to 1518 were as high as 50,000 *tonneaux*. In 1517 there were said to be as many as seven or eight thousand Englishmen within the Bordeaux area. In September 1532 the *jurats* resolved to send 20 *tonneaux* of the best possible wine to England to prove that it was still good: *Il était aussi bon que jamais*.

In Queen Elizabeth's reign British merchants were still as active as ever, and her successor James I, formerly King James VI of Scotland, kept an agent of his own in Bordeaux. We know too from literary evidence how strongly the wines of Graves were favoured.

A purchase of Graves by the innkeeper of the Mouth Tavern in Bishopsgate, is recorded in 1612: he bought one and a half *tonneaux*; and in a play by Thomas Heywood, *The Fair Maid of the West* (1632), one character says that 'sextons love Graves wine'. Six years later, Lewis Roberts in his *The Merchant's Map of Commerce* referred to 'those Graves wines which we esteem so excellent'. His knowledge of wine was better than his knowledge of geography, for he was seriously at fault in saying that the Graves wines came from 'the little village of La Grave'.

The sale of wine remained as closely controlled as it had been in the Middle Ages. Thus, an English order in council of 1633 laid down that 'the best Gascoigne wines' should be sold at '£18 the tonne and at sixpence the quart by retaile', a lower retail price than that charged for 'Canary Wines, Muskadells, and Alligant' or 'Sacks and wines of Malaga'. In 1672 a similar order stated that 'no Gascoigne or French wine should be sold by retail under eightpence the quart', two-thirds of the retail price of Rhenish wines. In the last of such price-fixing orders in 1679 and 1680 the figure was raised to 'twelvepence the quart' after a new duty of fourpence on a quart had been charged on all French wines.

One of the London inns in which Gascon wines were sold during the reign of James I, the Mouth in Bishopsgate, has already been mentioned; another was the Three Cranes in the Vintry, not far from the Vintners' Hall. The playwright Ben Jonson, with his keen eye for what was actually happening in London – below and above the ground – referred to it both in his *Bartholomew Fair* (1614), along with the Mitre and the Mermaid, and in his play *The Devil is an Ass* (1616):

> Nay, boy, I will bring thee to the sluts and the roysters,
> At Billingsgate, feasting with claret-wine and oysters.

The combination remained acceptable throughout the seventeenth century.

Throughout the sixteenth century the Irish and the Scots were increasingly entering the wine trade also. So, too, were the Bretons and the Dutch, who in 1579 began their revolt against Philip II of Spain. The Reformation had introduced a new factor into European economics and politics, and the Protestant Dutch Republic that emerged after 1581 and that played a major role in the *révolution des boissons* was to reach its period of greatest relative wealth and power in the seventeenth century. Its links with Catholic Bordeaux, where Calvinism was a minority religion, were very important to it.

The wine growers and merchants of Bordeaux themselves were looking for new markets still further away – as far east as the German Hanseatic League, the members of which were as willing to sell imported wine as to drink it; and even before the revolt of the Netherlands we learn of the wines of Gascony being drunk in Ghent and Antwerp. We also learn of them being drunk in France itself – for example, in Nantes.

Around this time the phrase *vins de France*, wines of France, was beginning to be used, as it is today, to mean all French wines and not, as it had in the past, only those wines produced in the Île-de-France, *Vina Parisina*. As Dion and others have claimed, before national sentiment had clearly and fully emerged in a period of protracted war, *'le sentiment d'une patrie française'*, a genuine French sentiment, was developing fully in the vineyards. They were beginning to be thought of as a jewel in the French crown.

It was against this background, never static, that the long line of Pontac proprietors of the Haut-Brion estate, one of a number of new vineyards, *bourdieux*, not only created an overseas market for their own wine but established its distinctive taste and reputation. They were drawn at first to the French market, however, and again there are several significant dates. One was 1518, when Arnaud de Pontac, father of the founder of Haut-Brion, dispatched 6 *fûts* (casks) of honey, 31 *tonneaux* of wine and 4,000 vines to Rouen. Another was 1525, when according to a nineteenth-century source, the *jurats* decided that 120 *tonneaux* of 'the best wine of the Graves' should be sent to King Francis I, the Queen and the royal children.

There is evidence from this time to suggest that the importance of ensuring the quality of particular wines and of identifying their place of origin was beginning to be recognized before the *grands crus* came to be identified as such, although the wine on offer was still, as it had been, new wine, the *vin de l'année*. Wine tasters in Bordeaux and in England – and Ireland (merchants from Limerick were mentioned in 1511) – were fixing prices after careful comparative tasting; and it was often stipulated in contracts, to quote the historian M. J. Bernard, that 'the wine mentioned in them should not only be described as coming from a particular parish but that the names of its proprietors should be specified also', '*du creu de las vinhes de son bordieu qui es en les Graves de Bordes*'. It may well be that one day a sixteenth-century contract will be found, British or French, that will mention specifically the name of the de Pontac wines of Haut-Brion.

Old Bordeaux

The château at Haut-Brion seen through the arch

The park of Haut-Brion

The vineyards

Gathering the grapes

Sorting

A crate of grapes

The arrival of the grapes at the chais

M. Delmas tasting in the laboratory

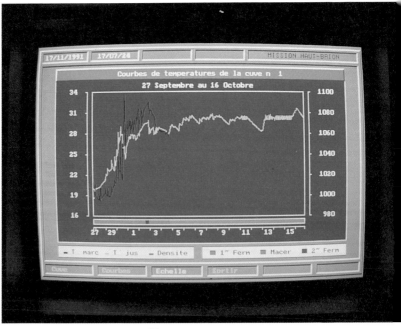

The computer screen

The cuvier

Wine in the barrel

Haut-Brion labels

8

The Pontacs

One of the most ancient and illustrious families of
the Guyenne.

Édouard Féret, 1888

Going back to the beginning of the Haut-Brion estate, Jean de
Pontac, who did not marry for the first time until he was thirty-
seven years old, fathered no fewer than fifteen children. When he
married for the third time, he was seventy-six. His new bride was
Isabelle de Léon, Dame de la Tresne. There were no children, yet
the name de la Tresne was to figure prominently in later Haut-
Brion history.

Jean's first bride, Jeanne de Bellon, brought with her as dowry
part of the Haut-Brion estate: her father, Pierre de Bellon, was
Mayor of Libourne, a smaller rival to Bordeaux four miles from St-
Émilion, which had enjoyed the privilege of sending wines direct to
England. A year after the marriage Jean is said to have acquired
his first Haut-Brion property, in 1526, from Admiral Philippe de
Chabot, one-time Mayor of Bordeaux. Chabot had served in Italy
with King Francis I of France and had been taken prisoner at the
battle of Pavia in 1525. In 1533 Jean acquired the seigneurial rights
of Haut-Brion from a Bordeaux merchant of Basque origin, Jean
Duhalde: he paid 2,650 francs bordelais for them. In feudal times
no land was left without a lord (*seigneur*), although the detailed
pattern of seigneurial rights was complex and frequently disputed.
They had also become transferable, and Duhalde was only a recent
holder of the Haut-Brion rights. According to folklore, they had
been acquired in 1509 by Jean de Ségur, head of a family that was
to play a key role in the history of the wines of Bordeaux. The story

has often been repeated, but we know that before 1509 packets of rights had been held by various proprietors, among them Robert Pey and Guillaumine Bernard, wife of an Eyquem who had been born a Pey. Both were mentioned in a document of 1474.

The Eyquems had been a rising family in Bordeaux far earlier than the Pontacs, and in three generations they had entered the nobility as the Pontacs were to do. Their name was to be associated with the name of a great wine, Château d'Yquem, although theirs was not the family that was to be responsible for it. The name of the Ségurs was to be connected with two other wines, but in their case the family was the agency that was directly responsible for the wine-making. In 1680 Jacques de Ségur was to plant a new vineyard at Lafite in an old *seigneurie* dating from the fourteenth century, and in 1695 Alexandre de Ségur was to acquire by marriage the fourteenth-century seigneurial rights to Latour.

Jean de Pontac's acquisition of seigneurial rights in 1533 was only one stage, if the most important, in a protracted process of appropriation during which Haut-Brion swallowed up many small properties that had been concerned with wine-making in the Middle Ages. There had been many such properties in an intricate network of feudal dues and obligations, but few of them were bigger than 40 *journaux*, a dozen hectares, and the grapes that they produced might vary greatly in quality according to the plot within the vineyard. Jean created a compact *domaine*, big enough to permit supervision and control.

The *Livre de Raison de la Famille de Pontac* is an indispensable contemporary source that covers Jean's life. It refers to the crucial Duhalde purchase, and goes on to list some of Jean's other purchases, among them a piece of land acquired from Nicolas Peyron in 1533. Later purchases included are one in 1540 from the wife of 'Johan de Lafite' for 16 francs and one in 1542 from a labourer (*laboureur*) in the parish of St-Eulalie, the nearest Bordeaux parish to Haut-Brion. Jean paid 20 '*francs bourdellais*' for the latter. The prices varied widely. In 1559 Jean bought two pieces of workable land (*terres labourables*) in the parish of Pessac, one 'behind my warren' ('*derrière ma garenne*'), also for the price of 20 francs. He had already bought one piece from the same seller.

Two of the new parcels of land were acquired from blacksmiths, several from Pierre de Lestonnac, a *jurat* of Bordeaux, member of a family that towards the end of the sixteenth century was itself to consolidate and extend an estate as *seigneurs* of Margaux. There had been a fortress at Margaux since the thirteenth century, and according to one source the *domaine* had once belonged to an English king, Edward II.

The ambition to be called *seigneur* had moved many Bordeaux merchants during the Middle Ages: they had taken it for granted also that growing vines was a part of the pattern of business in a *ville de vin*. Jean de Pontac, however, seems to have been interested in acquiring seigneurial rights less in order to secure revenues in cash or in kind (*arrières*) than to create a compact estate at Haut-Brion. He was willing to exchange land, therefore, as well as to purchase it. He conceived of an estate dedicated solely to the production of wine in an area where wine had long been produced by small proprietors or by the Church. The first mention of a '*chay*' in the *Livre de Raison* unfortunately does not give the date, but by 1560 Jean had a *chai* in Bordeaux itself as well as at Haut-Brion.

Jean was an innovator, but he must have been familiar with the manner by which the Archbishop of Bordeaux's vineyard at Pessac had been – and still was – managed through direct exploitation: *vignerons* worked under the direction of an episcopal agent. And this was to be the first working pattern that the Pontacs followed. Haut-Brion was not the only property that Jean owned. Indeed, by the time that he died, he was lord of ten different estates. In accumulating his various properties, wherever they were, he always seems to have had his eye on their potential as vineyards and not on land acquisition as such. Half of his properties were situated in what is still wine-producing territory. One was as far away as the Agenais in old wine territory, the *haut-pays*. Another was at Pez, St-Estèphe, the most northerly area in the Haut-Médoc, an area which did not yet figure prominently on the wine map. A third was in the Bas-Médoc, no more associated at that time with wine than the Haut-Médoc was. It included Lalande, Mont-Plaisir, and Belin, a nodal point where highways, including a main highway, met. There Jean could collect tolls.

It was at Haut-Brion that he built a new château in 'the place called Montcuq', the place name that had figured in fifteenth-century documents. At the time, as well as in retrospect, this was the first great event in the history of the Haut-Brion property. The contracts that survive – and they were drawn up not with a mason, but with a carpenter and a tiler (*couvreur*) – were signed in 1549 and 1550. The work was probably carried out by Jean Cheminode, a master builder who worked with Jean on other properties and with other rising merchant families. The medieval castle, about which we know nothing, had probably been situated some small distance away from the present château, but wherever or whatever it was, it was soon forgotten.

The new château, as Paul Roudié has pointed out, was in complete contrast with the old buildings of the district. It was not a stronghold, but rather an early example of a castle that was explicitly designed for wine-making, 'authentiquement vinicole'. Its creator, who obviously needed both a central point for his enterprise and a home for his large family, sold his wines at a good price: by 1543 they were fetching between 50 and 64 livres per tonneau.

Jean lived in a time of opportunity that was also a time of trouble – the two usually coincide – and although the Pontac family was to be correctly described in the late nineteenth century as 'one of the most ancient and the most illustrious families of the Guyenne', it rose not through inheritance but through late fifteenth- and early sixteenth-century enterprise. By the late nineteenth century, when the claim could be made that the family name had figured in 'each page of the history of this province', the family stood out (as it still does) as an aristocratic family, 'still worthily in evidence', although no longer holding Haut-Brion.

By the late nineteenth century there was a fashion on both sides of the Channel for looking back in carefully compiled genealogies to times long before the age of Jean, the age not of the noblesse de robe but of the noblesse d'épée, the men of the sword. Men were men then, and honour was honour. There had been a Guillem de Pontac, it was stated, 'around the year 1060', before the Norman conquest of England, and as early as 1375 a French king, Charles V, had granted Antoine de Pontac and his heirs the privilege of incorporating the Royal Star in their coats of arms. Antoine had been awarded the privilege for driving the English out of the castle of Mortagne, in Saintonge, which they were then holding, and the Latin letters patent were said to have spoken of the English as 'our enemies'.

It was not with Antoine, however, but with Jean de Pontac that Édouard Féret, historian and specialist in the study of wine topography and production, rightly chose to begin in the late nineteenth century a collection of brief biographies of individual members of the Pontac family. There were by then diverse branches of the family, members of which had served many kings in many different fashions, but they all could recognize in Jean a common founder, '*un auteur commun*'.

An 'illustrious lineage', the phrase that André Simon used to describe Haut-Brion, applied equally aptly, therefore, to the Pontac family. But it is only part – and not the most important part – of the necessary description. The origins of the family were undoubtedly ancient – in a little town in Béarn with the same name, not far from Pau, and there it can be traced back to the eleventh century – but the later development of the family was associated more with the urban and mercantile life of Bordeaux than with the rural countryside.

Jean's father Arnaud, *bourgeois* and *marchand de Bordeaux*, the founder of the fortunes which Jean was to put to good use, rose through business acumen rather than through the advantages of birth. He was obviously a man of influence, but his influence derived primarily from his wealth, and in this he was representative of a number of new families that were not only ousting some of the older merchant families of Bordeaux, but were challenging the power of the often debt-ridden Gascon nobility. The shifting social background is fascinating to a historian.

So also is the economic background. As a merchant and shipowner, Arnaud was also interested in wine, as his 1518 shipment to Rouen suggested. He sold vines, exported wines and imported cloth, but he also purchased a vineyard (*bourdieu*) at Taillan, the wines of which, we know, were already appreciated in England. In addition, he owned windmills and a *chai* in the newly developing business district of Bordeaux: Les Chartrons. He belongs to a period before *marchands* (merchants) had become *négociants* (dealers), as they were to be in the golden age of the Chartrons in the eighteenth century, yet he was already prepared to make deals that involved risking his capital. His attitudes and his achievements substantiate the view advanced two generations ago by R. H. Tawney that 'the sixteenth century took its character from the outburst of economic energy in which it had been born'. Like later members of his family, Arnaud was drawn to public office, so that we have more details of him than would otherwise have survived. He was Mayor of Bordeaux in 1505 and in 1525, and eight years before his son Jean's first marriage he became Controller of

Accounts (*contrôleur du Roi en la comptabilité*), an influential and lucrative position. His rise to wealth and power was expressed in an escalating sequence of local descriptions of his social standing: '*honneste homme*', '*honorable homme*', '*noble homme*'. His career has rightly been deemed to illustrate the working of the motto *requesses noblessent* (riches ennoble).

Jean, Arnaud's oldest son, was one of six male and two female children and, in what was soon to become a family pattern, he inherited from his father the Controllership of Accounts. In 1529 he became an active tax farmer, practising what was then the most lucrative type of farming in Bordeaux. Taxes were a burden to those from whom they were collected, but a boon to those who collected them for an agreed sum. The system of tax farming appealed to kings and their servants in that it substituted a certain income for a fluctuating revenue, but by its nature it could never make tax farmers popular. At best they were tolerated. One of Jean's relatives, Louis de Pontac, also a tax farmer, had his house in Talence sacked by peasants in violent riots against the salt tax (*gabelle*). The *grande coutume* which Jean farmed was a very special prize, however, since, as has been explained, it had been at the very heart of the medieval complex of local taxes and privileges in Bordeaux, some of which were to survive until the French Revolution.

There were, of course, other than monetary rewards for representing authority. Louis, with financial interests in Armagnac, was made a member of the *Parlement* at Bordeaux in 1543, and from 1522 to 1589 Jean was Civil and Criminal Registrar of the Court, a key legal position based on the *Parlement*, already the most prestigious body in Bordeaux. He held office under six kings: Louis XII, Francis I, Henry II, Francis II, Charles IX and Henry III. Their fortunes fluctuated: his rose.

The *Parlement* of Bordeaux, a supreme court, hierarchical in structure and influence – misleadingly translatable as Parliament – was served by a large number of officers. It had medieval origins, some of them, it was said, going back to 1451, eleven years before a *Parlement* with significant authority was summoned by Louis XI; and throughout the sixteenth, seventeenth and early eighteenth centuries successive *Parlements*, stronger or weaker, continued to provide financial, political and social opportunities for local families seeking to acquire noble status, as did the Pontacs. For those who acquired such status there were continuing privileges: offices might – and often did – pass from father to son. The Pontacs, in particular, made the most of such hereditary succession in the seventeenth century until one of them, François-Auguste, the Pontac who came to London, deliberately rejected it. Such succession was taken for granted until the *Parlement* was dissolved in the French Revolution – with one descendant of the Pontacs playing a prominent part in the final stages of its history.

In its beginnings the *Parlement* had succeeded in representing local interests while at the same time serving the needs of centralizing monarchy, yet during the seventeenth-century troubles of the Fronde, which began with a movement within the Paris *Parlement*, it passed from reconciliation to rebellion. Leading opposition to the Royal Governor, the Duc d'Épernon, it actually raised an army in 1650 against the young King Louis XIV's Regent, Cardinal Mazarin, when Bordeaux was in open revolt. By the end of the seventeenth century – and by then the Pontacs had withdrawn from it – it had lost some of its power, but it was active, if ultimately unsuccessful, in asserting its claims in the reign of Louis XV.

The members of the *Parlement* constituted a Bordeaux élite, linked by intermarriage and renowned for their wealth, at least as influential an élite as the *Jurade* had been when the English kings ruled Bordeaux. Meanwhile, the *Jurade* continued to exist until the French Revolution. Like the *Parlement*, it was also a law court, in its case a court of first instance. By the late eighteenth century it consisted of six *jurats*: two noblemen, two advocates, and two merchants, headed by the Mayor. Both *Jurade* and *Parlement* influenced and were influenced by the development of the wine trade. In the middle years of the eighteenth century almost three-quarters of the gross landed incomes of the families represented in the *Parlement* came from wine.

That was far in the future, long after Jean came to depend on wine. He lived for most of the year in Bordeaux, but the château that he built at Haut-Brion was more than a symbol of what we would call upward mobility. As a *château vinicole* it stood out in a district where most of the neighbouring vineyards remained small. Yet it had few pretensions. A rectangular building, with a tower at each corner, its measurements were originally calculated in feet, *pieds*: 50 feet by 22 feet. Its walls were bare and undecorated, and its windows simple, but it had a high slate roof and corner turrets.

One tower has not survived, neither has an outside staircase. The chapel as such has disappeared also, although there are signs in an upstairs room, now used as a bedroom, of where it once was. A second wing was added, at right angles, in the seventeenth century.

The chapel obviously mattered deeply to Jean. He was a devoted Catholic in an age of religious and political conflict, and his own activities during 'the wars of religion' were as much political as economic. Politics in the sixteenth century in France as elsewhere were very much the politics of religion. In Jean's own region Calvin had won over many early disciples, as zealous in their Protestant faith as he was in his Catholic faith. Some of them held positions of power, and their ambitions were opposed bitterly by the Catholic League, one of France's most powerful organizations. Within this context the chapel at Haut-Brion was more than a place of family worship for Jean. It was at the heart of his faith. At a time and in a place where there are said to have been many switches of religion (*croyances flottantes*) Jean's allegiances were firm.

The years 1588 and 1589 were among the most exciting in modern French – and modern European – history. Indeed, events moved as quickly then as they were to do two hundred years later at the time of the French Revolution or, in our own time, in the late 1980s. In December 1589 Catherine de Medici, the Dowager Queen and one of the most remarkable women of her time, died; her third son, Henry III, had been murdered by a fanatical friar in August. In the previous year, the year of the Spanish Armada, he had himself arranged for the assassination at Blois of the leaders of the Catholic League, the Duc de Guise and his brother Louis, the Cardinal de Lorraine. His own murder was almost as dramatic.

It was in the light of the events at Blois that Jean de Pontac, as a leading Gascon notable, joined with his son Thomas in a plot designed to hand over the city of Bordeaux to the Catholic League, but he died in April before the failure of the plot could affect him. This was four months before the coming to the throne of the Protestant King Henry IV, Henry of Navarre, whom Henry III, when dying, had recognized as his successor. It was a new turn of the wheel when Henry IV joined the Catholic Church in 1593. '*Paris vaut bien une messe.*'

A local lawyer, who was also a member of the Bordeaux *Parlement*, Estienne de Cruzeau, wrote at the time of Jean's funeral (omitting the complex politics) that he died 'suffering neither from gout nor from gallstones, in good health, speech and hearing, unimpaired up to the last breath, and the richest man in the city'. He was buried in appropriate style in the Church of the Carmelites in another chapel that he had founded and endowed, and all the members of the Bordeaux *Parlement*, including those who had disapproved of his politics, were said to have been present at his funeral. The Carmelites had, of course, been producing wine long before the Pontacs dealt in it, and in years to come there were to be wrangles between them and the owners of Haut-Brion.

With a touch of historical irony the Haut-Brion estate passed neither into the hands of Jean's eldest son, who had died before him, nor into those of his second son, Thomas, who had been a Deputy to the Estates General in Blois, but into those of his fourth son, Arnaud, then fifty-nine years old and a priest. Ordained in Rome when he was twenty-seven years old, Arnaud had later become Bishop of Bazas, the small city about thirty-five miles west of Bordeaux which under the English had been a *filleule* of Bordeaux, a fortified city sharing the privileges of Bordeaux and looking to it for protection. Its cathedral had been built in 1233, and while he was Bishop Arnaud spent time and money restoring it. Religion now figured even more prominently in the story of Haut-Brion than it had done before.

Other members of the growing Pontac family – increasingly dispersed throughout Gascony – were important in local life in various places, and wherever they lived they were now beginning to live in style. Indeed, by then they clearly constituted a dynasty. In his *Nobiliaire de Guienne et de Gascogne* (1858) O'Gilvy was to give a long list of the diverse tasks that the members of the family had performed. The titles of their offices were high-sounding. After Jean, for example, there were four Pontacs who were registrars, three who were procurators and two who were tax receivers. One, Jean's eldest son by his second marriage, was Dean of the Cathedral in Bordeaux. Yet Arnaud stood out among all the members of the family. One of his ecclesiastical titles, from 1580 onwards, was Dean of the Chapter of St-Émilion, a town where pastoral care and the care of wine went naturally together.

When Arnaud died in 1605, his funeral was an even greater event than Jean's had been. The cortège was said to have been so long – nearly ten miles, according to one estimate – that the head of it entered the Cathedral at Bazas before the Bishop's body had left the

Château des Jourbettes fifteen kilometres away. In his will Arnaud left 12,000 écus to complete restoration work on the Cathedral, and a plaque in the Cathedral fittingly commemorates him. Yet of his imposing tomb there is now no trace. Like Jean's chapel at Haut-Brion, it has passed into legend. Arnaud was one of the most cultivated men of his age – one of his languages was Hebrew – and he was to be given more space in Féret's brief biographies than his father Jean. He was to be remembered, however, less for his vines than for his charities, his books and what his contemporaries called his wide range of knowledge ('*vastes et profondes connaîssances*'). He had assembled a huge and wonderful library, the cataloguing of which was not completed until 1663, fifty-eight years after his death. 'Of all the roads that lead to glory,' wrote its compiler, l'Abbé Machon, in a dedication to Arnaud, 'I know of none that is more certainly secure than that of Letters.'

After Arnaud's death, the destinies of his books and of his wines were to be intertwined, just as his pastoral and intellectual activities had been intertwined during his lifetime. The first owner of Haut-Brion after him was Arnaud's nephew, Geoffroi, said to be twenty-nine years old when he inherited it (we do not know his exact date of birth) and he had also inherited the Bishop's library. He had already moved to the château at Haut-Brion by 1605. Six years after inheriting Haut-Brion – and with nine manor houses at his disposal – he ordered the building of a magnificent new mansion in Bordeaux. It was to become the Maison Daurade, originally '*la maison dorée*' (the golden house), the site of which had been acquired by his father, Raymond de Pontac, the older brother of the Bishop, in 1579. The new house, built and decorated over a period of years, beginning around 1611, contrasted as much as any large house could have done with the simple and undecorated château at Haut-Brion. Situated in the Rue de Saint Rémy, in a new aristocratic quarter of Bordeaux, it was one of a number of imposing new *grandes maisons*. One of them, the Maison du Chapeau Rouge, belonged to the Pichon family, related by marriage to the Pontacs; another belonged to the grandfather of Montesquieu. There was no doubt, however, that even among the *grandes maisons* of Bordeaux the Maison Daurade was exceptional: a contemporary observer, Pierre Bergeron, who travelled in Italy, described it in 1612 as a wonder of the age. Almost everything in the house was of gold or covered in gold leaf. There were also magnificent ornaments and tapestries. The King's daughter, Mademoiselle d'Orléans, had sent paintings. The splendour of the Maison outdid that of all the other former merchant families who had risen to wealth and power in Bordeaux.

When Geoffroi died in 1649 at the age of seventy-three, his son Arnaud, 'Haut et Puissant Seigneur de Salles, Hautbrion et Autres Places', was already nearly fifty years of age; and four years later he was to have added to his title the even more resounding words 'Messire le Premier Président du Parlement de Guyenne'. His father had been only a councillor (conseiller au parlement) from 1596. The presidency was the most prestigious of all local and regional offices.

Arnaud resided in what became a still grander Maison Daurade, and acquired an additional nearby property from his aunt, Ysabeau de Chassaigne, 'dame de Bataille, des Jauberthes et de Salles', which provided him with a new kitchen, a bureau, other extra rooms – and, not least, cellars. His prestige in Bordeaux was acknowledged, outside Bordeaux also, for in 1632 he had married a daughter of the President of the Parlement of Paris, providing a family link between the Parlement of Bordeaux and the Paris Parlement from which it had derived. Such a link was socially and politically significant.

Arnaud's years as President were turbulent years in the politics of Bordeaux and must have absorbed a great deal of his time. Yet money interested him as well as power. Like his father before him, he bought further properties, including farm land and pine forests, and he lent money as well as made it. He became President of the Parlement at a time when France and Oliver Cromwell's England were at war, and he seems to have appreciated clearly that England would become a major market for his wine: perhaps he knew that Oliver Cromwell loved wine as much as any Englishman. In 1663, three years after the King of England had returned to London, the most important of the French King's officials in Bordeaux, the Intendant of the province, estimated Arnaud's annual income at 25,000 livres francs. This was at a time when the workers in his vineyards at Haut-Brion were earning 10 or 12 sous a day. (There were 20 sous to a livre franc.)

Charles II of England, restored to the throne in 1660, reigned for another twenty-one years before Arnaud died, years of importance in the history of wine-making at Haut-Brion. At his death Arnaud left behind him an inventory of his possessions at Haut-Brion and at the Maison Daurade which had been prepared for legal reasons: it was associated with his testament that had been drawn up in 1677. The inventory of Maison Daurade, which covered the contents of thirty-three rooms, took six days to prepare, although it did not deal in detail with the great library which Arnaud had inherited from his great-uncle. The shorter Haut-Brion inventory listed what was to be found in its twenty-three rooms and in the wine *chai*: in the latter there were ten vats, five of which were said to contain 24 *barriques* of wine.

The master bedroom at Haut-Brion was then on the ground floor; it had a huge red bed with three down mattresses and a red taffeta counterpane. Next to it was a valet's antechamber. Madame's bedroom was on the western side of the house, and it too had a maid's antechamber. The dining room contained a long walnut table, complete with nineteen chairs covered in red cloth, and there was a tapestry with a hunting scene on the wall. Red was the predominant colour everywhere, including the bedrooms, one of them a room for guests known as the Red Room. There was a billiard room on the first floor. Over the fireplace in the salon was a picture of Christ. Obviously religion continued to be taken very seriously in this noble household, which had separate chaplain's rooms. The chapel itself displayed more than twenty paintings, including a painting over the altar of the Virgin holding the dead Christ in her arms.

On his death Arnaud did not leave his affairs in the tidiest of conditions. Nor was he alone in his untidiness. Already his only son, François-Auguste, had contracted substantial debts – an accepted feature of the aristocratic way of life, very different from the way of life of the medieval merchant – and there was an unsavoury argument between him and Arnaud's widow, who continued to live in the Maison Daurade. She had been a benefactress to the Carmelites of Bordeaux – as had Jean de Pontac and his father – and with her powerful family connections, must have been a woman of considerable influence. The argument centred on the question of the ownership of some of Arnaud's possessions that had been listed in the detailed inventory that François-Auguste had called for. The widow had complied, but significantly she had signed the document listing them not with the name Pontac, but with her own maiden name. Even after her death, it took more than ten years and more than one lawsuit to settle the problems of the Pontac properties, ten years when conditions at Haut-Brion were in a critical state.

François-Auguste, born in 1636, was the last Pontac in direct line to own Haut-Brion, and the contribution that he made to its history through London, not Bordeaux, was, as we have already seen, of a very different kind from that of any of his predecessors. He was uninterested in the affairs of the *Parlement* in Bordeaux, which remained disturbed and controversial, although his father, in line with tradition, had spent 27,000 livres francs to buy him the *Présidence au Requêtes* (the Receivership of Requests) in 1653, when he was only seventeen: this was more than one year's income. François-Auguste sold it back in 1662, and apparently moved to England then. This was at a time when Bordeaux was exporting about 44,000 *barriques* of wine a year for Englishmen to drink.

How long François-Auguste stayed in England is not clear, although there is one reference in a pamphlet of 1671 to 'Sprightly Pontack', 'the best of the sort', which suggests that François-Auguste was still singing its merits. The annual import of wines from Bordeaux to England had risen to 68,000 *barriques* by 1667 and 88,000 five years later. There was political trouble, however, in Bordeaux itself, where there was an uprising in 1675 – the cry was *'vive le roi sans gabelle'* (long live the king but without the salt tax). The uprising was followed by military occupation of the city.

At the time of his father's death in 1681 and the compilation of the inventory, François-Auguste was in Bordeaux, and he was married in the same year in the chapel of Haut-Brion. His bride, Marie-Félice de Crussol d'Uzès, was twenty years younger than he was, and through her he acquired a new title: Comte de Caubon. The marriage obviously did not affect his travels, for he was back in England again in 1683, nearly twenty years after he had first set up Pontacks. It was there that he met the diarist John Evelyn later in the year. The chef at Pontacks is said to have come from the Maison Daurade.

When Evelyn wrote about 'Pontacque', sophisticated English tastes were strongly influenced by France. Indeed, in the same year as he wrote about it he wrote also with admiration of the 'new French fabrique of French Tapissery' (even the spelling of the words was Frenchified) and of 'rich and splendid' new French furniture. It was Henri Misson, a Frenchman living in London, who wrote in the late seventeenth century of 'our famous Pontacks' where people who would 'dine at one or two guineas a head' were 'handsomely accommodated'. Apart from praising the merits of the wines of Haut-Brion, Evelyn praised equally carefully the merits of the members of the Pontac family. Arnaud he described as 'the famous and wise Prime President of Bordeaux'. François-Auguste, however, he thought had been 'made mad' by 'much learning'. He had 'studied well in philosophy, but chiefly the Rabbines and was exceedingly addicted to cabalistical fancies . . . and half distracted with reading abundance of the extravagant eastern Jewes'. Obviously, François-Auguste de Pontac was not a conventional tavern keeper. Nonetheless, Evelyn's final verdict was not completely unfavourable: 'For the rest he spake all languages, was very rich, had a handsome person and was well bred; aged about 45.'

Given Evelyn's description, it was ironic that it was a philosopher totally unimpressed by 'cabalistical fancies', John Locke, who has left us the fullest accounts of 'President Pontac's vineyard at Hautbrion'. They were written in 1677 and 1678 while Arnaud was still alive, but after François-Auguste had begun to popularize Haut-Brion wines in London. Apart from mentioning the poor soil and the ditch, Locke described how some of the vines were 'about 4 or 5 foot high' and had stakes, while others were 'direct along upon the ground, not above a foot from it, between little, low stakes or laths'. The old branches stood on each side with 'the root like a pair of armes spread out towards the south'. The vines 'were laid out in rows and cropped as perfectly as decorated hedges'. He could not find out 'the reason of this different way of culture' since the workmen spoke only Gascon.

On his second visit in 1678, when France and England were on the verge of war and after the English Parliament had prohibited all trade between the two countries, Locke visited the smaller vineyards of the Graves, 'all sandy with small stones among', and this time he concentrated on the poverty of the small local proprietors. Observing that 'the present prohibition in England' was much 'troubling' the merchants and wine growers, he realized the marked difference between Haut-Brion and the rest, a difference which Jean de Pontac would have appreciated. Most wine from the Graves was worth 'but 25 écus per *tonneau*, which formerly sold here for between 40 and 50'. Yet Pontac was selling for 80 or 100. In 1684 the difference between the two prices was even greater: four times.

Although François-Auguste's publicity may have been responsible in part for this, he was in trouble at Haut-Brion itself soon after
his marriage. One of his two brothers-in-law had the château seized
because of a legal argument about debts, and in 1683 – the year
Evelyn dined at Pontacks – François-Auguste had to pay 15,000
livres to have seals removed from it. Six years later, an account of
his expenses records that he was employing a secretary who cost
him 200 livres a year; a *valet de chambre* who cost him 120; a
sommelier (100); a cook (90); and eleven other servants. He had
two carriages, and his expenditure on Haut-Brion accounted for
only 3,000 livres out of a total of 18,000 livres. He certainly must
have made Haut-Brion wine ('Pontaque' and 'Obrien' Evelyn called
it) as well known in Pessac and in Bordeaux as in London. In the
same year he himself spent 4,500 livres on *vin de table* and 600 on
vin du commun. This was lavish drinking.

François-Auguste seems to have passed as much time in Paris as
in London and to have left the daily management of Haut-Brion to
his energetic agent, Bertrand Dubut, who served as his *régisseur*.
The Haut-Brion vineyard then covered 120 *journaux* (around 38
hectares) and was only a small part of the total estate (825 *journaux*) and even of the *seigneurie* (228 *journaux*). It was a smaller
area than the total area cultivated by those peasants and *bourgeois*
in Pessac who owed seigneurial dues to the Pontacs. There were
132 other *journaux* devoted to wine, mostly in small lots. Few
vineyards were more than three *journaux* in size, most less than
one.

With very limited resources at his disposal, Dubut skilfully
organized the labour force, developing the new techniques for
wine-making that made it possible to meet London's growing
demand for acceptable wine. He had one *chai*, equipped with
cuveaux (vats) and *vaisseaux vinaires* (wine-making vessels), along
with *truilhs* (the old word which in this case seems to have meant
presses) and *maietz* (troughs). He had only one pair of oxen, however, and one cart, and there was only one full-time *vigneron* in
charge of the vines. One *bouvier* (drover) and one *tonnelier*
(cooper) completed the full-time establishment. In consequence,
Dubut seems to have depended for the most part on temporary
labour, even at times other than the *vendange*. Thus, in 1689 for
example, we find him signing on a team of eight *vignerons*, seven of
them from 'Tondut' and one from Pessac. All these were nameless,

like their wives, who were themselves often part of the casual labour force. Given all the restraints on Dubut's enterprise, it was possible for him, nonetheless, to introduce innovations, like improved *ouillage* and *soutirage*, the two seventeenth-century arts of wine-making which made possible a revolution in vinification, carrying it for the first time beyond its old medieval limits.

Ouillage, topping up, was discussed far more frequently by eighteenth-century writers on wine than any other topic. There is some evidence that the importance of regular 'topping up' of casks – as often as once a week – had been recognized even in the Middle Ages, particularly as wine travelled, but topping up, later called in English 'refilling', was not dealt with systematically until the late seventeenth century. Racking, *soutirage* – the racking of the wine off the accumulated lees, '*tirer au fin*' as it is still called – guaranteed for the first time the production of a *vin clarifié*. It not only got rid of sediment but allowed carbon dioxide to escape from the barrels and the wine to be purified.

Records kept at Haut-Brion in 1689/90 include such genuinely innovatory entries as 'three barrels were opened and in order then to fill them a fourth barrel was pierced. The rest of the barrel was drunk in the cellar.' In the same year, there are references also to 'last year's wine', with suggestions that wine was being quite deliberately kept at Haut-Brion. By the middle of the eighteenth century such references were commonplace. Racking seems to have followed the seasons. The first racking occurred in March and the second at the end of June, coinciding with the flowering of the vines.

There were economic incentives to develop new techniques, independent of questions of quality. Apart from a deterioration in the quality of untopped wine, there was also a clear loss of the amount of wine in the cask. *Ouillage* saved money. As for *soutirage*, it enabled wine to be stored. There was also an incentive to improve the barrels in which wine was kept, and Bordeaux began to import oak for making casks from places as far away as Stettin and Lübeck. Wine was kept in cask for longer than it was to be at a later date. Later the oak was to come from Spain, or from France itself. It was best for it to be new, for this made for cleanliness.

There were some dangers in the improved processes, however. The opened barrels might be filled with wine from different sources, and since the Pontacs owned more than one vineyard there could be a confusion of identities at best, and at worst adulteration rather than purification. It is interesting that on the first occasion that we hear of the adjective '*grand*' being applied to wine – in a text of August 1690 – it was being applied to Pez, the Pontac wine from St-Estèphe that sold for half the price of Haut-Brion. The same text, however, described improvements in the arts and techniques of wine-making, notably *ouillage*, at Haut-Brion: three *barriques* of Pez had been prepared not at Pez but at Haut-Brion. The text also makes it clear that the wine had been cleared of all dregs. It was wine that was ready to be kept.

At the time, the late-seventeenth century changes, *ouillage* and *soutirage*, were deemed far more important than corking and bottling. As Warner Allen wrote in his *History of Wine*, 'the ageing of wine in bottle', now thought of as a great breakthrough, 'does not seem to have been a major preoccupation of growers and merchants'. Perhaps they believed that those who had the money to purchase *grands crus* also had the money to keep their wine in personalized bottles, as Pepys did or as Thomas Jefferson was to do. In 1663 Pepys described how he had seen five or six dozen of his own bottles with his crest on them. Happily they 'were filled with wine'. Such bottles, often beautiful, served, like decanters, for holding wine drawn from the cask when it was brought to the table. In the time of Dubut wine drinkers were beginning to buy handsome 'wine-related objects', 'objects of desire' as they were to be called in the twentieth century, some in glass, some in silver. Hitherto most wine-related objects had been tools, although there were pitchers and wine-tasters, some of them medieval, and cork had been used exceptionally to stopper some early bottles. In Shakespeare's *As You Like It* Rosalind tells Celia to take the cork out of her mouth 'that I may drink thy tidings'. Nonetheless, a gross of corks cost four shillings in 1653. It was from Spain that the first cork reached Bordeaux.

Innovations, like *ouillage, soutirage* and eventually corking, pointed to the future. Yet the decade of the 1690s, when Dubut was active, was no easier a time for the wine industry than it was for the de Pontac family. To the problems of war already outlined – and these became far worse – were now added the problems of weather. These were years of misery, as Enjalbert has called them, when exports languished, and in Bordeaux itself it was difficult in 1692 to sell Haut-Brion even to tavern keepers. Then came four disastrous harvests in a row, from 1692 to 1695, years when Bordeaux actually had to import wine from Languedoc for its own use. There had been floods in 1691, and now there were famines.

Export possibilities were restricted by taxation as well as by war. Even before 'the Glorious Revolution' of 1688, when William III of Holland and his English wife Mary ascended the throne, turning England and Holland into Protestant allies, there had been a divergence of attitudes to France between the Court – and London society – and the countryside; and there were English landowners, some of them in Parliament, who believed that trade with France was 'detrimental to this Kingdom'. For this reason, therefore, there was a pressure to increase the duties on French wines, and in 1693 duty on French wines was raised to £22 10s a *tonneau*, or two shillings a gallon. Five years later there was a further increase to £47 a *tonneau*, the equivalent of over a shilling a bottle, as compared with a duty of 1s 8d per gallon on Portuguese wines. Not surprisingly, only two *tonneaux* of French wines were imported in 1697 as against 4,774 *tonneaux* of Portuguese. The writing on the wall had been there earlier. When times had been more propitious, the great Colbert, who recognized the importance of 'the quality wine trade' of Bordeaux, had imposed increased French taxes on imported goods, inevitably provoking sharp fiscal retaliation against Gascon wines.

In the long run, the wine trade was to survive war and taxation. Yet in the years after 1688, 'the jealousy towards every thing French' (as Cyrus Redding, a Victorian authority on wine, put it) was bound to affect wine. Writing with hindsight, he condemned 'the laying on of enormous duties' on French wine by the legislature, who were not wise enough to reflect that those wines must have been exchanged for British commodities of one class or another.

In 1692, one year before the first increase in taxes, the château at Haut-Brion had been seized for debt for the second time. François-Auguste sent his wife from Paris to Bordeaux by herself to face his creditors, a trip that took six days each way. Two years later, he himself was dead. His funeral in January 1694 was a modest event, quite unlike those of his father and great-grandfather. The worst troubles for the wine trade were still to come.

There remain elements of mystery about François-Auguste. One year after his death, Nicholas Luttrell reported in London that 'Mr

Pontack, who keeps the great eating house in Abchurch Lane, has been examined before the Lord Mayor for being author of the late report that the King was missing, and gave bail to answer the same.' Who was this Mr Pontack? Was he really a Pontac? There is a touch of mystery at the Bordeaux end also, for, according to one document, long before François-Auguste's death his father, Arnaud de Pontac, is described as being broken-hearted at the loss of his only son. Given such mystery, it seems entirely fitting that François-Auguste was 'exceedingly addicted to cabalistic fancies'.

Some facts are certain. François-Auguste was childless, and his goods – and his debts – were passed not to his wife, who soon remarried, but to his one surviving elder sister, Marie-Thérèse, and to the one surviving son of his other sister, Marie-Anne. The major part of the Haut-Brion inheritance, two-thirds, went to Marie-Thérèse, who, like her sister, had been left 100,000 livres by her father. The other third went to François-Auguste's nephew, Louis-Armand Lecomte, Baron de la Tresne, a President of the *Parlement* of Bordeaux, who also inherited Bishop Arnaud's library. Old ties were thus restored.

In 1654 Marie-Thérèse had married Jean-Denis d'Aulède de Lestonnac, a member of what was now deemed one of the oldest and most prestigious families in Gascony, the family with which Jean had been associated in the early sixteenth century. She was obviously a highly eligible heiress, since along with Haut-Brion she inherited the Château de Pez at St-Estèphe. The Pontac name thus ceased to be heard at Haut-Brion (and at Pez) just at the time when it was most famous in London. Moreover, the two families that acquired a stake in Haut-Brion – the Lestonnacs and the la Tresnes – had a stake in other vineyards too. Jean-Denis d'Aulède de Lestonnac, the new owner of Haut-Brion, was owner also of Margaux, a property in the Médoc. It had been acquired in 1590 by Jeanne de Montaigne, the sister of the great essayist, and bequeathed to her son Guy de Lestonnac at a time when the wines of the Médoc were little renowned even in Bordeaux. In 1612 the estate had passed into the hands of Pierre d'Aulède de Lestonnac, the father of Jean-Denis. Marriages, carefully planned, played as big a part in wine history as enterprise.

Margaux was to join Haut-Brion as a named *grand cru* in the early years of the eighteenth century, but Jean-Denis d'Aulède was not to see this happen. In another surprising twist of history he too died in 1694, only eighteen days after François-Auguste de Pontac. Unlike François-Auguste, he was buried in style.

The Baron de la Tresne, the other inheritor, belonged to a family that during the sixteenth century had become even richer than the Pontacs. One of the *Livres de Raison* of the mid-seventeenth-century Baron survives and records that he had an income of 36,576 francs in 1663 and spent 31,450 of them. Yet even though his house in Bordeaux was modest, on occasion la Tresne too could get into debt. The family's *Livre de Raison* also shows that he owed Arnaud de Pontac 28,000 livres for the purchase of the office of Receiver of Requests that François-Auguste had not wanted. The Baron already owned vineyards in the Graves and elsewhere when he acquired his share of Haut-Brion.

Whatever the dynastic vicissitudes, the name 'Pontacks' survived in London. Prices there had never been cheap. One early visitor spoke of 'five shillings a head', when one of the heads in question on that occasion was the head of an earl, the Earl of Orrery. In 1722, however, the journalist, traveller and novelist, Daniel Defoe, author of *Robinson Crusoe*, a man with an eye for a bargain and a taste for food, was to write in his *Journey through England* that at Pontacks 'you might bespeak a dinner from four or five shillings a head to a guinea or what sum you please'. Defoe singled out the wine as well as the food. The Pontacs, he said, had given their name 'to the best French clarets'.

From the start Pontacks was obviously a very different place from the Royal Oak in Lombard Street which Pepys had visited in 1663 or the Three Cranes, a 'narrow dogg-hole' where he had dined a year earlier and had been served with a meal (claret-wine *and* oysters) that he called 'a sorry poor dinner'. It appears to us an odd combination, but then so do many of Pepys's mixed drinks, like raspberry sack and lamb's wool. A century before Pepys, there had been a saying in Tudor times that 'claret is a noble wine, for it is the same complexion that noblemen's coats be made of'. In the late seventeenth century in London, the largest city in Europe, there was increasing sophistication and an accessible demand for a wine that stood out both for its colour and for its flavour. Noblemen bought Haut-Brion, but noblemen were not the only arbiters of taste. Society was more complex than it had been, and many people who were not noblemen were developing sophisticated tastes.

Literary references to 'Pontacks', spelt in various ways, are common in later generations than those of Pepys and Evelyn, for love of wine was beginning to be treated as a mark of 'civilization'. Thus, Richard Steele in his *Lying Lover* (1703) makes Latine say 'I defy Pontack to have prepared a better [supper] o' the sudden', and in *Reflections . . . on the Vices and Follies of the Age* there is a description of a knighted fop dining at 'Pontacks' on French *ragouts* and claret at disastrous expense. Steele, along with Addison, wrote most of the pieces in the new the fashionable periodicals the *Tatler* and the *Spectator*, first launched in 1711.

In the same year, Jonathan Swift, England's great satirist, who sang the praises of wine – and, on occasion, of 'honest claret' in particular – was a regular visitor to Pontacks. 'I was this day in the city, and dined at Pontacks,' he wrote in 1711. 'Pontack told us, although his wine was so good, he sold it cheaper than others; he took but seven shillings a flask. Are not these pretty rates?' Swift was thrifty in most things, but he was never thrifty in wine. When he became Dean of St Patrick's in Dublin, succeeding Dean John Stearne, he or an Irish friend wrote two well-known but very non-heroic couplets:

> In the days of Dean John those who came here to dine
> Had choice of good meat, but no choice of wine,
> In Jonathan's days those who came here to eat,
> Have choice of good wine, but no choice of meat.

In Swift's correspondence there is frequent mention of the wines of Bordeaux, and his letters show that he watched carefully the reports on each year's vintage. The relatively low price of claret in Dublin until 1735 (as compared with London) greatly appealed to him. 'Remember that I drink French wine twice as cheap as you do port,' he wrote to the poet Alexander Pope in 1723. By then the consumption of port in England had tripled since 1700.

It had been possible to dismiss port in the early 1690s, when the following dialogue was offered in 'Farewell to Wine' (1693):

'Some Claret, boy!'

'Indeed, Sir, we have none: Claret, Sir-Lord, There's not a drop in town. But we have the best Red Port.'

'What's that you call Red Port?'

'A wine, Sir, comes from Portugal; I'll fetch a pint, Sir.'

The boy's facts quickly give way to the customer's judgements when the drink brought to the table is actually tasted:

'Mark how it smells; methinks a real pain
Is by its ardour thrown upon my brain.'

The taste of port was not to be dismissed quite so quickly or so easily in the future, even by lovers of claret, but the port of 'Farewell to Wine' was as yet unfortified. The idea of 'vintage port' had not yet been born.

English merchants were already operating in Oporto, however, and were building up a new trade with its own style. It was to develop its own pride also and to become in a short time what Susan Bradford – and others before her – have called 'the Englishman's wine'. Yet it always had its critics. 'Port sapped our brains,' wrote Angus Reach in his book *Claret and Olives* in 1852, adding for good measure that men who preferred port to claret had no souls to be worth speaking about. It is fair to add that he observed also that there were clarets and claret: 'the ordinary Bordeaux is very ordinary indeed'.

The most famous eighteenth-century satirical reference to Pontacks was a dubious compliment paid by William Hogarth in the third plate of his *Rake's Progress* series in 1735. One of the pictures of Roman emperors that had adorned Tom's room after he had lost all his innocence had been removed to give place to a picture of Pontack, described in accompanying words as 'an eminent French cook, whose great talents being turned to heightening sensual, rather than mental enjoyments, has a much better chance of a votive offering from this company, than would either Vespasian or Trajan'.

By that time the Royal Society was holding its dinners elsewhere. From 1743 onwards there was an almost continuous record of weekly dinners at the Mitre, 'over against Fetter Lane', which remained a tavern eight years longer than Pontacks – until 1788, on the eve of the French Revolution.

The eighteenth-century story of claret drinking in Scotland and Ireland was different from that in England. There was always greater demand there. 'Ye maun leave port and punch to the likes of us,' a Scots tavern keeper is said to have told the local lairds, 'it's claret that's fit for you lairds.' And eighteenth-century Edinburgh was said to have shown as discriminating a taste in claret as any city in Europe. The wines of Gascony had made their way to Leith, port for Edinburgh, in the Middle Ages, when Scotland was an independent kingdom; and claret was already sufficiently prized in Scotland for an Act to have been passed in 1431 requiring that half the price of salmon exported to France should be paid in Gascon wine. In the eighteenth century medieval vaults in Leith were used for claret auctions arranged by the President of the Vintners' Guild. When a cargo of claret arrived at Leith, the citizens of Edinburgh were informed by a horn blown by the attendant of a horse-drawn cart carrying the hogshead. Judges took bottles of claret into court, and it was the favoured drink in the clubs of Edinburgh and Glasgow until 1780, when new duties were imposed.

The duties were extremely unpopular, and inspired an epigram that was much admired by Sir Walter Scott:

> Firm and erect the Caledonian stood;
> Old was his mutton, and his claret good;
> 'Let him drink port!' the English statesman cried –
> He drank the poison and his spirit died.

It should be added that the duties were no more popular in England either. An earlier eighteenth-century writer had talked of 'Foreign wines of every sort / From costly French to common port', and it was taxation that was blamed for the fact that by 1785 French wines in general represented only 3 per cent of all the wines imported into England. What statistics there are must, of course, be treated with caution. Smuggling was a major industry, with the smugglers often establishing dashing reputations as popular heroes.

Smuggling was a major industry in Ireland also, where, as Constantia Maxwell wrote in her delightful book *Dublin under the Georges, 1716–1839* (1936), there was an 'abundance of wine'. She quotes the philosopher Bishop Berkeley, who had observed that while in England many gentlemen with £1,000 a year never drank wine in their houses, in Ireland this could hardly be said of any who had but £100. 'Was there any Kingdom in Europe,' Berkeley asked in *The Querist*, 'that was so good a customer at Bordeaux as Ireland?' Samuel Madden considered Ireland a land that 'flowed with wine as much as the land of Canaan with milk'.

If London showed Pontack's Head, eighteenth-century Dublin had a Shakespeare's Head, an Addison's Head and an Isaac Newton's Head, while at the Rose, a favourite rendezvous of Swift, the customers were said in a poem to 'swallow down wine like fishes'. When the fourth Earl of Chesterfield was Viceroy in Dublin for eight months in 1745/6, he estimated that 5,000 *tonneaux* of wine each year were being imported into Ireland. For his part, however, Chesterfield, friend of Montesquieu though he was, expressed himself as horrified rather than pleased: he was concerned that excessive drinking of claret was calculated to destroy too often 'the constitutions, the faculties and the fortunes of those of superior rank'. His opinion carried no weight. Decades later, in 1807, the Scots author 'William Thomson' (the Reverend J. Hall) described claret as 'the common wine of all tables', although he was critical in a less forbidding way than Chesterfield had been: he believed that the claret drunk in Scotland and Ireland was inferior to that drunk in England.

In England itself, where some of the claret arrived via Ireland and a proportion of it to ports other than London, there was increased interest in the wines of Bordeaux in 1786, following William Pitt's Commercial Treaty with France. The interest was fanned by the presence in Bordeaux of a by then established group of English, and Irish, merchants, some with a stake in viticulture, and it was they who welcomed the Treaty most warmly. When in 1787 Arthur Young paid a brief visit to Bordeaux on a tour of southern France, he was told that the Treaty was 'a wise measure equally advantageous to both nations'. He collected precise data about wine and other products and also formed personal impressions. French wines were now to be imported into Britain on the same terms as those of Portugal, but in Bordeaux itself Young was informed that 'the English take only wines of the first quality' and that most producers of claret would not be able to benefit, therefore, from the lower duties. He was informed, too, that an English attempt to sell beer in Bordeaux had failed! His own conclusion was that the increase in the sale of wine to England, admittedly over a very short period, had not been as great as the negotiators had hoped.

Among official papers relating to the 1786 Treaty, one Foreign Office paper of 1786 is particularly interesting in that it distinguishes between first growths and second and third growths 'for the London market' and gives some details of annual production. Even at that date, at least two-thirds of the 'first growths' came to England, the paper states. Other statistics were set out in the paper. Recent production of 'Pontac', still so called though the Pontacs had left Haut-Brion, was given as 40 *tonneaux* and for another year 86, in both years less than half the production of Margaux and Lafite (100 and 225 *tonneaux*) and less also than that of Latour (50 and 89). Mouton figured by name among the second and third growths, as did Pez. The author of the Foreign Office paper took an optimistic view of the potential English demand for claret, which confirmed that the port of London accounted for only a part of British imports of wines from Bordeaux. Boulogne and Guernsey were mentioned too, as Boulogne had been in an interesting note by the English novelist Tobias Smollett, who met British merchants there when he visited the port in 1766. As late as Smollett's time it remained difficult to separate literature and wine.

9

The Rise and Fall of the Fumels

There is an obvious relationship between great families and the quality of wines produced.

R. Boutruche, 1966

If we hear relatively less of Haut-Brion as a wine in the eighteenth century it is largely because of the end of the male Pontac line and partly because of the divided inheritance of the Haut-Brion property after the death of François-Auguste de Pontac. Marie-Thérèse's son, Pierre-François-Delphin d'Aulède de Lestonnac, Baron de Margaux – and later Marquis – who became owner in 1694 and died in 1747, was happier singing the praises of Margaux than of the wine of the Pontacs. This was the period when at last the Médoc began to be developed and when the *Intendant* in Bordeaux, Bazin de Bazons, noted the *furieuse quantité des vignes* then being planted.

Surprisingly, the Médoc came into its own during the long War of the Spanish Succession, which lasted from 1702 to 1713. Neither war nor taxation – nor the rise of Oporto and the port wine trade – completely held back the demand in London for what were now called 'new French clarets': those that came from the Médoc as well as from the Graves. Indeed, the fact that in war conditions they were hard to find in London stimulated publicity for them. Moreover, while legal trade was banned, trade in wines captured at sea was well advertised. In 1703, for example, the very year of the Methuen Treaty with Portugal, which greatly favoured the trade with Oporto, there were notices in the *London Gazette* of auction sales of claret, some of them described as 'sales by the candle'. Ironically, many of them took place in London coffee houses.

The year 1705 seems to have been of special importance in a mounting publicity for the 'new French clarets'. Haut-Brion was now no longer alone. In May of that year 200 hogsheads of 'Neat Choice New Red Obrian and Pontack Prize wines (just landed)' were advertised in 'Two Hogsheads a lot'; and in the following month '207 hogsheads of New Pontac and Margouze wine' were also on offer in London. They had been seized by the Royal Navy from foreign ships on the high seas and brought to England unracked. Later advertisements of 1707 described a wide range of 'lately landed' clarets, all named, among them 'Laffitt, Margouze and La Tour'. Some customers expressed preferences for one, others for another, with Haut-Brion fetching £60 a *tonneau* as against £18 for 'ordinary' Gascon red. Spelling – and doubtless pronunciation – proved more difficult than drinking. The French themselves long had difficulty with Haut-Brion. Now a wide range of other misspellings and mispronunciations became familiar.

Noblemen's account books are as revealing as advertisements in tracing the history of Haut-Brion. From one of them we learn that John Harvey, first Earl of Bristol, frequently bought Obrien, Lafite, La Tour, Margose and Pontack. Two hogsheads of Obrion cost him £56 in 1707 and six dozen bottles £12 12s in 1714. Despite war and taxation, Haut-Brion and the other newly named *grands vins*, wines that were deemed 'the most exquisite and the most expensive', were in the long run profiting from a persisting, even increasing, élite demand. There was a more general demand also. As Bernard de Mandeville, born in Holland, put it in 1714 in his influential work *The Fable of the Bees*, 'those [Englishmen] that cannot purchase true hermitage or pontack, will be glad of more ordinary French claret'.

When Mandeville wrote, Margaux was as popular as Pontac in England. The *domaine* there, well managed by an innovative *régisseur*, M. Berlon, accounted for almost a half of d'Aulède's total holdings. It was because of d'Aulède's wealth and enterprise – rather than his lineage – that he was both able and willing to make substantial investments in the rapidly developing region of the Médoc at what proved to be exactly the right time. There was no other château in the Médoc to compare with Margaux, where d'Aulède lived, and he had another house and a park at Mérignac, not far from Haut-Brion. He also had town houses in Bordeaux and Paris. Yet in 1744 he sold the Maison Daurade with its courtyards and garden to two Bordeaux bankers, Thomas and Philippe Clack.

Other dynastic changes were affecting the rapidly developing vineyards of the Médoc where the *grands crus* were made. One year after d'Aulède inherited Haut-Brion in 1694, Marie-Thérèse de Clauzel, heiress of Château La Tour, married Alexandre de Ségur, who was then twenty-one years old, and another of the *grands crus* of the Médoc was in the process of establishing itself. Through an earlier marriage in 1670, Alexandre de Ségur's father Jacques had married the heiress of Lafite, Jeanne de Gasq, a friend of Arnaud de Pontac, and from the time of her death in 1704 Alexandre owned both Latour and Lafite.

In 1719 the second son of Marie-Thérèse and Alexandre, Nicholas-Alexandre de Ségur, born in 1697, whom Louis XV was to make a marquis, also acquired Mouton. He preferred, however, to live at Lafite when he was in the Médoc. Indeed, he ran Latour from it. When he died in 1755 he was the richest man in Bordeaux, a *'prince des vignes'*, whose fortune was valued at 2,400,000 livres. He bequeathed it to his four daughters, the eldest of whom married a cousin. From 1760 onwards Latour and Lafite were separated again, but until 1785 they shared the same manager. He, not the proprietor, was in control.

In a letter of 1732 Latour, Lafite, Margaux and Pontac are all described as 'topping wines', and the Bordeaux *négociant*, J. Bruneval, who wrote it, noted that an offer of £1,600 that he had made (on behalf of King George II) for 71 *tonneaux* of that year's Haut-Brion had been turned down. He observed that more 1723 had been produced than 1722, for which he had paid a higher price.

Such glimpses of the early *négociant* in action reveal that Haut-Brion was in demand whatever was happening elsewhere. There were, in fact, important dynastic changes at Haut-Brion also. In 1747 Margaux and the two-thirds of Haut-Brion that Pierre-François-Delphin d'Aulède owned passed on his death to his son, another François. He left no children and, when he died, the estate was acquired by Cathérine d'Aulède, a grand-daughter of Arnaud de Pontac. She had married at the age of twenty-two, in 1682, only one year after her uncle François-Auguste, and she is said to have carried with her an enormous dowry. Her husband was Count François-Joseph de Fumel, about the same age as herself. They quickly produced four children.

The story of this intricate dynastic network explains how the Fumels came to dominate the eighteenth-century history of Haut-Brion, although the remaining third of the property continued to be held by the heirs of the Marquis de la Tresne. For this reason Thomas Jefferson mentioned both the la Tresnes and the Fumels when he described his purchases of Haut-Brion. The Fumels provided a new proprietorial name, but not a new kind of proprietor. The contribution of François-Joseph de Fumel himself, however, was not to last long. Six years after his marriage, he was assassinated in the street at Réole, his native town. He died before his own father. At times there was as much violence in the eighteenth century as there had been in the seventeenth, although 'civilized' people did not like much to talk about it. They preferred to talk about wine.

This was to be only the first of the Fumels' family tragedies, for of the four children of François-Joseph, born in rapid succession, the third had died as a child and the second was killed at the Battle of Oudenarde in 1708. The heir was the eldest son, Louis, who inherited sufficient money to maintain his estates properly. He also secured an even larger sum as dowry when, advised by two powerful aunts, he married Cathérine-Thomas de Béthier at Toulouse in 1712. The final tragedy was the guillotining during the Revolution of François-Joseph's grandson – a Fumel with the same name, Joseph.

The Fumel family had their origins in the town of Fumel in the Agenais, and the Barons de Fumel had the right, which they retained until 1789, of carrying the Bishop of Agen into the city on their shoulders when he entered the capital of his see. Yet François de Fumel, a contemporary of Jean de Pontac, had been the first of them to be designated '*messire, noble, haut et puissant seigneur*': in 1547 Henry II sent him on a diplomatic mission to Constantinople to try to persuade the Sultan, Suliman the Magnificent, to break a treaty that he had made with the Holy Roman Emperor. Like the Pontacs, the Fumels were drawn into the Wars of Religion, many of their vassals having become Calvinists; and François-Joseph de Fumel was not the first person in the family to be assassinated: in 1561 François de Fumel had been murdered as a 'tyrant'.

The eighteenth-century Fumel succession at Haut-Brion was not straightforward. Louis de Fumel, who died at Haut-Brion (not at

Margaux) in 1749, only two years after taking over the two estates, had drawn up his will at Haut-Brion before a Bordeaux notary: of his three sons, it was the third who inherited. His first son, who had served at the court of the King of Spain, was already dead. His second son was a bishop, was to refuse an archbishopric and was to live until 1790: he did not follow in Bishop Arnaud de Pontac's footsteps. His third son, Joseph de Fumel, who became heir to the Fumel share of the property, was a soldier.

Born in Toulouse in 1720, Joseph had served with distinction in the French army before inheriting Haut-Brion. He had fought in several battles, among them Dettingen, in 1743, the last battle in which an English king, George II, took part – on the other side – and in 1781 was to be awarded the Grande Croix of St-Louis. It was appropriate, therefore, that one of his later titles, after he had become a marshal, was that of Governor of the Château Trompette in Bordeaux, which he acquired in 1770. Nonetheless, Fumel sold his wine to the English as cheerfully as he fought against them – George II himself ordered it, as the Bruneval letter shows – and he was to perish not at the hands of the English, but under the guillotine – in 1793 – at the hands of his fellow countrymen. Fumel might well have lost the Château Trompette even if there had been no revolution, for there was a plan in 1785 to demolish it and replace it with an impressive Place Ludovise.

After the end of the Seven Years War in 1763, Joseph de Fumel seems to have spent much of his time at Haut-Brion, where he improved the château at the same time as he developed the vineyard, adding a beautiful *orangerie*, smart new outbuildings and a great park; and in February 1789, a few months before the French Revolution, we find him exchanging pieces of land with his vassal and neighbour, Jean-Baptiste Vigneras, who also worked la Tresne land, so that he could get rid of a path (*chemin*) that separated two rows of his own vines.

Haut-Brion must have been a crowded château when he was in residence, for after his marriage in 1748 to Marie-Élisabeth de Conty d'Hargicourt – from distant Picardy – several relatives lived there with him. There was an active social life, which had a touch of Versailles about it. The vineyard, however, was at the heart of it, and Haut-Brion was now making its way to most parts of Europe. One interesting market was Sweden. Three visitors to Bordeaux from Stockholm reported in 1755 that 'wines are the principal element in the commerce of Bordeaux' and that among them '*le cru de Pontac*', much esteemed in 'the restaurants of Sweden', was outstanding: it was, indeed 'a unique wine much sought after'. One of the visitors was Hallman, a correspondent of the great European savant Linnaeus, and he added that because so much Pontac made its way to England, it was a rare treat in Bordeaux, where people gave away a few bottles to one another as presents. Nonetheless, in 1767 a great tribute was paid to the quality of Haut-Brion in Bordeaux itself by Nicolas Baujon, described as '*un mécène bordelais*', who favoured Pontac at his own table. When he died, he left in the cellar of his Paris house, bought from Madame de Pompadour, 280 bottles of the wine.

Publicity played its part in the development of domestic consumption in the eighteenth century as it had done in international trade with England in the seventeenth; and it was publicity, too, that is said to have started at the top. In 1758 the Duc de Richelieu, great-nephew of the Cardinal, then sixty-two years old, had become Governor of Guyenne and Gascony: he had defeated the English at the battle of Fontenoy in 1745, and he was now enjoying the delights of living for a part of the year in Bordeaux. Claret was one such delight, if not the chief of them. The most celebrated *libertin* of his age, Richelieu was also known as '*le plus bel enfant de la cour*', the best-looking child of the Court.

Richelieu's predecessor as Governor, the Comte d'Eu, had been self-effacing. Richelieu was flamboyant, and since he remained Governor until 1788 his influence was considerable. His dinners were as famous as the gardens of his palace. Pariset writes of his *politique de grandeur et de prestige* (his grand and prestigious policies). He is said to have treated the *jurats* like lackeys and to have humiliated the *Parlement*. One story – surely legend – claims that when Richelieu arrived in Bordeaux he was a devotee of Burgundy and could be made to taste claret only when it was transferred into a Burgundy bottle with a faked label. (The props seem wrong.) Another happier legend claims that once he had tasted claret, the Duc was so taken with it that he presented a bottle of Lafite – or was it Graves? – to King Louis XV with the words: 'I must tell your Majesty that I have discovered the secret of eternal youth.' The wine was an elixir.

A third story – perhaps not a legend – is that when the King presented the bottle to his mistresses Madame de Pompadour and Madame du Barry they were so taken by the claret that they would drink nothing else. The reason this may not be a legend is that Madame du Barry had real historical connections with Haut-Brion.

A few sets of genuine – and relevant – eighteenth-century statistics confirm impressions. The *Intendant* of the Auvergne bought five *tonneaux* of Haut-Brion 1764; Richelieu bought from the Marquis de la Tresne two *barriques* of his Haut-Brion 1765, a year when another eight *barriques* were transferred into 2,043 bottles; and the '*courtier* Loton' (Lawton), who was to become a French citizen just before the Revolution, bought one *tonneau* of the 1776.

Wine was then being kept in the *chai* for a number of buyers, and there were links with Bordeaux *négociants* also. Two of them, each referred to in letters of the 1780s, were called Copinger and Féger, and both of them were to be mentioned by Thomas Jefferson also. Another, whose name still means much in Bordeaux, was Barton. The increasing references to 'bottles of wine' point to one of the biggest changes in the wine trade of the period.

De Gascq, Baron de Portets, last of his line, who had sold his office as President of the Bordeaux *Parlement* in 1778 and who owned the vineyard that became Château Palmer, kept a cellar list, details of which have been described by Florence Mothe. In addition to 1,500 bottles of unspecified 'Graves de Bordeaux' it included 920 bottles of Haut-Brion; and like Pepys's list of more than a century earlier it also included Rhenish wine and wines from Cyprus and Hungary. There were also 118 bottles of Château d'Yquem. The natural son of Portets, Valdec de Lessart, a minister of Louis XVI, kept an even broader range of wines in his cellar, and Haut-Brion was prominent among them.

In December 1783, two days after Christmas, the Comte Joseph de Fumel, then owner of a large part but not all of Haut-Brion, had written to Servat, described as *chargé d'affaires* of the city of Bordeaux in Paris, telling him that he had asked his relative d'Hargicourt to sell 1,500 to 1,800 bottles of his wine in Paris at the Bordeaux price: 'the lowest price that you can at present quote to him . . . 55 sous a bottle, including the bottle, the glass, the case, corks, the wax, and the export duty'. Fumel added – and it was a revealing comment – 'Paris merchants have no idea about how to treat these wines.'

The du Barry connection with Haut-Brion, mentioned earlier, was contrived not by Fumel, but by his daughter and only child, Marie-Louise-Élisabeth. Born in 1749, she was heiress to a great fortune and might have married anyone. As it transpired, she married a captain of the Swiss Guard who had fought in the Seven Years War: Jean-Baptiste-Guillaume-Nicolas du Barry (or Dubarry), usually known as Élie, the brother of one of the most famous – and last and loveliest – of Louis XV's mistresses. The marriage provoked both gossip and satire, for after the death of Louis XV the name du Barry ceased to carry with it any immediate advantages, and the Comtesse du Barry, who had herself had no right to the title, was banished from the Court. Du Barry himself was heavily in debt and wanted to take over both the name of his wife and her fortune.

When the Fumel family refused to comply, the newly married couple decided to call themselves the Count and Countess d'Hargicourt, the maiden name of Marie-Louise-Élisabeth's mother. Hargicourt was far away from Bordeaux, in Picardy, but the du Barrys, whose name the Comtesse herself had appropriated, were Gascons who had made their fortune out of war contracting. After their marriage the Hargicourts spent much time at Château Margaux and at a house in Bordeaux in the rue des Trois-Contils. Their life together was to be short. Like her father – and the Comtesse du Barry – Marie-Louise-Élisabeth, a woman of spirit, was to make her way to the scaffold in 1793.

Joseph's younger sister, Marguerite, married in 1750 to the Comte de Giverzac, had lost her husband three days after their marriage, and thereafter is said to have given up her life to good works – Haut-Brion was her base – while Joseph's youngest sister, Marguerite-Laure, had become an abbess in 1766 and stayed at the Abbey of Savre-Bénète until the Abbey was suppressed after the Revolution. Another Fumel relative, Jean-Georges, had fought with the French in India and had been taken prisoner by the British after the capture of Pondicherry. He was lucky to die in Toulouse one year before the Revolution.

When the Revolution began – and the story of the Revolution in Bordeaux had many twists and turns – Hargicourt, who had made the most of his feudal privileges before 1789, emigrated to England, leaving Marie-Louise behind. As a result, Margaux was seized by the state in 1792. Another exile from the Haut-Brion estate was

Vigneras, who had exchanged land with Joseph de Fumel only a few months before. The la Tresne family, who in 1770 had built a new *chai*, called the Chai Neuf, lost their land also. It was sold in 1797 for 70,000 francs *en assignats*, dubious paper money, to the Marquis de Catellan, and remained separate from the rest of Haut-Brion until 1840, long after the Revolution. By that time, the Marquis de Catellan was dead (1838) and all the Fumels had come and gone.

We have fascinating evidence both of wine-buying and of wine-making at Haut-Brion on the eve of and during the first stages of the French Revolution. The Jefferson papers tell us about the first: letters from the *régisseur*, Louis Viallon, who served the divided estate, tell us about the second.

In his very first month in Paris in 1784, Jefferson had written to John Bondfield, American commercial agent in Bordeaux, asking him to send '1 gross such wine as he drank at Dr F's [Benjamin Franklin's]'; and a few months later Bondfield had dispatched to him in a brig called the *Fanny* four cases each containing thirty-six bottles 'of our first growth'. In February 1786 Bondfield had also bought for him two hogsheads. In the same year, the first regular postal service by sea was inaugurated between Bordeaux and the United States, and Jefferson was communicating about wine with Francis Eppes, back in Virginia, long before he sent him via Captain Gregory – 'just sailing for Portsmouth' – six dozen bottles of Obrien, 'the very best Bordeaux wine', in May 1787. His cellar then included 374 Burgundies and 239 Bordeaux.

Jefferson believed that 'genuine wines can never be had but of the *vigneron*', even though in 1788 one direct order of his for 125 bottles of Haut-Brion was lost through 'inattention', making its way not to Britain but to 'the Isle of France'. Later, he discovered that Fumel no longer had enough of the Haut-Brion 1784 to supply him: 'I offered him 600 livres for one of them, which he refused.' Perhaps for this reason Jefferson compiled an interesting list of the wine merchants in Bordeaux, picking out some of the English merchants, among them Barton, Johnston and Copinger, and some of the French, among them Féger, Nérac and du Verget, having been assured that they never mixed the 'wines of the first quality' with any other wines 'to improve them'. 'In Bordeaux,' he added, 'the only introduction, and the sufficient one, is cash.'

Viallon's letters deal as much with money – and with the times – as with harvests and vintages. Thus, in a letter of 24 November 1785, which is concerned primarily with sales of wine, Viallon leaves to a postscript the thought: 'Sir, the *vendanges* have greatly disturbed me and have affected my health.'

The world of wine-making and of wine-selling was by then almost as complex as that of politics, for Bordeaux was selling wine everywhere, including huge quantities of cheaper wine to the West Indies. On the eve of the Revolution more wine was being exported there than to Britain. Viallon was disposing of an expensive wine, which still kept its British market, but it was wine from different vintages, selling at different prices at different times. Some was sold through *courtiers*, some direct. The Chartrons as well as Haut-Brion was therefore part of Viallon's world. The most expensive wines he could offer, such as his 1785 and 1786, were wines of a good quality that kept well even if the price of some of them, as he wrote in July 1790, was sometimes so high that only the English would pay it. In the middle years of the century Haut-Brion had been priced at 1,500 to 2,000 livres a *tonneau*, more expensive than Margaux. Other wines of Pessac were described then as fetching between 800 and 1,200 livres.

As the decade went by, many wines were in short supply; and when in 1790 a merchant tasted the 1788 and told Viallon that it lacked body (it had *un petit corps*), he was advised briskly that if he wished to buy it he could have no more than three *barriques*. It did not help Viallon that one of his distant proprietors did not approve of his sales policy, and in November 1786 he offered his resignation after receiving a letter, now lost, which must have compared his policy – he used the word '*police*' – with that followed at Latour and Lafite. Viallon's own letter was angry in tone – there was little deference in it – and threatened that if the policy were to be reversed, 'the merchants would keep away from your *chai*'. Affairs were patched up – grudgingly – and Viallon was back in his post in January 1787. Later in that year, after the harvest, he described himself as angry that it had not been more abundant, but then 'God had willed it so'. He hoped that there would be compensation another year. There were times when He could be merciful. When a great storm hit Bordeaux in June 1788 and even at Pessac huge hailstones smashed windows, it left Haut-Brion untouched.

Viallon described 1789 as the saddest year that he had seen at

Haut-Brion in thirty-six years of service. He was not thinking of the Revolution, however, at least in the first instance. The main reason was that there had been 'perpetual storms' in the Bordeaux region and that the Haut-Brion 1789 was 'without body and aroma' (*parfum*) and had little colour as well. He drew the same conclusion as that which Jean de Pontac would have drawn: 'God is irritated with us.' He added, however, that if the wine was poor so was the bread – and that could be bought only at a high price. The poor were suffering. In a correspondence that is shot through with religious references, this is the only time that the poor figure in the letters.

A year later, in September 1790, Viallon was complaining of the price of oxen – and of feedstuff. And by then there were only three *barriques* of wine in the *chai*: one each of 1785, 1786 and 1788. Soon he was to have no wine for himself. 'I shall do all that I can,' he went on movingly, 'to make as much wine as possible without doing anything to compromise quality.' Four to five *tonneaux* would be produced, but locally they would be paid for not in solid cash but in *assignats*. There was much 'misery' (*misère*) around, and *assignats* were among 'the greatest miseries'. Earlier in the year, in April, Viallon had noted that nobody was prepared to lend. He made that observation in the same letter in which he reported that Fumel had been made Mayor of Bordeaux: '*Il a accepté sous la loi.*' ('He has accepted under the law.')

Viallon himself was in poor health in 1791 when he grumbled about excessive heat, and within a few months a man called Prax was working in his place. In his letter of April 1791 he had complained, too, that he had broken his spectacles and could not see properly. There was better news around the corner, however, although it was soon to be followed by far worse. The wine of 1791, he reported in April 1792, was excellent wine in colour, taste and *finesse*, '*d'une couleur admirable, d'un goût supérieur, et d'une finesse admirable*'. In the same year Fumel, to whom he regularly referred, had produced fifteen *tonneaux* of wine and La Mission, referred to for the first time, eleven.

There is an undated note by Fumel himself, probably much earlier, on the governance, administration and culture of Haut-Brion (*régie, manutention et culture*), which describes in more detail than Viallon did the organization and pay of the labour force employed. It deserves to be set alongside Dubut's account at the end of the previous century. After the *vendange* twenty-eight 'good workers' were kept on to clear and restore the vineyard. They were paid 21 sols a day. Another ten women and children were paid half that amount. Work began on 15 October. Eight days later, they were to turn their attention to the vines. Some of them were to prune and others to prop them. If any worker left one particular *parcelle* of land in order to find a better one, the *chargé d'affaires*, Giraud, had to take down his name, and if the worker left Haut-Brion altogether he was to be paid less than the rest if he ever returned. Giraud himself was paid 600 livres and his son, who helped him, 300 livres. Were the output of the vineyard to exceed 50 *tonneaux*, Giraud would receive a bonus of 200 livres; if it reached 80 *tonneaux*, 300 livres. For more than 100 *tonneaux* (the peak figure mentioned in the Archbishop of Bordeaux's accounts for 1361), the bonus would be 400 livres.

Joseph Fumel's instructions to the *chargé d'affaires* reveal a business sense that never forsook him, and he was at first undisturbed when the Revolution arrived in Bordeaux. With the abolition of feudal privileges, however, his position became an awkward one. Yet he remained behind, an important figure in Bordeaux, still Military Governor of the Province of Guyenne and still at the same time deeply involved in the wine trade. During the early years of the Revolution, he made all the right gestures and gained rather than lost. Thus, he opened the drawbridge into the Château Trompette and handed over the keys of the arsenal, allowing a citizens' guard to muster behind the impressive château walls. In addition, he renounced his official pension of 12,000 livres, and sent part of his gold and silver to the Treasury in Paris as a 'patriotic contribution'. When his gifts were announced to the National Assembly, there was said to have been general applause.

Joseph also donated 12,000 livres to the city of Bordeaux and 2,000 to the village of Pessac, telling his workers in the vineyard to carry to the village square baskets of wheat and rye for the local inhabitants: they had suffered severely in the years of bad harvests that preceded the Revolution. Perhaps it was not surprising, therefore, that in April 1790 he was elected Mayor of Bordeaux, defeating the son of a Montesquieu who was the rival candidate. A year later, in April 1791, he was made Commander of the 11th Military Division. He was then seventy-one years old.

In 1771 Joseph had survived the dissolution of the ancient *Parlement* of Bordeaux, which a year earlier had defied the King in protest against the dissolution of the *Parlement* of Paris. Indeed, it was Joseph himself, deputizing for Richelieu, who dissolved it. He was involved with the *Parlement* again in 1784, this time deputizing for the Maréchal de Mouchy, when the *Parlement* was forced in 'military session' to submit to royal pressure. Joseph had survived also the dissolution of the more ancient *Jurade*. The post-revolutionary municipal council, of which Fumel now became first mayor, was the product of a new constitution, although its original membership remained socially restricted. The mayor's two chief officers, one of them his deputy, were lawyers whom Fumel knew well.

None of Fumel's early involvement in the revolutionary process in Bordeaux was to save him. His mayoralty soon came to an end, and in June 1791 he lost his command and returned to Haut-Brion. By then the Church in Bordeaux, a rich institution with substantial seigneurial rights of its own, was already finding itself in increasing danger. The municipality had made an inventory of ecclesiastical properties in Bordeaux which were now to be proscribed, and many of these were properties that had been traditionally supported first by the Pontacs and then by the Fumels. The Carmelite convent at Les Chartrons was soon to be turned into a market-place, and the Carmelite church where Jean de Pontac was buried was soon to be destroyed – along with the Maison Daurade.

A royal decree of 1790, which changed the basis of the electoral system, was received unenthusiastically by the merchant community in Bordeaux, already disturbed by news of the slave uprising in San Domingo and the threat to the West Indian trade which had boomed during the previous decade. The issue of paper money in the form of *assignats* in the same year was a further blow to mercantile confidence; and Joseph, closely linked as he was both to the nobility and to the merchant class of Bordeaux, was doubtless glad to return to his estates, as a number of other people did. Yet as the Revolution passed through new phases, he was to find no peace there. Each new phase in the sequence was portentously proclaimed in the name of *principes* and of *régénération*. Joseph could never think in such terms.

There were many divisions of opinion in Bordeaux, not least among the revolutionaries themselves. Most of them were expressed in the newly founded Committee of Public Safety in Bordeaux, and from the committee rooms made their way back into the streets. In July 1792 two priests who had fled from the city when their churches were destroyed were brought back, only to have their throats cut by a revolutionary crowd in the courtyard of the Archbishop's Palace.

The Terror began in Bordeaux in October 1793 with the establishment of a military commission headed by Jean-Marie-Baptiste Lacombe, the subject of a recent revisionist historical study by Dr Bécamps; and Marie-Louise-Élisabeth was one of the first to be taken prisoner: on 3 December 1793 she was forcibly taken away from Haut-Brion, to be followed three days later by Joseph and other members of their family. At first they were lodged in the same gaol, but they were not allowed to communicate with each other. Meanwhile, seals were affixed to the doors of Château Haut-Brion. No one was allowed inside. An age had come to an end.

Marie-Louise-Élisabeth was accused, among other things, of having permitted a religious marriage ceremony to be held in her house in the Rue des Trois-Contils in Bordeaux the previous June – in defiance of revolutionary laws of March 1793. The bride was her chambermaid, the bridegroom a wigmaker, and the ceremony had been conducted by a priest who had refused to swear allegiance to the Revolution. Joseph was denounced by one of his valets, Jean Lafon, who, not knowing how to write, had made his mark on a deposition that read: 'Jean Lafon, Haut-Brion, has declared that a priest is saying Mass in the house of Citizen Fumel.' Accompanying the deposition was a letter from Citizen Barbe to the Committee of Public Safety which began with the salutation, 'Republicans, my brothers'. 'I write to advise you,' Barbe went on, 'that at Haut-Brion an unsworn aristocrat says Mass for Fumelle. The bearer of this letter will give you details. He is from the staff of Haut-Brion, our national property. Let me grab this black animal on the spot. *Salut.*'

News of Joseph's arrest provoked protest in Pessac, and a letter of complaint signed by thirty people was sent to the Military Commission. 'We do not fear asking for the liberty of this true father of the poor,' they declared. 'After the last harvest he saved many people from famine by having distributed without charge twenty-four baskets of grain to the people of our Commune. Give him back his liberty. We ask it out of humanity.' The citizens of Pessac sent a second letter, too, in February 1794, after an investigating magistrate had interviewed Joseph's employees at Haut-Brion and had taken testimony from eighty-two witnesses.

Joseph's dossier, thirty pages long, suggests that there was little basis for charging him: the most serious complaint was that he had refused to permit hunting on his property. The fact that mattered most was that he was an aristocrat. It did not help him either that he was rich. The militant revolutionaries of Bordeaux were particularly contemptuous of 'the aristocracy of the rich'. This was the time when the Marquise de la Tour du Pin was hiding in a lonely cottage not far from Haut-Brion.

Joseph was not silent in his own adversity. In the same month, February 1794, he asked for the seals to be lifted at Haut-Brion so that he could send someone into the château with money to pay his employees; and he also petitioned the Commission, outlining his conduct since 1789 and requesting that he should either be set at liberty or, if this request were not granted, be transferred to the Orphélines prison. There he could be in the same place as his daughter, his sister, his niece and his nephews, and they would have 'the sad consolation of mixing our tears together'.

This last request was granted, but there were to be many more private tears. Two weeks before Joseph moved to the Orphélines, in the second year of the new French Republic, '*le treize Pluviôse, l'an deuxième de la République Française une et indivisible*', his daughter, then forty-five years old, was sentenced to death. The sentence was pronounced by Lacombe's Military Commission. The Commission had not yet fallen under the influence of Marie-Antoine Jullien, sent to Bordeaux two months later almost as a personal agent of Robespierre in Paris. Before he arrived in Bordeaux, 104 people had already died under the guillotine. After he arrived 198 others were sent there, two-thirds of the Bordeaux total, before Thermidor, Year II (August 1794), brought the Terror in Bordeaux to an end.

Corrupt, it seems, as well as arbitrary, although lenient towards some of his fellow revolutionaries whose views he disliked, Lacombe was not capable of administering even revolutionary justice when *aristocrates* – the term was used loosely – and priests were concerned. The crime Marie-Louise-Élisabeth was accused of committing – arranging the 'clandestine' marriage – had not always been considered serious enough for capital punishment even in revolutionary Paris, but this did not deter Lacombe from describing Marie-Louise as a person who had 'given a thousand proofs of her hatred of liberty'. There could be neither peace nor truce ('*ni paix, ni trêve*') in dealing with such aristocrats, 'the enemies of the Revolution'. The judgement pronounced, Marie-Louise-Élisabeth was dragged from prison through the streets of Bordeaux to the Place Nationale and beheaded. An attempt was made later to have her declared a martyr. The main charge against her had related to religion, it was argued; she had 'spilt for Christ blood more red and more pure than the best of our wines'. For the revolutionaries she was guilty, above all, of '*fanatisme*'. The reference to 'the best of our wines' was an oblique reference to Haut-Brion.

There was little hope, thereafter, for Joseph, although in May 1794, he wrote a third petition to the Committee of Public Safety, now framed in the humblest possible terms. 'Citizen Joseph Fumel, age seventy-four, weakened by infirmities, has been held for five months in prison. His detention was necessary, without doubt, according to the circumstances, and he is not complaining.' Could he not be 'reunited in the country at Haut-Brion with his old and infirm sister, and with his young niece and his nephew, all of them held many months in the Orphélines, their care and aid being necessary to the re-establishment of his health'?

There was no response; and only four days before the Military Commission in Bordeaux was itself brought to an ignominious end and its members arrested, Joseph was called peremptorily before it, 'convicted on all counts' and sentenced to death. The judgement on him was not signed by Lacombe, but the language was the same as Lacombe would have used and which Jullien, a passionate believer in equality, always insisted upon. Joseph belonged to 'the class of enemies of the Revolution', and he had been in touch with the English. For all the historical links between Bordeaux and England, this could be deemed the most serious of all crimes at a time when there were hundreds of French *émigrés*, ecclesiastical and aristocratic, some of them Joseph's relatives, in England. The same charge had been made against Marie-Louise-Élisabeth. It had been stated of her that she had advised her father to send money to the two Fumel *émigrés*, her husband and her brother.

Led out of prison and into the tumbrel, Joseph moved off to his death through streets that were now silent. He was one of the 198 people who went to the scaffold between 4 June and 31 July 1794, by no means all of them aristocrats and some of them treated far more cruelly than were the Fumels. Among the other victims were the owners of La Tour and Lafite. Lacombe himself was to fall from power before the Terror ended.

As part of the Fumel punishment, all Joseph's goods were duly 'confiscated to the profit of the Republic', a decree not without irony in that it was the English who had done most to ensure that Joseph's goods had increased substantially in value during the years when Haut-Brion had prospered. The informative *Documents relatifs à la Vente des Biens Nationaux* describe him as holding 228 *journaux* of land in Pessac, of which 120 were vineyard and 47 *bois taillis*. His whole estate was valued at 382,298 livres, and other estates in Talence, including a house, at 33,048 livres.

Other confiscated vine-growing properties in Pessac included at the other end of the scale around two or three *journaux* held by Millet. In Talence, La Mission property (just over 45 *journaux* of vineyard) was valued at 100,000 livres. It fetched more, 302,000 livres in paper money. The purchaser was Martial-Victor Vaillant, an important – and rich – citizen of Bordeaux, who had been responsible since 1776 – at first along with others – for lighting the city. Along with La Mission he acquired strategic properties in the city itself, including a mansion which he rented for gaming, for entertainments and for the use of an influential masonic lodge. Given the opposition of the Church to the freemasons, there was special irony in this. Vaillant could do more, but one thing that he could not do was to establish a dynasty. He had no son and only one daughter, who was married to a *Conseiller Général de France*. The couple lived in Paris, and in October 1821, with the wars of the Revolution and of Napoleon long since over, they were to put up the property for sale.

When Joseph de Fumel went to the guillotine, his nephew, Jacques Pons, a twenty-one-year-old soldier, now Comte de Fumel for those who recognized the title, was still in gaol. So also was his formidable eighteen-year-old sister, Augustine-Laure, who later in the year was to marry a still more formidable husband, Joseph-Hector, the Baron de Branne, a former officer of the *Parlement* of Bordeaux. In the wake of the reaction to the Terror they were both soon released, in September 1794, and returned to the château, where they had earlier lived and where parts of the building and estate had been declared state property.

After their return, an auction of Joseph's properties and possessions, one item in the great sale of '*Biens Nationaux*', was
stopped, and Haut-Brion, including the confiscated parts, was
returned – very briefly – to the family. So, too, was Margaux. At
the same time the father of the *émigré* Vigneras, Jean Vigneras,
bought back the land in Pessac which had been confiscated and
which he was to sell to Catellan in 1802. We have one record of a
sale of Haut-Brion that belongs to the period of turbulence. On 2
Pluviôse, Year VIII, Citizen Élisée Nairac bought for a *négociant*
124 bottles of Haut-Brion for 434 livres and 72 bottles of La Tour
for 252 livres.

The man then in charge at Haut-Brion, Jacques Pons, Joseph's
nephew, was soon to sell it and was to make his mark in Bordeaux
only after 1815, and then as a soldier in a Bourbon regiment. He
was to remain loyal to the Bourbons even after the revolution of
1830, and he did not die until 1850. Augustine-Laure's life was
more colourful. She divorced Baron Hector de Branne, who fled
from France in 1796, and in 1801 married a *négociant* of Bordeaux, Frédéric-Guillaume Langsdorff. For a time she held Margaux, although she sold it for 654,000 francs a year after her new
marriage to Bertrand Douat, the Marquis de la Colonilla – the title
was Spanish – and it remained in his hands until 1836. Augustine-
Laure died in 1813.

Many estates were in trouble (economic as well as political)
during these years, in both war and peace. Everywhere in Europe
the amount of land devoted to wine-growing fell during the long
wars which began in 1793, and so too did the average price of the
wines of Bordeaux, including that of the *grands crus*, which was
almost halved. Great vintages – 1795, 1798, 1801, 1802 – came
and went; and, as the 1793 had done, some of the 1795 even made
its way to England in a year of discontent when food was in short
supply in England itself. The 1801 and 1802 were also sold in
England during the interlude of the Peace of Amiens. One fact,
however, persisted after 1799. As Penning-Rowsell remarks suc-
cinctly, 'Napoleon drank burgundy'.

Charles-Maurice de Talleyrand-Périgord, Prince de Bénévent, so
closely involved in the politics of the period, bought Haut-Brion
from the Fumel heirs for 255,000 francs, on 9 Ventôse, Year IX
(28 February 1801). If there had been some doubt about Bertrand

Douat's title – and antecedents – there was none about those of Talleyrand. Doubt centred instead on his consistency. Born an aristocrat in 1754, the son of the Comte de Talleyrand-Périgord – and by first vocation a priest – Talleyrand was consecrated Bishop of Autun in 1788. Yet as a member of the Constituent Assembly in 1789 it was he who successfully proposed that Church property should be appropriated and it was he who in 1790 helped carry the Civil Constitution of the Clergy. He had influenced what happened at Haut-Brion, therefore, before he acquired it.

During the Terror Talleyrand emigrated first to England and then to the United States. Otherwise, he might have shared the fate of Joseph de Fumel. When he returned to France with a fortune that he had accumulated abroad, he quickly became Foreign Minister first under the Directory (1797–9) and later under Napoleon, both as First Consul and after he had become Emperor. He retained the post until 1807. It was because Talleyrand had amassed considerable funds before he ceased to serve the Directory, most of them held in assets abroad, that he was able to bid for Haut-Brion. And while his negotiations for Haut-Brion were continuing, France was engaged in the complex negotiations leading up to the brief Peace of Amiens with the English.

Thereafter, as before, Talleyrand proved himself a survivor, for in 1814 and 1815 – before Elba and after Waterloo – he represented Bourbon France at the Congress of Vienna, and after yet another French Revolution in 1830, served for four years as French Ambassador in London under Louis-Philippe. The diplomatic strain in the Talleyrand-Périgord family was old: it was claimed that an ancestor had tried to persuade the Black Prince and the King of France not to join the Battle of Poitiers in 1356. When Talleyrand died in 1838, Britain was already being ruled by the young Queen Victoria.

It was to Talleyrand's English biographer, Alfred Duff Cooper, first Viscount Norwich and first British Ambassador to France after the Second World War, that Hilaire Belloc dedicated his well-known *Heroic Poem in Praise of Wine*. Duff Cooper told his son, John Julius Norwich, on his fifteenth birthday that there were only two liquids generally to be avoided 'in your drinking life. One is water, and the other is milk . . . Stick to alcohol.'

There is no documentary evidence that Talleyrand, a *bon viveur* as well as a speculator, ever visited Haut-Brion. Nor is there any evidence to support the statement that the great chef, Carême, was involved at any point. There is evidence, however, that when in 1805 he sold the property for 300,000 francs to Pierre-Narcisse Michel, a Paris banker, his sister was apparently involved with him in the deal. This was the year of Trafalgar, and the fortunes of the Bordeaux wine trade were at as low an ebb as Haut-Brion had been at at the end of the eighteenth century. Yet Talleyrand made a profit of more than 50,000 francs on the sale.

Three years later, when Napoleon briefly visited Bordeaux in 1808 on his way to Spain and commiserated with the merchants about the state of their business, he might have had Talleyrand as his host at Haut-Brion if the chronology had been slightly different. Instead, Michel was now the proprietor, and he was still in charge when an English army, commanded by Marshal Beresford, appeared in March 1814 before the gates of Bordeaux.

Michel had seen a financial opportunity in Haut-Brion just as Jean de Pontac and Joseph de Fumel had done in the sixteenth and eighteenth centuries and as Talleyrand himself had done in 1801. So, too, indeed, had the Marquis de Catellan, then called Citoyen Catellan, who bought the second part of the Haut-Brion property (then called Chai-Neuf) from the la Tresne heirs nine days after Talleyrand bought the château and main *domaine* of Haut-Brion.

Proprietorship has meant different things at different times. In a time of trouble Jean de Pontac, acquiring seigneurial rights that disappeared entirely with the French Revolution, conceived the creation and development of a compact and growing estate, geared to wine production; and in the process he combined what are often thought of as peasant qualities with entrepreneurial ones. In the eighteenth century the Fumels, apparently secure in their nobility, displayed managerial qualities that are not usually associated with the pre-revolutionary French aristocracy. So, too, did the Marquis de la Tresne. Now bankers entered the vineyards – not for the last time. Of course their motives could be mixed too. There were – or could be – profits not only in buying and selling property as an investment but in a *grand cru*. In the latter case there was prestige also, the kind of prestige that later in the nineteenth century was to attract the Rothschilds. Baron James de Rothschild, who acquired Lafite for more than 4 million francs after an auction in 1868, was never to visit the château, but he was to establish a new kind of dynasty.

Some of the most interesting mid-nineteenth-century deals involved the acquisition by bankers of properties which after the Revolution had passed into the hands of *courtiers* and *négociants*. Thus, Beychevelle, which had been acquired by Pierre-François Guestier in 1825, was sold in 1874 to a Parisian banker, Armand Heine, whose daughter had married into the influential Fould family. Eight years earlier Madame Demarolles, grand-daughter of another Guestier, Daniel, who had acquired Batailley in 1819, sold it to another banker, Constant Halphen. Mme Demarolles was herself married to a Lawton. The story of Haut-Brion, as always, is part of a bigger picture, not all the details of which have yet been filled in.

10

Through Wars and Revolutions

Like all human institutions, [vineyards] are subject
to the laws of time and must at certain times be
rejuvenated and kept abreast of progress.

Cocks et Féret, 1868

The fortunes of Haut-Brion were as mixed between 1805 and 1836
as were the fortunes of France; and in 1825 Pierre-Narcisse Michel
sold the property to two partners, Louis-Nicolas Comynet, a stock-
broker, and Jean-Henry Beyerman, a well-known Bordeaux wine
merchant of Dutch origins, the former taking up a two-thirds share.
The price was said to be 525,000 francs. Michel had made a good
profit. Beyerman, whose ancestors had built up what still remains
the oldest wine business in Bordeaux – it had been founded in 1620
– managed the estate and sold the wine, for which he paid Comynet
an annual rent of 25,000 francs. These were times when perhaps
the best people to control a vineyard were dealers in wine; and
when Comynet went bankrupt in 1830, Beyerman bought out his
two-thirds share. Yet in 1835 Beyerman died suddenly at the age of
fifty-three and his widow, left with eight children, was forced to
auction Haut-Brion. The notice of the sale on 12 March 1836
survives.

The new purchaser in 1836 was a Paris banker, Joseph-Eugène
Larrieu, who paid nearly 300,000 francs for the property, more
than the pre-auction estimate of its value, 250,000 francs; and in
1841 Larrieu bought the remainder of the Haut-Brion estate, that
part which had belonged to the Marquis de Catellan, from his
daughter the Comtesse de Vergennes and her husband. This time,

the price was 60,000 francs. Haut-Brion was one property again for the first time since 1746.

Although Joseph-Eugène Larrieu was to spend little time at Haut-Brion, the property was to remain in the hands of the Larrieu family for almost as long as it had remained in the hands of the Fumels – until 1922. The word 'dynasty' was to be applied to the Larrieus, therefore, just as it had been to the de Pontacs and the Fumels, and it was under their ownership, supported by capable and energetic *régisseurs*, that the red wine of Haut-Brion was judged second to none and often the best of all. A high point came in 1855, with the official classification of Haut-Brion as one of the *grands crus*. It was then producing 100 to 120 *tonneaux* of wine a year, the same figure as Margaux, which had been bought for 1,300,000 francs in the same year as Larrieu had purchased Haut-Brion. La Mission across the road, then in the hands of Célestin Chiapella, was producing 30 to 40 *tonneaux*. Both Haut-Brion and La Mission won acclaim at the London Exhibition of 1862.

By then, Joseph-Eugène's son, Amédée Larrieu, had succeeded him (in 1856). Born at Brest in 1807, he had spent two years in the United States after studying law in Paris, two years which are said to have strongly influenced his attitude to politics and possibly to business. He was defeated by five votes in a Bordeaux election of 1846, the victor being the political economist, Adolphe Blanqui, said to have been the inventor of the phrase 'the industrial revolution'. Thereafter Amédée was twice elected to parliamentary bodies – on the first occasion, as a Republican, to the National Assembly created in 1848 after the revolution of that year. He was a follower of the poet–politician Lamartine. The second occasion was years later, for he consistently refused to support Louis Bonaparte either as President in 1848 or as Emperor in 1851, and quickly lost his parliamentary seat. He played no further part in politics until Napoleon was about to fall, but after his fall – and having once more been elected to the National Assembly – he was given the important post of Prefect of the Gironde. He was said to incarnate '*l'esprit des Girondins de la révolution*', a proud description in Bordeaux.

Amédée's work as Prefect won him great respect: an obituary referred both to his 'wise administration' and to the fact that 'he had affable relations with all sides'. In his own family, however, Larrieu did not always have his own way. His brother was an admiral, and his wife is said to have been uneasy about some of his Republican visitors. On one occasion, Amédée himself is said to have told a fiercely political guest that his wife had locked away the silver.

Amédée spent much of his time not at Haut-Brion but at his country estate near Châtellerault in the Vienne. His son and successor Eugène, a militant royalist, was born at Haut-Brion in 1847 and after he took over from Amédée he used to send his grandfather a hogshead of Haut-Brion *vin de presse* each year. During the German siege of Paris in 1871 he served as a gunnery officer, and according to Bertall tried to introduce the same discipline among the labourers in the vineyard as he had inculcated into soldiers in uniform. 'A regime of liberty' was a mad regime, he told Bertall, particularly at harvest time. Rules had to be obeyed without question.

He and his father were alike, however, in promoting their wine and protecting it against people who used the name Haut-Brion on their labels. Both prospered, too, under political regimes of which they did not approve. The Second Empire was a golden age of wine, when small proprietors might benefit from the price rise as much as large ones. It was during these years that Charles de Lorbac published in 1866 his book *Les Richesses gastronomiques de la France*, which covered both wine and food and which included a section on '*Vins de Graves des environs de Bordeaux*'. Lorbac paid a special tribute to Larrieu, who was proclaiming the merits of his '*cru d'élite*' at a time when the cheaper wines of Bordeaux were being sold in huge quantities both in Europe and in Latin America. Exports to the Argentine increased by 600 per cent between 1859 and 1869 and those to Mexico by 500 per cent.

In 1860 the story of claret consumption in Britain took a new turn, although it was hailed as a turn away from the élite when, in the wake of a new Anglo-French commercial treaty, the Cobden Treaty, William Ewart Gladstone, then Chancellor of the Exchequer, boldly reduced the duty on French wines of all descriptions from 5s 9d to 3s a gallon. With claret in mind, particularly cheap claret, Gladstone successfully persuaded Parliament that 'there is a power, I will not say of unbounded demand, but of an enormously increased demand, for this most useful and valuable product'. At the same time, he reminded his fellow members of Parliament that 'taste was not an immutable, but a mutable, thing'.

Whatever was said about the Englishman's preference for ale over wine, he went on, nothing was 'more certain than the taste of the English people at one time for French wine' – and by that he meant the wines of Bordeaux. 'It is idle to talk,' he added, 'of the taste for port and sherry, and the highly brandied wines as fixed and unchangeable.'

Amédée, well aware of the importance both of the British and of the French market, modernized the *chai* and carefully supervised the making of the vintages. He was disturbed in his tasks, however, by disasters that plagued the growing of vines during the Second Empire. So, too, was his son after him. Routines were broken. New challenges were presented.

Coping with the diseases of the vine required more than toughness, although toughness was not irrelevant. The first disease to strike in the 1850s, oidium, drove Amédée to carry out a large-scale programme of replanting vines and training the new vines on wires. According to Cocks et Féret, he replanted half the vineyard, making possible a production of 120 *tonneaux*. Then came phylloxera. It reached the Graves region in the late 1870s, and by 1882 138,000 of the 141,500 hectares of wines in the *département* of the Gironde were affected. It was Eugène, like his father a lawyer by training, who had to deal with late-arriving phylloxera. At first he did not believe that it would affect Haut-Brion: '*il n'ose pas se présenter içi*' ('it would not dare to present itself here'). It did, however, and Eugène's first way of trying to cope with it was to contain it with the use of chemicals. This did not succeed, and Eugène had to follow the way of his father and replant many vines, some of them so recently replanted, now using American rootstock. He had to deal, too, with mildew which hit Haut-Brion hard in the mid-1880s and destroyed the quality of the wine.

Because the reputation of Haut-Brion was so high, because demand for it remained buoyant, because the Haut-Brion property was substantial and because the Larrieus did not have to seek capital from outside, they were able to avoid serious financial difficulties during these years of strain, when the proprietors of small vineyards were in deep trouble. The price of pre-phylloxera Haut-Brion, carefully kept in the cellars, was higher than it had ever been. It had risen sharply during the oidium years and in the years of speculation that followed. Moreover, when the general price level, which had also risen significantly during the mid-nineteenth century, began to fall during the 1870s and fell sharply during the last years of the century, the price of Haut-Brion did not fall correspondingly. The Eschenauer firm of Bordeaux *négociants*, founded in 1821 by Louis Eschenauer of Strasbourg, enjoyed a monopoly of the sales of Haut-Brion in many of these years, and was able to report in 1875 that a record price of 100 francs had been reached for a single bottle of wine.

For the years 1876 to 1878 the diary of Sanchou, Larrieu's *régisseur* and *homme d'affaires*, provides valuable evidence of work in the vineyard. Like Viallon, Sanchou had to keep his proprietor informed both about the state of the vintage and about conditions in the wine market. It is sad that the record does not cover a longer period. One outside source, Bertall, confirms, however, that when Amédée Larrieu was at Haut-Brion he marshalled children as harvesters not just because their labour was cheap. He preferred 'a well drilled corps of children . . . clean and orderly and not allowed to eat too many grapes'.

The flowering was excellent, Sanchou reported in June 1876, and there would be little *coulure*. Yet the weather varied – one fine day, one foggy day to follow. By 19 September the grapes had matured well. There was a new moon. He had gone to a local orphanage that day to try to employ female pickers aged twelve to fifteen. They would sleep on straw and receive 60 centimes a day plus food. Those girls who emptied their baskets into the *douilles*, where the grapes made their way, would receive 75 centimes a day. This reference points to the source of the Bertall story, Sanchou himself.

There is a more intimate note in the Sanchou letters than there had been in the letters of Viallon. He sends baskets of fruit for Larrieu to collect at Châtellerault railway station, along with his proprietor's pipe which he had left behind. He has the roses cut and sent to be sold at Bordeaux market. He describes how the bullocks which were used in the vineyard had 'swollen feet', but adds that ploughing must begin in two or three days. He explains how a visitor who had come to taste Haut-Brion and to have lunch with him in the château had eaten first at La Mission before arriving. 'The servants had to eat the food . . . They were not displeased.'

References to the state of the vineyard are common. He sends weather reports, describes new terracing at the Chai Neuf, complains about the pump being out of order, and reports on the staff. When a labourer leaves Haut-Brion to work at La Mission, he writes: 'We lose a good labourer, but his wife is worth nothing.' There are details, too – although they are not systematic – of sales of wine, with cross-references to the prices of Latour and Lafite. In January 1877 Louis Eschenauer comes from Bordeaux to rack his wines. All Larrieu's 1874s had by then been sold: Eschenauer was tasting his 1875 and 1876 and was surprised to find that the former were not yet bunged. In 1878 Calvet and Meller came – separately – to taste the 1875s. They also gave Sanchou reports on Lafite and Margaux.

Unfortunately, there are no cross-references to La Mission, which the Chiapella family sold to the Paris firm of Duval in 1884. Chiapella had ordered the great iron gates that still stand firm outside the property, but he was thoroughly familiar with everything that went on behind them. Indeed, he was interested in other vineyards, including Cos d'Estournel where the soil was as gravelly as at La Mission. He raised its quality and its price. There were Haut-Brion links here, for the first Delmas to be employed at Haut-Brion had previously worked at Cos d'Estournel. There were American links too. Another Chiapella, Étienne, who lived in Louisiana, had a daughter who married Toutant Beauregard, a Creole general who was one of the full generals in the armies of the Confederacy during the American Civil War. The general was a flamboyant character who, after returning to Louisiana, made a fortune as a railway director and as manager of the state lottery. Étienne himself was a successful shipowner, and all his descendants were American.

La Mission deserves its own history as do the great firms like Eschenauer and Calvet. Another firm which had a monopoly of Haut-Brion sales in particular years during the 1870s was Cruse and Son (1871). The firm's founder had arrived from Schleswig-Holstein in 1819. It was successfully managed during the 1860s and 1870s by Herman Cruse and later by his son Adolphe. Herman acquired the vineyard of Pontet-Canet in 1865 and later the vineyard of Taillan, which has already figured in this history. When Adolphe died in 1892 he left a fortune of over 30 million francs.

Merchants had fewer worries during these years than proprietors, who often saw their profit margins narrow. Yet recovery of the vineyards at Haut-Brion after the phylloxera years was complete by the end of the nineteenth century, and after two particularly bad years, 1897 and 1898, the year 1899 produced a great vintage. Eugène had died in 1896, a bachelor who left no heirs, and once again, therefore, the future of a dynasty of proprietors was in doubt.

Characteristically however, Eugène had tried to ensure that the past of the dynasty, at least, was not forgotten. In his will he left 150,000 francs to the city of Bordeaux to provide for the making of a statue in memory of his father. The sculptor, Raoul Verlet, was chosen by a jury, and the work was completed in 1900. The dynasty that he could not perpetuate was honoured still further when the square where the statue was erected had its name changed from the Place Pessac to the Place Amédée Larrieu. Eugène also asked for a plaque to be attached to a Delacroix painting of the Convention in the Municipal Museum of Bordeaux, indicating that it was a gift from his father. Again, it was a gesture of filial duty, not of political loyalties, for Eugène was the last person to have any reason for wishing to perpetuate the memories of the French Revolution. It was more difficult for him to know what to do with Haut-Brion after his death than it was to honour his father; and it seems to have been by an oral deposition made on his deathbed that the château and the *domaine* were bequeathed to a nephew, Jacques-Norbert Milleret, and to a niece who later became Mme Georges Taconet.

For all the outstanding Haut-Brions that were produced between 1896 and 1915, life was not easy for the new proprietors, and they were drawn into all kinds of new business deals, not all of them as successful as a long-term, ten-year exclusive contract drawn up in 1907 for the sales of Haut-Brion; the monopoly was granted to the Bordeaux firm of Richard and Muller. The contract was signed at a time when there was a serious overproduction of the cheaper wines of Bordeaux. These were years, indeed, when the fortunes of the producers of the cheaper wines of Bordeaux and those of the proprietors of the *grands crus* diverged more sharply than they had done since the by then largely forgotten years of the *ancien régime*. Wine was also facing new competitors abroad, particularly whisky, publicized by 'whisky barons' who blended whiskies and gave them names. There were many signs, indeed, of a *bataille des boissons*, with distillers pitted at a distance against vignerons.

Before the ten-year contract term was over, the First World War had intervened, and in 1918 Milleret was killed in action, in its very last stages. Once again, there was a Franco-American link, this time in death, for Milleret was serving alongside the 78th Division of the American Expeditionary Forces. The business outcome was bizarre. Milleret's share of the château and estate, whose prosperity had been heavily hit by the war, now reverted to his father and to his two brothers. They borrowed heavily (and fought one court case in May 1920) in order to buy out Mme Taconet's share for 4 million francs, 3 million to be paid at once. They succeeded, but at such a high cost that they were obliged to sell off a large part of the park to building speculators. Even more alarmingly, they aroused nasty rumours that they would sell the rest. Eventually their bank, the Compagnie Algérienne, then at the height of its influence, foreclosed on them. They had become entirely dependent upon it. This was a difficult time for proprietors in the Graves, and the last descendants of the Larrieu family were so preoccupied with money that they could not run their vineyard effectively.

The Compagnie Algérienne had no desire to invest in undercapitalized Haut-Brion – or to manage it – and it was happy to sell the property to the Société des Glaciers de Paris. And that is when and how André Gibert came into the picture. The son of a Bordeaux tailor who had made a fortune in Algeria, Gibert was one of the bank directors, and in 1923 he decided to retire from the Entrepôts de Grenelles de Paris and took Haut-Brion and a large sum in cash in exchange for his stake in the company. It is said that his fortune had been made during the First World War, when the Entrepôts de Grenelles business sold cheap Algerian wine to troops. Now he had a *grand cru* at his disposal.

In any history of Haut-Brion, Gibert should never be dismissed quickly. He was genuinely interested in wine-making and in enhancing the reputation of his own wine. Several visitors to Haut-Brion, including Maurice Healy, found him knowledgeable as well as entertaining. He was, nonetheless, an eccentric character with more than a touch of meanness in him. After bicycling out from Bordeaux to Pessac, he would turn out the electric lights in the *chai* and urge men on the bottling line to finish just one more barrel before they stopped work. This must have been more irritating to workers in the vineyard than Eugène Larrieu's discipline. But it was not only workmen who could rouse Gibert. When the local water company offered him a free supply of water for thirty years in exchange for permission to build a water tower, he is said to have demanded free water in perpetuity. The company then offered water for ninety-nine years, and when he again refused he was taken to court and compelled to pay in future for all the water that he consumed.

There seems no doubt that Gibert, who unlike the Larrieus had no legal training, was a man who actually enjoyed litigation. He certainly spent much of his time trying to protect the exclusivity of the name of Haut-Brion in expensive and usually abortive legal proceedings against a number of vineyards, near to and far away from Haut-Brion, that used Haut-Brion as part of their trade name. One legend relates that when he heard of a restaurant in Germany that was selling wine in a pitcher and calling it Haut-Brion, he set off at once – not this time on his bicycle – found the restaurant, filed suit, and actually won. A number of nearby vintages were not allowed to use Haut-Brion on their labels. These included Fanning-la-Fontaine-Haut-Brion, the name of which was blocked out of Cocks et Féret in 1926 after it had gone to the printer. There was nothing that Gibert could do – or tried to do – however, about La Mission Haut-Brion. An able and energetic new owner, Otto-Fredéric Woltner, had purchased the property in 1919 from Victor Cousteau, who had acquired it from Duval in 1903.

Woltner dealt in Pol Roger champagne as well as in La Mission, and it was his son Henri, an early graduate in oenology from the University of Bordeaux, who restored the fortunes of La Mission as a wine-producing centre. Known everywhere as a good host, he warmly welcomed visitors to La Mission, recorded their names in his visitors' book, offered them a choice of wines to taste, and displayed to them an excellent, if incongruous, collection of holy-water stoups and religious statues, housed in the old chapel which he turned into a museum. He also collected Delft dishes, brought to Bordeaux by Dutch merchants who had enjoyed La Mission wines in the eighteenth century. Above all, Woltner did everything that he could to ensure that the quality of the wine that he offered his own visitors was good: in Edmund Penning-Rowsell's words, he was 'one of the most infectiously "committed" Bordeaux château owners'. Penning-Rowsell was writing after the Second World War. One very special occasion in the Woltner calendar had happened long before that, however. In June 1926 a great garden party had been held on the occasion of the third national congress of Conseillers du Commerce Extérieur. In the same year, Henri installed glass-lined steel fermentation vats, a remarkable and controversial innovation for the period.

Four years earlier, Woltner had acquired through rental from the widow of Victor Cousteau, who died soon after he had sold the La Mission, rights to another vintage – that of the adjacent vineyard of La Tour-Haut-Brion, eight hectares in size; and on the death of Cousteau's widow in 1935 Woltner took over completely this valuable property which Madame Cousteau had bequeathed to his wife in her will. From 1928 onwards he had also produced a dry white La Tour-Haut-Brion, after having planted four hectares with Sauvignon and Sémillon. Meanwhile, the red La Tour-Haut-Brion had come to be thought of (wrongly perhaps) as a second wine. The white Laville-Haut-Brion was a delightful wine in its own right, 'nerveux et distingué.'

There was a possible argument on two fronts about the name of La Tour-Haut-Brion. Latour stayed out of it, but Gibert foolishly did not: La Tour-Haut-Brion was one of the names he chose to attack. The vineyard, which he called Latour de Rostaing des Esquivants, was allowed to keep its full name, and in 1953 it was to be among thirteen red Graves that were classified.

There had been an even longer history behind La Tour-Haut-Brion than there had been behind the Château of Haut-Brion itself, although it was not until the nineteenth century that the then proprietor of La Tour, Jérôme Cayrou, a Bordeaux merchant, added the name Haut-Brion to the wine that he was producing in the same *chai* as La Mission. In 1850 his production amounted to 25 *tonneaux*. The owner of La Tour during the Revolution, Madame Saige, a member of the great mercantile family of Pessac, had chosen not to emigrate, but her son was the first person to be guillotined. Thereafter, other Bordeaux merchants held the property in the nineteenth century.

Soon after taking over – and on occasion later – Gibert had to protect his own name as well as the name of the wine that he produced. He was accused by journalists of seeking to sell the whole estate of Haut-Brion for building development. In fact, it was the Millerets, backed by their bank, not he, who had issued a brochure drawing attention to the 'diversities' of the Haut-Brion estate; and it was the bank, not he, which had sold off significant parts of the property – '90 hectares of meadow and woodland' – for urban development.

Rumours about Gibert's intentions were at their height early in 1925, when the newspapers *L'Intransigeant* and *Figaro* (16 January 1925) suggested that the vineyard itself would disappear. Very quickly *Le Matin* (18 January), followed by *L'Oenophile* and by *L'Intransigeant* itself (22 January), quashed them, but the damage had been done and obviously had to be repaired. Apologies were made, and in a second article *Le Matin* quoted a reporter who had decided to visit Haut-Brion in order to find out just what was happening. What he saw came as a surprise. 'The old Haut-Brion is not dead', he concluded. 'Perhaps it has never been better managed.' He had been assured by people in the know that 'the Haut-Brion vineyard would never lose any of its *noblesse*'.

The editor of *L'Oenophile*, who had published an article on the history of Haut-Brion in March 1922, added that 'we know the love that the new proprietor of Haut-Brion has for viticulture' and the '*grands vins*'; and Gibert himself was quoted in *Le Petit Journal* as saying: 'I am Bordelais, I love the soil, the vine, the wine also, and I am not ready – even for dollars or pounds sterling – to hand over to others this national treasure.' Gibert was determined, too, to produce limited qualities of white wine, believing rightly that it had good prospects. His zeal – and his white wine – won the approval of Paul de Cassagnac among others. Haut-Brion, he said, was 'in good hands' and its wines were 'worthy of the most glorious successes' of the past.

Dollars, not sterling, were to count in the future, but it was *The Times* of London that took up the claim made in *L'Intransigeant* on 17 January 1925 under the heading 'A Threatened Vintage', when it spoke of the grave danger that Haut-Brion might become extinct. So also, later, did the *Observer* ('Suburb or Vineyard?'). The young member of Parliament, Alfred Duff Cooper, later to be Talleyrand's biographer, in the same month wrote an article in the *Evening News* headed 'The Rape of the Vineyard'. *The Times* retracted three days later; Duff Cooper, however, did not: 'perhaps a gallant battalion of sturdy wine lovers', he mused, 'will have to march down to Haut-Brion and having dug a trench, not on, but round, the sacred soil of the vineyard, will hurl defiance at the burghers of Bordeaux from under the shelter of a wine-red standard inscribed with the old proud device "*ils ne passeront pas*" '.

*

The 'sacred soil' was worked by a team of people whose duties were described on paper soon after Gibert took over. The high-level full-time staff at Haut-Brion then consisted of the *régisseur*, the accountant (*le comptable*), the keeper of the vines (*le maître de culture*) and the keeper of the *chai* (*le maître de chai*). Neither of these last two offices was known to Dubut. Nor was either of them referred to by Sanchou, although they probably then existed. The *maître de culture* was assisted by an under-keeper, his *contre-maître*, and by fifteen workers, including a carpenter, while the *maître de chai* was served by his *contre-maître* and two full-time workers. Some workers were still employed casually on a day-to-day basis, as they had been in Dubut's time, and the accountant visited the château only for a few hours each week when he was required. For this he was paid a fixed sum.

The *régisseur* was the man who really counted. He is described clearly in the document as 'an agent with technical knowledge who gives his orders to the *maître de culture* and to the *maître de chai*'. It was he, too, who was responsible directly for the sale of the wine. He was paid a percentage on sales and other revenues as well as salary. The arts of marketing were different from those of the 1890s yet, like his predecessors, both he and his successors had to deal regularly with *courtiers, négociants* and *commerçants*.

'*Le propriétaire*', it was stated in a further briefing note, 'has only a general relationship with the administrative staff.' It was through his manager that the good order of his estate was maintained, and it was his manager whom he would provide with necessary funds and to whom he would delegate the pricing of his products. Other servants were under the *régisseur*'s control: the proprietor often did not know them personally. The accountant, however, was required to submit regular statements of income and expenditure directly to the proprietor himself.

The *maître de culture* was a 'workman, son of a peasant and a peasant himself'. He had secured his job on merit (*par sa valeur*) and it was he who gave orders to the workers in the vineyard. For carrying out these duties he received a monthly payment of 250 francs, along with free lodgings, light and 'wood for his fires'. He also had the kitchen garden, which he had to cultivate himself. The *maître de chai* was paid the same amount and was given the same perks. 'He receives the fruits of the harvest and turns them into wine,' the note went, 'his role is important and is not lacking in responsibility.' One of his responsibilities was to receive those *commerçants* and *courtiers* who visited the *chai* to taste the wines of Haut-Brion. It was he who kept the keys of the cellar, who ensured that barrels and bottles were in good condition, and who decanted wines before lunches and dinners.

The workers who were under the orders of the *maître de culture* fell into different categories: *vignerons*, who were called upon to carry out any tasks concerned with the care of the vines ('such as planting, pruning and spraying, etc.'); carters (*charretiers*), who might be called upon to carry anything, including barrels and timber; and general manual workers (*manœuvres*) who might be called upon to do anything from cleaning the rows between the vines or making stakes to heaping compost. There was an eight-hour working day, starting at seven in the morning.

Women were employed for a variety of less heavy forms of work: they were often the wives of the male labourers. It was as true in the twentieth century as it had been in the seventeenth that the family, not the individual, was the unit with which the vineyard had to deal. There were marked differences in pay. Women were paid 5 francs a day, men 13, or, if they were on the payroll, 200 francs a month.

Gibert was interested in the processes of wine-making, but he had little capital at his disposal. This accounts in part for his reputation for meanness. It also accounts for the setting up in 1927 of La Société Fermière de Bordeaux, which had an initial capital of 100,000 francs, divided into 200 blocks of 500 francs each. Gibert himself was president, and at the annual meetings each year, when the accounts were presented, it was he who communicated his own version of the harvest and the prospects. Bossuet, a Bordeaux lawyer, drew up the legal documents, and Fernand Ginestet as a *négociant* represented the business affairs of the *Société*. Since Gibert insisted on selling wine direct from the château he was lampooned by most *négociants*; indeed, they even produced a picture of an Haut-Brion bottle with a dead mouse inside it.

Gibert was never rash in his communications to his *Société*. The year 1929, for example, so significant in world history, was not at once announced as 'a great year' for the vintage. All that Gibert chose to say was that 'we are left with a waiting ticket'. In 1930 he stressed that 'the poor state of our affairs along with the painful situation of our commerce . . . depreciates the value of our harvest even when the harvests are good'. Sales remained low, and in 1931 costs were cut to the minimum, and would remain cut, Gibert added, until the crisis was over. From the annual accounts presented at the meetings of the *Société*, culminating in an extraordinary meeting held in May 1935, it is possible to trace the process of further decline, during which Gibert, always '*un personnage inquiet*', set out to sell Haut-Brion to Clarence Dillon. He dreamed of going to Switzerland, as he was to do eventually ten years later.

In 1934 Gibert had made one last dramatic gesture – not unlike Churchill's gesture in 1940 at the moment of greatest disaster for the Europe of the west, when he offered the French government a full union of the French and British peoples. Ill, old and childless, and anxious to dispose of Haut-Brion, Gibert now offered it to the city of Bordeaux on condition that it gave a guarantee that it would maintain the vineyard 'in perpetuity'. No such guarantee was forthcoming, and it was only after this local bid had failed that the international bid succeeded.

On 13 May 1935 Clarence Dillon, an American millionaire who headed the great American investment banking firm of Dillon, Read, bought Haut-Brion for 2,300,000 francs (about US$160,000) after months of negotiations. The deal was concluded in the office of Maître Buguet, the lawyer, and the sum provided covered the château and the vineyards, the *chai* and the cellars, the gardens and the park, and a group of workers' houses. When Gibert told the annual meeting of the *Société* in 1932 that 'the early opening of the American market gives us a little hope', he had customers for Haut-Brion wines in mind, not purchasers of Haut-Brion. Did it ever cross his mind that American help of a different kind might one day arrive?

Whatever happened on the road from Bordeaux to St-Émilion in 1935, it was Henri de Fonroque-Mercié, former ship's purser and later Secretary of the Académie du Vin of Bordeaux, who after talking to Gibert had made contact with Dillon's Paris partner, William Lindsley Fiske, regarding Haut-Brion. He had been told that Dillon was interested in acquiring a *grand cru*, and he was anxious to help. Dillon had turned first to Château Margaux, then managed by a syndicate headed by a Bordeaux banker, Pierre Moreau. One member of the syndicate was said to be willing to sell for 4 million francs, but this price was pushed up to 5 million francs when the proprietor learned that Fonroque-Mercié's client was an American. That particular deal was off, if it had ever been on; and it was a well-known Bordeaux figure, who had been involved with Gibert in the Société Fermière, Fernand Ginestet, who from 1935 onwards began to buy out the other members of the Margaux syndicate.

For more than one reason a possible Dillon purchase of Cheval Blanc was also off. It would have cost 2,500,000 francs. Later, Dillon was to say that Fiske knew that Haut-Brion was Dillon's favourite wine. He was interested in the property, his nephew Seymour Weller recalled later, not only because of the vineyard but because it was close to Bordeaux, because there was attractive riding and hunting country nearby, and because the château itself was empty except for one shabbily furnished room where Gibert slept during the harvest season. 'It was a place', Weller wrote, that he could 'restore and refurnish *à son goût*'.

Whatever Dillon's motives may have been – and they were doubtless mixed – at the time that he was informed by Fiske that a deal might be possible, he showed immediate interest. He was on his way back to the United States when he received a shipboard cable telling him that he could get it if he 'acted fast'. His immediately cabled reply revealed that he wasted no words: 'Act fast.' Behind his speed of reaction, however, was the 'thoroughness' of his research, picked out by a classmate of his as his outstanding quality: 'if he wanted to buy a cow, he would read up everything on cows, and before the deal closed he would know more about the animal than the farmer himself'. In 1935 what had been said about a cow now applied to a vineyard.

Born in San Antonio, Texas, in 1882, Dillon had been educated at Worcester Academy in Worcester, Massachusetts, and at Harvard, and his early career had been well described in an article in the internationally famous *Review of Reviews* in 1926. What he now offered to Haut-Brion was something it had never had since the mid-nineteenth century: secure finance that would permit continuity of investment even in difficult times, investment backed also by financial know-how. Dillon had good French connections too. His mother was part French, and he and his wife had chosen to spend their honeymoon in Paris after their marriage in 1908. It proved a long honeymoon that was to last for two years. Indeed, as far as France was concerned, it was a honeymoon that was to last for the rest of Dillon's life.

He joined the old and comfortable banking house of William A. Read and Company in 1916 – with good prospects of success – and there was more than a touch of drama in the fact that, on the very day he joined, Read was struck with a fatal illness, was carried to his home and died within a week. Dillon's long-term prospects were strengthened, and his experience was greatly extended when he worked for a time with the outstanding American financier Bernard Baruch, acting as his personal aide in the War Industries Board. This was a perfect apprenticeship. On returning from Washington to New York, Dillon became president of W. A. Read, which in 1921 became Dillon, Read, and very soon he established his respected reputation as a businessman who knew how to act fast, the quality that was to be needed most in 1935: he was famous too for 'stealing business from under the nose of the Rothschilds'. Once he is said to have put through in two hours a deal that involved the largest cheque ever written: this followed the sale of over a million shares of common stock of the National Cash Register Company. Along with a respected reputation came the laying of the foundations of a great personal fortune. Based largely at first on international dealings, his fortune was greatly increased after the Wall Street crash of 1929, at a time when other Americans were losing theirs. His story, a journalist noted in 1929, had more of the 'ingredients of romance' in it than that of most of 'the Napoleons of finance of the last century'.

In the same year Dillon rented an apartment in Paris, where he spent part of each year, an apartment which he was to transfer to his Haut-Brion company in 1935. From the start he drew in his family. It was his granddaughter, Joan, who was to restore the château imaginatively *à son goût* in the 1970s, but long before then, on their annual visits to Haut-Brion during the 1930s, Dillon and his wife Anne had set about improving and refurnishing the château. Clarence had been told by his friend Dolly Hoffman, who knew France well and visited the château at his invitation in 1935, how unattractive, even sinister, it seemed to be. She was a decorator by profession and gave him invaluable help in transforming it. They bought Louis XIII pieces for the salon, including a great game table, hired weavers to produce hand-loom upholsteries, and summoned potters to fire and to decorate china. They even created an entirely new entrance to the property, designed by Dolly Hoffman's husband, Burrall, who also built the entry gate at Haut-Brion and designed a house for Clarence in Jamaica. Only Americans would have applied themselves to these tasks with such vigour and enthusiasm – and they brought in American plumbing too.

Meanwhile, under Dillon's orders, Seymour Weller, the son of his wife's sister, had become president of the newly formed Société Vinicole de la Gironde, and worked as Dillon's personal agent, arranging for the tidying of the park, the pruning of the trees, the cleaning of the *chais*, the introduction of new wine-making equipment and the modernization of the electrical system. Fluent in French, which he spoke with a strong American accent – he said that his palate had been formed too soon – he was on good terms with Gibert and wisely retained Gibert's *régisseur*, Georges Delmas, and all the families already working in the vineyard, many of whom had experience stretching back to the Larrieu years.

A report prepared for Weller includes interesting questions, sometimes with answers noted in the margin. For example, against the description of *collage*, the 'putting of fresh whites of egg in each cask', the pertinent question is asked, 'How many?' Against the months of May and July are references to the importance of getting rid of butterflies: 'must keep a machine going through the vineyard which destroys butterflies'. Against the dates 25 September to 10 October there is the single instruction: 'Hire about 50 to 70 extra people.'

Another description was clearly written by Weller for Clarence Dillon to read. After an introductory quotation from André Simon, it went on to describe how sixteen men and nine women were then working in the vineyards and *chais* at Château Haut-Brion, and living 'in minor Châteaus on the property – Bahans, Chai Neuf, Maillot – and two smaller houses'. In addition, there were a gardener and his wife, and Marie-Lise, the cook. Marie-Lise was the widow of a former cellar-master at Haut-Brion, and she died in 1989, at the age of ninety-nine, while I was writing this book. She belonged to a dynasty of her own.

The annual sequence of activities as described to Dillon would not have surprised Sanchou, Dubut or the Pontacs. During the winter, from November to March, each of the 320,000 vines was cut down almost to the soil. One area 'slightly over two-acres square' was replanted each year. The life of a vine was set then at about fifty years. Locke had believed that the oldest vines with the fewest grapes made the best wine, and the belief still held.

'Early in June,' the report went on, 'the vines begin to flower. If the weather is favourable, the vines flower for about ten days. If the weather is cold and stormy, the flowering drags on and the crop is reduced. Once a week from May to the end of August the vineyard is harrowed to aerate the soil and eliminate grass or weeds.' The time for gathering the grapes was said to vary from 15 September to 15 October, and last for about ten days. 'Fifty to seventy additional pickers are hired, men and women from sixteen years up. The grapes ripen best when there is little rainfall from July to the *vendanges*. It is very important to have a good amount of sunshine in August.' At the *chai*, several men wearing rubber boots 'shovel the grapes from the platform where they have been dumped' into a machine which takes off the stems, throws them aside, and then pumps the squashed skins, pips and juice into large vats, each holding 4,400 gallons.

It ferments for about ten days. During fermentation, the skins of the grapes give the red colour to the juice. After this fermentation, the juice is drawn from the vats into barrels holding about 288 bottles each. These barrels are kept in another room. During the first year, the juice from each barrel is drained off every two months into another barrel. The second and third year, the wine is drained from the barrels less frequently. Once during the second year, each barrel of wine is fined with whites of fresh eggs, eight eggs to a barrel.

The wine of Château Haut-Brion is bottled on the average three years after the *vendanges*. The wine is drawn from the barrel into a bottling machine which fills up the bottle, inserts the cork and puts on the label and cap. The bottles are then put in cases branded with the name Château Haut-Brion and containing 12 bottles and/or 24 half bottles and/or 6 magnums.

The bulk of the crop is normally sold the year following the *vendanges*. The crop averages about 140,000 bottles, some years more and some years less. When the Château decides to sell, the four principal Bordeaux wine brokers are called in and give their opinion as to what price the crop could be sold to the thirty or so Bordeaux wine merchants who year after year have been buyers of Château Haut-Brion wine, and these Bordeaux wine merchants then distribute the wine to their clients throughout the world.

Weller ran a Paris office, at 39 rue Cambon, and sold Haut-Brion through a new company, Granvins, with offices on the Quai des Chartrons in Bordeaux, where stocks of Haut-Brion were held. At that time there was little room at the château. One of his first salesmen was Lichine. Simon dedicated a book to him.

When the Second World War broke out, in September 1939, the Dillons, who had stayed at Haut-Brion earlier in the year, were in the United States. They were unable to return to Bordeaux for six years. Yet on 10 September 1939 – long before the United States entered the war – Dillon offered the French government the use of the château as a hospital for wounded soldiers and sailors, adding that he would pay for any necessary alterations. Meanwhile, Weller, who had become a French citizen, was in charge of all the arrangements, and on 10 May 1940 he was instructed by Dillon to do all that he could to protect the property.

The story of the short-lived hospital and of the way in which it was converted in 1940 into a Luftwaffe rest home is well known in Haut-Brion and Bordeaux. Less well known, however, even in Bordeaux, is the story of how in June 1940, at the time of the fall of France, Dillon gave 500,000 francs to a small committee set up in Bordeaux to help refugees who were fleeing despairingly *into* the city. The committee included Daniel Lawton, Adrien Marquet, Emmanuel Cruse, Émile Calvet and Louis Eschenauer – all very familiar names at Haut-Brion as in the city – and it handed over Dillon's gift to the Archbishop of Bordeaux, the President of the Protestant Presbytery and the Chief Rabbi, asking them to make the best use of it.

Before the eventual conversion of Haut-Brion into a Luftwaffe rest home, most of the furniture was removed and stored under Weller's direction in houses of neighbouring French families, and the best of that which still remained was hidden by the staff. The German airmen proved to have their own taste, however, re-upholstering the remaining chairs and sofas in pink and lavender-striped satin, and painting the old stone fireplaces 'warm brown', doubtless in order to make the château *gemütlich*. They also re-legated the game table to the sheds and amused themselves with indoor shooting. They were never permitted to interfere with the wine, however, which remained safe in the cellars, the entrances to which had been hidden behind piles of rubbish. Nor could they drink any of the new wartime wines, some of which were to prove remarkably good, or participate in the annual process of wine-making. Doubtless, high-ranking Nazis like Goering and Ribbentrop – the latter a wine merchant by original occupation – wished the stocks to be preserved for their private consumption after victory.

In the absence of its proprietor, the continuity of daily life at Haut-Brion was maintained by the *régisseur*, Georges Delmas, who was even able to make improvements during the war. It was a sign of his abundant skills in all circumstances that what many judge to be the vintage of the century was produced in the long-awaited year of Allied victory, 1945. (One of the wartime visitors had been Gibert. He came to get vegetables, not wine.) During these often frustrating, sometimes challenging, years when his son Jean was a boy, Georges and his wife knew exactly how to deal with the Germans. Soon after the Germans had moved into the château they began eating fruit from the garden. Unafraid, Madame Delmas told their commanding officer to ask them to stop doing so since the fruit was for her little boy. Next day, seeing them still in the garden, she returned to their commanding officer and said: '*Mon Capitaine*, there must be some mistake, because certainly your men would not disobey your command, but they are still in my garden.' Later that day, her husband, unaware of what had happened, demanded to know what was 'going on in the garden'. There were patrols there with fixed bayonets, 'marching up and down and around the garden, letting nobody in'.

The Delmas's son, Jean, was to succeed his father as *régisseur* in 1961 and become managing director of the whole enterprise. Meanwhile, Seymour Weller had become mayor of the town of Neaufles-St-Martin in the Eure and had bought a house in Amboise half-way between Paris and Haut-Brion. The Dillon family had returned as soon as possible to Haut-Brion. It was a memorable moment in 1949 when Dillon's mother, then in her eighty-seventh year, blessed the vintage in French ('*Que Dieu bénisse*'): 'God bless this soil which produces this good wine.' Thérèse Weller, Seymour's wife, who had worked for a time with Granvins before she married Seymour, stood with her husband beside Clarence Dillon and his wife. Clarence's sister Jeanie Dillon was there too.

A year later, the first post-war ball was held at Haut-Brion. It was a glittering occasion when garlands of grapes decorated the arches above the platform on which the dance band played. Jacques Chaban-Delmas, the young Mayor of Bordeaux, was one of the chief guests. Joan Dillon, Clarence's granddaughter, remembers the evening well. It was her first visit to Haut-Brion. She also remembers a 1957 dinner in the Bordeaux restaurant, the Chapon Fin, where she heard Chaban-Delmas talking of the return to power of General de Gaulle. Joan was one of the members of the Dillon family who moved to Europe in 1955, becoming in time the Dillon family representative at all Haut-Brion occasions, and then representing Clarence Dillon's son and daughter, Douglas and Dorothy. In 1967 she married His Royal Highness Prince Charles of Luxembourg, Prince de Bourbon-Parme, Prince de Nassau – and a direct descendant of Henry IV. He too served on the Haut-Brion board until his death in 1977.

Like his father, Douglas Dillon, born in 1909, was a Harvard graduate. He became a member of the New York Stock Exchange in 1921 and a director of Dillon, Read in 1938. After the Second World War he had an outstanding career in American public service, first as Ambassador to France from 1953 to early 1957 and then as Under-Secretary of State for Economic Affairs under President Eisenhower from 1957 to 1959. He went on to serve as Secretary of the Treasury under Presidents Kennedy and Johnson from 1960 to 1965. Dillon knew much about France – and much about international business.

The company Domaine Clarence Dillon SA was founded in 1958, with Weller as president, to be succeeded by Joan Dillon then Duchess of Luxembourg, in 1975. After years of depression and war the Dillon stake in Haut-Brion was at last beginning to justify itself in economic terms. Clarence Dillon last visited Haut-Brion in 1967 – 'I will not come back', he is reported to have said – and he died in 1979 at the age of ninety-six.

Joan, born in 1935, the same year as Jean-Bernard Delmas, made the most of her inheritance. She stayed in Paris after her father had left the Embassy and enjoyed a fascinating spell in publishing with the *Paris Review*, of which she became Assistant Paris Editor. At Haut-Brion it was the château, not the vineyard, that first engaged her attention in 1973 and 1974. Entirely redecorating it was a sound investment. So, too, was the purchase of pictures and furniture. She made it a far more beautiful place than it ever had been, even in the days of Joseph de Fumel. With the help of a knowledgeable friend, Mme Lucie Vieyres, who was an excellent bargainer, she combed the antique shops and markets of the world to find just what she wanted. She discovered near at hand, in Bordeaux, the portrait of the Grand Dauphin that hangs over the chimney of the salon, a symbol of living history. Much of the furniture was also bought, as she wished, in Bordeaux, where she found that items that had hitherto been 'not for sale' suddenly became available for the château.

The two days a week that Joan spent at Haut-Brion were always busy, and she also got to know the Paris office well. In a pre-computer age her one accountant, M. Thorin, worked in an apartment office behind her kitchen in the rue Barbet-de-Jouy, in a house which she kept there from 1957 to 1978. Thérèse and Seymour Weller took care of her, and Mme Weller remains close to the family today.

After the death of her husband Charles, family portraits and furniture were brought in to Haut-Brion from Luxembourg and Italy, adding a further family touch to the château. They are the property of Charles's and Joan's children, HRH Princess Charlotte and HRH Prince Robert. The portraits include those of the Duc de Bordeaux and his sister Louise de France, children of the Duc de Berry. Louise married the Duc de Parme. One portrait of Charles's great grandfather the Duc de Parme shows him wearing a Stuart kilt, sign of a dynastic connection going back to Mary Stuart. There is a royal and a European influence, therefore, as well as an American one, in contemporary Haut-Brion. Douglas Dillon's sister Dorothy, half-owner of Haut-Brion, has always loved the château and its park and during the 1960s, while married to Sidney Spivack, spent entire summers there.

Outside the château immense improvements have been made since the 1960s. The huge gardens have been reduced to working size, old trees have been chopped down, and new trees and shrubs planted. There are sculptured stone lions outside the front door. These were bought for herself by the Duchesse at the age of twenty-two and ended up at Haut-Brion. The razing to the ground of the old château at Bahans and the planting of vines on the cleared site, the taking in of the adjacent property of La Passion Haut-Brion, the extension of the *chai de la première année*, the building of a new *cuverie* and reception bay, and the construction in 1974 of a large new underground *chai de la deuxième année* below the central courtyard were all symbols of enterprise. The last of these replaced rented cellars in Bordeaux.

In 1978 Princess Joan married the Duc de Mouchy, one of whose ancestors, the Maréchal de Mouchy, had been Governor of Gascony in the eighteenth century. The Duc and Duchesse remain today at Haut-Brion, themselves symbols of what in 1927 Gibert's lawyer had called correctly, but modestly, *'une hérédité terrienne importante'*. The value of the property has risen so much over the years since the dark days of 1935 that Gibert and his lawyer would have been even more amazed at the outcome than Jean de Pontac himself.

In promoting Haut-Brion the Duc and Duchesse have travelled round the world. One particularly remarkable journey was to Texas, where in 1986 they were entertained in style on the Overton ranch and were offered by their generous hosts no fewer than ninety Haut-Brions old and new (1899 to 1985, both reds and whites; thirty of them were whites). The Duchesse told Overton that Clarence Dillon 'could never have imagined that his granddaughter would return one day to his native state to taste more vintages of his wine than were preserved at Haut-Brion itself'.

One of the great occasions in the history of Haut-Brion took place in London in 1985. It was a dinner arranged by Michael Broadbent of Christie's to celebrate the fiftieth anniversary of Clarence Dillon's acquisition of the property. The dinner was attended by 500 guests, including members of the Dillon family – among them Douglas, Dorothy and the Duchesse – Lord Soames, Andrew Lloyd-Webber and Auberon Waugh. Chaban-Delmas flew in from Bordeaux. There were two tents, the first decorated with statues of Roman emperors in *faux-marbre*, the second hung with Louis XIV tapestries that the king himself used when he entertained in tents away from Versailles. They were borrowed in great secrecy from the Garde Meuble Nationale and were back safe and sound in Paris the following day.

As part of the celebration, which brought London into the centre of the story of Haut-Brion as it had been three centuries before, there was a special sale of Haut-Brions. And these brought Jean-Bernard Delmas into the centre of the picture, for as far as the wine-making process at Haut-Brion is concerned, the success of the enterprise owed most to what Harry Waugh, a director of Latour, called Delmas's 'able direction of Haut-Brion'. He succeeded, Waugh claimed – and he was an extremely knowledgeable observer – in 'often rivalling and frequently surpassing the other first growths of the Médoc'. It is important to add that Waugh, like most other observers, had good words to say also about Henri Woltner at La Mission across the road: he was 'a veritable wizard among wine makers', particularly in off-vintage years. Clearly, Waugh was equally at home in Pessac and Talence.

There would have been few overseas observers, however knowledgeable, who would have forecast in 1971 that within just over a decade Delmas himself would be equally at home on the two sides of the road or that another '*hérédité importante*' – with a very different history – would pass into the hands of the Domaine Clarence Dillon. How it did is not the least interesting of all the tales of Haut-Brion.

Henri Woltner died in 1974 and the properties passed to various members of the Woltner family: his daughter, his brother Fernand's son and daughter, and his sister Madeleine, who operated through a Société Civile des Domaines Woltner that in 1977 disposed of its wine merchandising business in Bordeaux. It was from this *Société*, then managed by Fernand's daughter Françoise and her Belgian-born Flemish husband Francis Dewawrin, that the Domaine Clarence Dillon SA acquired La Mission Haut-Brion in 1983 along with La Tour-Haut-Brion (the château by then was rented to an old people's home) and Laville-Haut-Brion.

The negotiations for 27 hectares of precious vineyard, divided though the property was by road and rail, were protracted; and Michel Delon, manager of Château Léoville-Las-Cases, considered to be the best arbiter in Bordeaux, was engaged by the Dillons as their arbiter. His patience as well as ability was needed in order to complete an intricate transaction with different elements in the Woltner family. The former owners retained the 1982 crop: that of 1983 was included in the final price they were paid.

After the deal was concluded, Dewawrin and his wife, having already launched a wine-importing business in California and acquired co-ownership of a Californian vineyard, extended their interests across the Atlantic in the Napa Valley. Franco-American connections of many different kinds and at many different levels recur in the histories both of La Mission and of Haut-Brion.

*

The first La Mission produced after the two properties converged has been rightly described by David Peppercorn 'as a true La Mission just in case anyone should have thought anything else'. That was the 1984, an excellent wine in a poor year – a wine to remember. The subsequent record has been impressive. So, too, is a new *chai* that pre-dated a new one at Haut-Brion itself that was brought into use as part of a major reorganization of the property in 1991. 'People think that things don't change in Bordeaux,' Peter Sichel wrote in 1989, 'but they do all the time, especially recently.' Haut-Brion proves his point.

Sichel was writing in *Decanter* for a knowledgeable British readership. In France Michel Dovaz focused directly on Haut-Brion in the *Revue du Vin de France*. The château, he noted, had always been exceptional not only because of its wine, but because its proprietors and managers had been the 'intellectual leaders' of a '*Gotha bordelais*', ceaselessly innovating, ceaselessly carrying out experiments, 'today more than ever'.

In the design of the *chai* at Haut-Brion lessons were learnt from the new one at La Mission, but the scale of the operation was different. The *cuvier* was twice as large, as was the range of facilities it was required to provide. There are now twenty-two new vats. The six stainless steel vats installed by Delmas in 1961 have gone. In their place are a huge bottling plant and depot. There is also ample room for stocks and a greater provision for mobility within the premises, together with a new reception area for visitors, a room for tasting, a *tonnellerie* (coopering plant), and a workshop for tractors and other equipment. A new laboratory has followed. From a reception room on the top floor of the *chai*, where visitors can taste Haut-Brion in style, there is a superb view of the vineyard. There are pictures, too, of some of the key figures in the history of the vineyard, a sign that tradition counts at Haut-Brion. So, too, does the presence of an archive room within the new complex.

The exterior of the *chai* has been so carefully designed that it is difficult to believe that it was not always there; likewise, the extended new courtyard. Everything fits – better even than in the past. The right word to describe the result is the word applied to the wine itself: harmony. The château itself, which looks better than ever, benefits from the new plan, which includes a harmonizing new tower. There are many new angles.

If the view of the vineyards from the reception room is superb, the view from the central control room of what is currently happening inside the *chai* – a view never possible before – is the view that matters when the wine is being made from the grapes brought in at the *vendange*. There are television cameras and screens, and an electronic internal communications system.

A description in static terms of the new *chai*, the kind of description that might be drawn up by or for an architect, is quite inadequate. The wine-making processes are what count, and that is why I felt that I was privileged as well as lucky to see the processes in action on the first day of the vintage in 1991. It was the first time round, and doubtless, as always, lessons were learnt – for example, about the reception and weighing of the intake of grapes, about overspill, about the operation of the conveyor belt and about the efficiency of the call system. The general impression, however, was of control rather than of bustle. This was an efficient plant, to use a word that over the years has been transferred from agriculture to industry. Everyone was told to follow orders that had been laid down: '*respectez scrupuleusement cette course*'.

The actual bringing in of the harvest reinforced the impression that good order matters. The sifting process, *triage*, was carried out in the vineyard by four *trieurs* who worked on a raised metal platform. Three of them were 'regulars' at Haut-Brion, but this year they were carrying out their traditional task – task number two after the grapes had been gathered in – in a slightly different way. *Savoir*, knowing, was being converted into *savoir faire*, knowing how to do it. My mind went back to Peynaud's wise words: 'Tradition is an experiment that has succeeded.'

The contracting work on the *chai*, which miraculously took only nine months to complete, began on the *cuvier*. The planning process had been very carefully discussed at every stage. I had the opportunity of listening to one of the discussions, which covered community planning questions as well as the arrangement of the new buildings. The Bordelais architect for the project was Michel Garros, and the cost in francs was substantial. There was a further cost, however, which few great vineyards would have been willing to pay: 30 ares of vineyard – an are is 100 square metres – had to be sacrificed. There was some compensation. Soil excavated from the earthworks was removed and carried to Talence on the other side of the railway. It was used to work a *parcelle* that had earlier been lost. Renewal goes along with change.

11

Times and Seasons

━━━━━

To everything there is a season, and a time to every purpose under the heaven.

Ecclesiastes 3: 1

Having traced the historical sequence at Haut-Brion from medieval times to the present – and having ended in a *chai* which looks forward to the future – it is sensible to complete the picture by examining the recurring cycles of life from generation to generation. The growing of vines follows the seasons; so does the selling of wines. Times change but they change within a pattern. Within the pattern, however, the wine produced varies from year to year. The final chapters of this book are concerned, therefore, with different vintages.

Any account of the annual round of the seasons at Haut-Brion must begin not with 1 January but with the wine harvest, a movable feast, often celebrated in poetry. It was a poem that Ribéraux Gayon, the oenologist, chose in 1958 to introduce his book *Au Service du Vin de Bordeaux*:

> *Quand le raisin est mûr, par un ciel clair et doux,*
> *Dès l'aube à mi-coteau, vit une foule étrange:*
> *C'est qu'alors dans la vigne, et non plus dans la grange,*
> *Maître et serviteurs, joyeux s'assemblent tous.*

This poem, by Aloysius Bertrand, describes the motley crowd (*une foule étrange*) that gathers in the vineyards on a day that has always been foreseen, but never precisely appointed. The grapes are ripe, the sky is clear; proprietor, managers, workers all assemble happily together.

Haut-Brion brochures of the 1990s set the scene in prose, taking less for granted:

> Summertime passes: the sun rises later and sets earlier as autumn approaches. Day after day samples of fruit show the rising of sugars and the lowering of acids. When this progression reaches a reactive stability the date of picking can [at last] be precisely fixed . . . The start of the harvest is full of suspense. Will the picking go well? Is it best to start now? The weather is marvellous, and nothing but a little light rain would make us repent having waited . . . Shouts from the pickers and the activity of the *cuvier* brings us quickly back to reality: the first of the Merlots have just been dumped into the *chai*.

I was lucky enough to arrive at Haut-Brion in 1991 on the day before the first grapes were picked, and I was up early in the morning when a very different crowd gathered for the picking from the *foule étrange* described by Ribéraux Gayon. Among the pickers were local inhabitants who had taken part in the same exercise for years, yet there were also students, some from the nearby University of Bordeaux, gathering in grapes for the first time. They were of different ages, and they were wearing a great variety of clothes, but they worked well together.

Writing in Victorian times, Angus Reach had described the vintage in the most fulsome of language, representative of his time, as 'the joyous ingathering of the fruits of the earth – the great yearly festival and jubilee of the property and labour of the Gironde'. The stress then as now was on 'togetherness'. 'From time immemorial,' he went on in Dickensian fashion, 'the season has typified epochs of planting and mirthful-heartedness – of good fare and good will.' Reach conceded, however, that the busy time of vintage had not always been quite so 'mirthful-hearted'. Ideal and reality often diverged. For all the folklore, there had sometimes been more of a sense of recurring routine than of special fellowship in the bigger vineyards, and 'property' and 'labour', *maîtres* and *serviteurs*, had not always been at one. Moreover, because everything in vineyards of all kinds depends each year on the weather there has often been genuine suspense. The sky has not always been '*clair et doux*' at the right time. Even if the weather had been good earlier in the year, a break in it during the harvest has often been disastrous.

The vintage is, of course, the climax to a year when there has often been a combination of both good and bad weather. At times in what seemed likely to be a good year there have been surprises. Of the 1862 vintage, for example, T. G. Shaw wrote:

> Independent of a vine disease or any similar infliction, sometimes a single night's frost almost destroys the best prospects. Last year (1862) was an instance, for rarely have the vines showed such abundance of fine grapes; but a night of frost in May and a few weeks of such heat as has been rarely experienced in Europe in July and August, caused such havoc that, instead of a remarkably abundant and fine vintage, it has been a very small one.

Sometimes such circumstances have led to price rises, as in 1830, when winter frosts ravaged the vineyards, but the summer was warm. Little wine was produced and 'rarity' forced prices to climb.

The annual round, as all observers have recognized, has been particularly difficult in years of epidemic, for when disease has struck vines it has broken, sometimes abruptly, the patterns of daily life. The fortunes of vines and of people have been interdependent. There has been no hope of a price rise then, for both quantity and quality have been adversely affected.

The people of the Middle Ages were directly aware of this interdependence long before wine could be stored, and the language they employed to describe it was often more stirring than Reach's prose. When poets sang the praises of the *vendange* in Gascon or in Latin, they were praising God as well as man. And so, too, generations later were the pioneers of Haut-Brion. Long after the Middle Ages, the vintage, whether good or bad, started with the ringing of bells. Everywhere there were prayers. They could, however, be prayers of thanksgiving or of supplication. Diseases of the vine, never uncommon, were thought of as being like epidemics affecting human beings. They could be treated either as God-sent trials or, more likely, as Devil-sent punishments, but in both cases the response was a call to prayer. As late as the harvest time of 1876, Haut-Brion's *régisseur* Sanchou reported to his *maître*, Larrieu, on 19 September that there was a new moon at Haut-Brion and that it was prayers offered in all the churches of Bordeaux that had made the awkward west wind subside.

In the Middle Ages, whatever the quality of the vintage, there was an acknowledged annual round of activities both in agriculture and in trade, closely interrelated just because the two great articles of medieval trade, wine and wool, were products based on nature. It was a round that at harvest time involved both the local gatherers of the grapes and the foreign seamen who arrived in Bordeaux, always in September, to carry the new wine back across the seas two months later. Meanwhile, there was hard work in the fields, and once the harvest had been collected there was exceptional liveliness and bustle in the city of Bordeaux. English merchants, travelling back and forth in ships to Bordeaux, spent eight to ten weeks there 'tasting and bargaining' before returning to England with their *vin de l'année* in good time for Christmas.

A second fleet arrived in spring, '*la flotte des vins de printemps*', collecting what remained of the *vin de l'année* in Bordeaux: most of it came from the *haut-pays*, the vineyards out beyond Bordeaux. From the month of January onwards, the Gascon vineyards were pouring their wines into Bordeaux. No ship leaving Bordeaux carried with it, however, the wine of one single place handled exclusively.

The rhythms of medieval trade were broken somewhat in the sixteenth and seventeenth centuries, when there was less sea travel by merchants in either direction and when large fleets were less common. Nonetheless, the rhythms of the seasons, based on the timing of the harvest, remained as influential in determining the annual round of activities as they had done in earlier centuries. Wine could now be stored in both Britain and Bordeaux, but the city still emptied at the time of the vintage and became busy once it was over. The *maîtres* were still as much involved as the *serviteurs*. The pattern persisted once the harvest began. Only a generation ago, 'everyone who is anyone in particular' was described as 'returning' to his country estate 'to superintend the vintage in person and to make the most of that joyous ever-recurring festival'.

There is one piece of striking seventeenth-century evidence about the impact of the harvest on the attitudes of people living in Bordeaux. When the young King Louis XIV was eleven years old, he wished to punish the Bordelais who then were in revolt during the *Fronde*. For him the *Frondeurs* were rascals, but to his surprise he found them willing to negotiate with him simply because the time of the vintage was close. Behind the scenes, however, the negotiators – the members of the *Parlement* of Bordeaux – quietly told the insurgents not to worry: 'We shall fight again after the harvest.'

In the twentieth century technology has given humanity what Michael Young has called 'a degree of independence from the sun'. The industrializing nineteenth century provided an energetic but confused prelude to the scientific and technological achievement. It has been only a *degree* of independence, however, and not total liberation. 'There are still proper seasons for ploughing and planting, for weeding and harrowing, and for harvesting,' Young wrote in 1988 in his book *The Metronomic Society*, which deals not with modern sequences of events but with modern cycles of activities. No longer do poor men, as in *Piers Plowman* (the medieval English poem), have such a grim winter time when 'they suffer much hunger and woe'. But cycles and seasons still have their hold.

Indeed, in some respects seasons were to become more important in nineteenth-century viticulture than they had been in the past, given that there was more emphasis than ever before on the quality as distinct from the quantity of the vintage. There were new interrelationships, too, between fluctuations of the wine harvest and fluctuations of the economy. Business recessions meant a decline in the demand for wine; booms pushed up wine sales. Trade cycles were identified; and the role of harvests – and even of what were called 'sun spots' – in 'causing' them, was a matter of serious debate among political economists. The English economist W. R. Jevons, more interested in coal than in wine, specialized in collecting relevant data.

Jevons was most interested, as were all political economists, in the influence of financial speculation on prices; and there could be as much of a speculative element in the wine market then as there was to be a century later. Thus, we read in the *Wine Trade Review* of January 1881 how, when

> the indifferent results of the previous vintage became known, comparative calm gave way to feverish activity. The quality of the 1879s never excited much enthusiasm, and rival first-hand operators commenced bidding against each other for the popular growths of 1880, whilst yet unmade. This unwise precipitancy led growers at length to demand such extravagant prices as to materially check the buying movement. As to the quality of the 1880s it is even yet premature to speak positively.

There had been an earlier burst of speculation, during the late 1860s, centring particularly on the 1868 vintage, not a good vintage, but one which was sold very early in the year. Yet not even the Franco-Prussian War, fought in a year when there was a very good vintage, reduced the prices of the *grands crus*. By then it was obvious that the fortunes of the wine trade depended not only on the harvest or on politics, but on the psychology both of wine merchants and of customers.

A century later, the 'extravagant prices' of the early 1970s provoked one British writer on wines, Clive Coates, to return to language that might have been used in the Middle Ages. In his words, 'greed overcame reason'. 'While the market was rising, any fool could make a lot of money by buying a name today and selling it later . . . The bubble, of course, burst with such savagery that there was hardly a merchant in England and France who was not wounded, and more than a few found themselves in acute financial difficulties.' As a form of investment buying, wine held dangers even for those who were knowledgeable.

The annual financial round in pricing began with the release of *en primeur* opening prices by the château in the spring or summer before the vintage and was followed by offers of wine in two *tranches*: the first larger in terms of quantity, the second with higher prices. No two years were ever quite the same. The rhythms favoured speculation as much as sales.

In relating the timing and selling of the vintage to sequences of dates in the calendar, it must be remembered that attitudes to time itself have changed. Not only was the medieval attitude to time different from our own – we have standardized it – but medieval dates were not the same as ours. Church bells not only ushered in the vintage: they told the time day by day, church time. And nature had its own time. Significantly, as late as the nineteenth century the age of wine was reckoned in Bordeaux by leaves (*feuilles*), the number of times the vine had flowered since the wine was made.

The birds follow their cycle too. Thrushes on their way from south to north cross the Bordeaux regions from the middle of March to the middle of May and on their way back from north to south in the months of the harvest, August, September and October. During the move north they pay their attention, as do the non-migratory starlings, to worms and small insects. There are at least thirty-nine insects that are known to attack the vine. On their move south, however, the migrating birds may themselves attack the grapes on the vines. Watching birds – and butterflies – in the vine-yards is as important, therefore, as watching leaves.

The word 'calendar' itself derives from the Latin *kalendæ*, the day when the accounts were due, so that it, too, relates as much to an annual round, in this case an economic round, as to a sequence; and when during the French Revolution there was a brand new calendar, beginning in 1792, with names and dates which broke deliberately with the past, the names of the months were directly related to the rhythms of nature. Year I of the Republic and of subsequent years was to begin not on 1 January but on 22 September, the date of the foundation of the Republic, around or just after the time of the vintage, and the first 'month' in the year was called Fructidor. The names of other months included Germinal and Floréal.

The revolutionary calendar, which was to be used only briefly, replaced the Gregorian calendar, named after Pope Gregory XIII, which had been introduced into France (but not into England) in 1582, when Jean de Pontac was at Haut-Brion. The calendar before that, the Julian, had lasted for centuries and the Protestant English did not change it until 1751, by which time the gap between the Julian and Gregorian calendars had widened to eleven days. This national difference in the acceptance of the new calendar, as awkward as the daily time difference of one hour is for travellers in the late twentieth century, makes it even more difficult to get seventeenth- and early eighteenth-century dates right than it is to get medieval dates right – and the dates matter immensely in the history of wine. It is awkward that we have to use the terms 'old style' and 'new style' for different periods in French and English history.

Nonetheless, to think of the calendar during these centuries, whether old style or new style, revolutionary or pre-revolutionary, in terms of daily and monthly dates that constitute a sequence of new 'events' can itself be misleading. As we have seen, diaries became popular only during the seventeenth century – and then mainly in England. Moreover, they were not necessarily kept day by day. Evelyn, for example, wrote up some of his entries later. Different dates had different significance in private and public history whatever the year, and some of the most important dates, Easter for example, which determined many other dates in the religious calendar, themselves moved.

There were always saints' days and festivals that had particular significance in the vineyards, and what happened on those days followed, with modifications, a recurring pattern. Most planting took place in autumn: spring planting produced worse results. Pruning traditionally started on St Vincent's Day in January: now it can start earlier. St Martin's Day, 11 November (our modern Remembrance Day), was a date never to forget in relation to the regulation of the wine trade in Bordeaux. For a long period no wines from the *haut-pays* were allowed to 'descend' into the city until after St Martin's Day.

St Martin, as the local saint of the parish of Pessac, was the patron protector of baptized babies, and another important local saint's day was that of St Jean. John was the most common boy's name in the parish registers. At Pessac there was excitement on other saints' days too, particularly St Mark's Day, when there were regular skirmishes between the Pessacais and the inhabitants of the adjacent parishes of Talence and Gradignac. The boundaries of the parishes met at Bardanac and men from each of them processed there, which frequently led to '*querelles de clochers*'.

The rhythms of the seasons went deeper even than any cycle of annual events. Significantly, the monthly distribution of births in Pessac was directly related to the character of the seasons. June was the month of the greatest number of conceptions – the pattern for the years from 1700 to 1709 was similar to that of the years from 1870 to 1879 – and the least fecund months were September and October, the months of the harvest. It was then that women were at work in the vineyards along with the men. February, a month of calm in the vineyards, was a favourite month for marriage in the eighteenth century, although November took its place in the nineteenth century.

For religious reasons, marriage was forbidden during Advent and Lent and, also for religious reasons, the favourite days for marriage were Tuesdays and Saturdays: marriages took place very rarely on Fridays. There were breaks in this pattern during the revolutionary years, and in the late nineteenth century economic changes were to influence the occupational distribution of men's and women's employment and to reshape family history. For this and other reasons, including transport and refrigeration, the significance of the food harvest diminished in importance relative to other events in the calendar. In the history of wine, however, it is still *the* event.

*

Within the framework of the seasons, in the Middle Ages there had been recognized differences between 'good' and 'bad' years – differences recorded earlier in the Bible – but any comparisons between the wine of one year and that of another had to be made from memory. There could be no comparative tasting of wines of different years. The main test of success was output. A second was value in money. Statistics of wine exports from Bordeaux to Britain looked quite different when they were expressed in barrels or in pounds sterling.

Details of particular vintages survive from the sixteenth and seventeenth centuries, even before the advent of the thermometer permitted precise measurement of temperatures. The year 1572, for example, was bad, 1566 good. Another bad year – and temperatures could now be measured – was 1675.

It was only after proprietors, *négociants* and *courtiers* had separated the *premiers grands crus* from the rest and had begun to store them in their châteaux or in the Chartrons that records of 'good' and 'bad' years for clarets, including Haut-Brion, began to be collected systematically, along with prices. And time itself acquired a new dimension in this connection as it did in reverse in the history of fashions in clothes. 'Fine wines' were not just the best wines of the year: they were carefully kept and tasted time and time again until they were 'mature', although long before that some of them were described, perhaps too often and too rapidly in recent years, as 'the vintage of the century'. In 1977 Penning-Rowsell wrote crisply that 'vintages of the century' occur roughly every five years.

Opinions have changed as vintages have aged, though by the time they are judged 'mature' little of them may be left. Some wines have failed to age. The 1912s, for example, deemed 'light and easy to drink at first', proved unable to stand long ageing. There are still arguments about the relative merits of the 1928s and 1929s. In the contemporary world, as Steven Spurrier has pointed out, whereas 'a fine wine, even if it is in relatively short supply, is not rare, mature fine wine is'.

Excellent records from the eighteenth century onwards include many that emanate from the vineyards themselves, beginning with notes on the weather and the date of the beginning and end of the *vendange*; and they often include informal reports by the *régisseurs*, for whom the most difficult of all their tasks was often the last – discussing the pricing and selling of wines with the owners, who took the decisions. 'It is quite essential for you, Monsieur, and for me to settle accounts,' wrote Viallon to his proprietor at Haut-Brion in 1785, reminding him that he had not yet sold the 1779. 'You know, Monsieur, that this year is poor. I have only seen one merchant, Monsieur Copinger, who will take no wine of our price. He took nine *tonneaux* at 2,000 livres in 1777 and he has not been back since.'

For the authors of such reports, the vintage was livelihood. And so it was also for the *courtiers* of Bordeaux, whose traditional task it became – and it was soon thought of as a 'traditional' task – to choose between wines, to set market prices and to profit from changing demand. Records, domestic and foreign, were an essential element in their business, and some of the most useful sequences of reports on vintages are kept in their private offices. It was their business to know. The Tastet and Lawton records, going back to 1795, are the best known. They have been used by many historians.

Knowledge could seldom be kept confidential at any time after the French Revolution, and the early editions of Cocks et Féret set out authoritative details of variations in the quality of Bordeaux wines after 1795, 'along with complete information concerning the time of the vintage, quantity produced, prices etc.'. At the same time, the authors realized that the detail of price movements could never be reduced to a simple formula, a conclusion reached by Cocks as early as 1846, even before he collaborated with Féret. For the years before 1835 he relied heavily on information collected by Wilhelm Franck in his *Traité sur les vins du Médoc et les autres vins rouges du Département de la Gironde*. Cocks stressed in 1846 that 'a considerable period' – a vague term – must 'elapse before any vintage can finally be pronounced upon', knowing that it was difficult to tell just how well a vintage would turn out, and adding that 'it has happened, more than once that the wines of certain years began to be appreciated only when there were but small portions remaining'.

Franck had assembled detailed accounts of particular early nineteenth-century *vendanges* and their aftermath, like that of 1826:

Summer had been cold and wet. The harvest was bad; white wines were thin and green; red wines lacked body and colour. Exhausted by purchases in 1825 [a year of considerable speculation in England and in France that hit Bordeaux hard], business

196

was completely uninterested in the 1826s which established their prices only very late and then only at moderate levels. Very little was now bought. The reds acquired a little more colour and body, but their quality as they aged remained mediocre. The whites remained obviously inferior.

It was perhaps fortunate that in the year 1826 the affairs of Haut-Brion were in the hands of a *négociant*, Beyerman, who knew what the trade could and could not bear.

In the nineteenth century Cocks et Féret divided past years according to seven categories of quality: exceptional (*excellente*); very good (*très bonne*); good (*bonne*); ordinary (*ordinaire*); mediocre (*médiocre*); bad (*mauvaise*); and very bad (*très mauvaise*) – a different, although related, classification from that which they employed in a section devoted to variations in quantity, where they distinguished between 'years of great abundance' (*très abondantes*); 'years of abundance' (*abondantes*); '*années moyennes*' (average years); '*années réduites*' (below average years); and '*années défi-citaires*' (years of dearth). Haut-Brion has followed a somewhat different classification, introducing the word 'average'; it has also assembled bundles of relevant meteorological statistics.

Whatever the classification, the peaks of quantity and quality did not always coincide. From 1795 to 1870 there were seven 'years of great abundance' as far as quantity was concerned, but only three 'exceptional years' in terms of quality. Between 1870 and 1926 the comparable figures were again seven and three. There was a higher proportion of poor harvests in terms of quantity in the period from 1795 to 1870 (47.4 per cent) than there was between 1870 and 1926 (34 per cent), but as far as quality was concerned there was a lower proportion: 21.5 per cent as compared with 40 per cent. Cocks et Féret drew no deductions from these differences.

The timing of harvests had not varied greatly. Between 1857 and 1879 all but three started between 14 and 26 September. Between 1795 and 1880 there had been only one August vintage (1822), a year with what was described as a 'very ordinary' yield, and there had been only thirteen October vintages, eight of them before 1825 (1797, 1799, 1809, 1813, 1816, 1821, 1823 and 1824). The latest vintage was in 1816, when the harvest did not start until 27 October, and the quality of the wine was subsequently described by the *Wine Trade Review* as 'detestable'. By 1880 the 'wine industry' was becoming better organized, but very soon after it was badly disturbed by vine disease.

Taking the long period between 1795 and 1926 as a whole, of the fourteen years that were identified as 'years of great abundance' in terms of quantity, only one was an 'exceptional year' in terms of quality, five were 'very good', five 'good', one 'ordinary', one 'mediocre', and one 'very bad'. This was a range of substantial variation, and problems in marketing followed inevitably from it. Yet different vineyards had responded to the conditions of the vintage in different fashions. As the *courtier* Amédée Tastet pointed out, 'a variety of capricious circumstances produce completely different results in the same year for different proprietors producing the same category of wines'.

The situation during the early years of the Larrieu regime at Haut-Brion, as described by Franck, was not much better than it had been in 1826. The eight years between 1835 and 1843 were in general bad for proprietors and particularly bad for the producers of *vins moyens* or of *crus classés*. England, which from 1837 to 1843 was in the midst of severe economic depression (not mentioned by Franck), the deepest since the industrial revolution, was, nonetheless, 'almost the only country consuming high-price wine: it paid very high prices, but only for a few privileged wines, and a few perfect vintages were enough to satisfy its demands'.

Like the year 1832, which had been a year of great political excitement in England, 1840 produced a plentiful vintage. As far as the *grands crus* were concerned, customers were then buying wines that were five or six years old at high prices deemed unjustified by Franck given their quality. There had been a run of four good harvests in the early 1830s, broken in 1835. The price of the 1836s fell and although there was a recovery, in Franck's opinion high prices were quite unjustified in the case of the 1838s, 'a mediocre year', and of the 1839s: 'we fear that these two years will never achieve a reputation that can measure up to the high prices that have been paid for them, especially for the 1839s'. Soon prices were to rise still further. A peak production figure of 125 *tonneaux* was achieved at Haut-Brion in 1841 as against another high figure, 118 *tonneaux*, in 1840; and a little later, the Haut-Brion 1844 was a wine much in demand. It was sold at 3,000 francs a *tonneau* when Mouton fetched only 2,600. In that year, however, Lafite, according to Cocks, fetched as much as 4,500 francs.

Writing in 1876, after the mid-century price rise, Féret noted how the value of money in the 1840s was only a fifth of what it had been in 1758 when the Duc de Richelieu had bought Haut-Brion at 2,000 livres per *tonneau*, the same price as in 1876 itself. Other red Graves were then selling at 300 to 400 francs. At a Christie's sale in 1844 the excellent 1834 sold for the same price as Lafite.

Only four vintages before 1900 – the 1798s, 1811s, 1874s and 1899s – are still thought of at Haut-Brion as 'great years', the last of them a year when Haut-Brion fetched 2,600 francs as against 2,200 for Margaux and 2,000 for Latour and Lafite. There is a case too, however, for the 1795s, which Franck thought better than the 1798s, and the 1802s, which he thought better than the 1811s. There are other unexplained gaps in the ratings of Haut-Brion – of historical interest only. Thus, there was a low yield, 104 *tonneaux*, in the year of revolutions, 1848.

The 1861 vintage was a particularly interesting one. There was a great frost on 6 May and the harvest was very small, but the wines were 'good and elegant' and 'fetched high prices'. The very abundant 1864 vintage was described in the *Wine Trade Review* as 'exquisite, extraordinarily soft, ripe, with fresh bouquet'. It lasted well into the twentieth century. The 1876 was still delicious in 1930, but, in Simon's words, 'so delicate as to be a little threadbare'. On a later occasion, when served with cheese, he found that it 'showed off beautifully': its remarkable qualities were 'too difficult to translate into words'. It was the delights of this particular bottle that encouraged those drinking it to plan the idea of a Saintsbury Club.

Other nineteenth-century vintages which have been judged outstanding are the 1871s, thought by both Simon and Warner Allen to be among the best Haut-Brions they ever tasted, and the 1875s, King Edward VII's favourite year, singled out by Cassagnac as in a class of their own. Of the last year of the century, 1899, there has never been any difference of opinion. The current brochure notes that 'the youth of this wine remains behind the wear of time'. It was being drunk with pleasure in 1930, although by then after 'entering with a stately bow, quite like the *Grand Seigneur* it departed' – in Simon's words – 'like a page boy'.

Lichine, who thought it 'one of the best for forty years', also mentioned the 1895s, a year with a very hot summer, when Haut-Brion (and Lafite) prospered; the 1896s, 'supple and distinguished';

and the 1898s, some of which, including Haut-Brion, were 'successes'. Prices were high in the 1890s. In 1891 Mouillefort, a professor of viticulture, spoke of a price *en primeur* of 5,500 francs and in the second year of 7,000 to 8,000 francs.

As, many years later, the 1965s and 1968s were to do, the 1895s seemed to bear out the somewhat dubious general proposition, advanced by Lichine, that Haut-Brion could do well with its wine even when other *premiers grands crus* did badly. Margaux, for example, could not château-bottle its wine of 1895. Yet all the *grands crus* prospered in 1899. The proposition stands or falls on the degree of dependence of variations in quality, as distinct from quantity, on local variations of weather.

It was during the first decade of the twentieth century, the *belle époque*, that the 1866s were being drunk at their best, although André Simon was happily drinking the 1871s thirty years later. Of the Edwardian vintages, the 1905 represented an example of a wine that had been criticized 'at the outset' but that had 'grown in favour', while the 1904 was deemed good from the start.

The oldest Haut-Brion under review at the remarkable tasting of thirteen vintages at Lockets Restaurant in London in 1972, a tasting attended by Delmas, was the robust and long-lasting 1906. It had once been judged unanimously to be 'a wine of rare power, body and flavour'; and as late as 1935 it had still been considered 'so powerful that it was recommended to be served only in winter and with game'. Healy had described it as 'a mighty wine, a first-class claret with a dollop of first-class port in it'. Daniel Lawton praised it consistently. Now in 1972, however, it was generally thought to be 'not as good as most of the others'. Time had moved on.

During the *belle époque* there had been one 'average year', 1901, and one 'bad year', 1902: 'little wine, little quality'. Other bad years, when many estates did not have any wine bottled, were 1910 and 1915, the latter a year deeply disturbed by the dislocations of war. In 1911, 'a year of mildew and pests unbridled', the Haut-Brion was better than most other clarets. For Healy 'it lacked little of the essence of a great claret', and Warner Allen, unprepared to share Healy's uninhibited enthusiasm, was nevertheless impressed in the late 1920s by 'its fine colour, body and warmth'. By then, the First World War had intervened.

The Haut-Brion of 1914, the year war broke out, was also

'good', while the 1916 was said to be 'very good' – 'the War cut down quantity, but the year was an over-all success – healthy, robust, full-bodied, very well coloured, well bred', even if its reputation was felt to be overrated, while the Haut-Brion 1918 created a sensation in Bordeaux when it was sold for 8,000 francs a *tonneau*, nearly three times as much as Lafite and Margaux. This was less because of its quality than because the fixed-price contract had expired and Eschenauer acquired and disposed of the vintage. The 1919, one of the wines tasted at Lockets in 1972, was felt to have 'kept very well': the year had hitherto been judged only 'average', and the wine 'thin'. Like the 1924, the wine of a 'good year', later thought by some to be 'a bit overrated', it had 'traces of acidity'. The 1922 was judged 'very supple' with a 'pleasant body' and a 'surprising bouquet'.

A long list prepared by Daniel Lawton picked out among 'exceptional' twentieth-century vintages that were produced before the Second World War broke out, those of 1921, 1923 (a year when Haut-Brion stood out) and 1926, when quantity was poor and quality good and when Georges Delmas shortened the period of maceration to less than ten days. The year 1928 was judged a good one for Haut-Brion, with an exceptionally hot summer. So, too, was 1934, Gibert's last year. The 'average years' were 1919 and 1922. The 1932s and 1935s were bad.

The 1929s can never be left out of the inter-war picture, for ironically in this year of dramatic falls on the stock market, followed by deep international economic depression, their quality was good. A hot dry year, the driest in the century, produced wine to last. The Haut-Brion was rich in tannin, 'powerful' and with a 'dense colour'. This was an *année exceptionnelle* in the vineyards as well as on Wall Street, although it was never without its detractors.

Lawton once made a number of general remarks about Haut-Brion vintages over the years. 'I have got to know the various Haut-Brion vintages from my youth onwards,' he wrote, 'and I believe that it is in large part due to my uncle, Henry Johnston, that I owe this.' Johnston's favourites had been the 1871s, 'light and elegant', and the 1870s, 'more bodied and *complets*'. In more recent years, 'thanks to the friendship always shown me by Monsieur Dillon and his colleagues at Haut-Brion', Lawton had followed 'year by year' the different vintages, convinced that 'by reason of the care devoted

to viticulture at Haut-Brion, to the harvest and to subsequent vinification, to barrelling and to bottling, the best possible product was
being prepared from incomparable soil'. There was no rule, Lawton
added, that would determine when to drink the Haut-Brion of a
particular year. Indeed, the best procedure was to return to the
same vintage over the years – *échelonner les dégustations* – to judge
the changes as the wine matured in the bottles. It was a mistake,
however, to drink any Haut-Brion before it was six or seven years
old, that is to say before it had been left for three or four years in
the bottle. Some were best left for fifteen or twenty years. When
tasted at Lockets in 1972, the 1959 was judged even better than the
1961, 'well balanced, very mellow, with a very fine perfume'.

Lawton judged the wines of Bordeaux on the spot, and Haut-
Brion usually at Haut-Brion. English connoisseurs had their own
canons of judgement, with Simon and Maxwell-Campbell, two of
the acknowledged connoisseurs, maintaining their own annotated
records of the vintages that they had been drinking at different
times with as great care as the management at Haut-Brion devoted
to wine-making. Michael Broadbent, who has described himself as
'an inveterate note taker and cuttings collector', is in the same
tradition.

The connoisseurs have made it clear that they have been concerned not with the qualities of summers and autumns that they
could not remember, but with the qualities of the wines that they
could compare for themselves in the glass. The vintage to them was
experience, backed but not dominated by history, and they took it
for granted that the details of particular vintages would be of
interest to their readers.

There was a wistful note of nostalgia, however, in Simon's foreword to his book *Vintagewise*, written while the Second World
War was still in progress, that applied both to wine and to language:

> There is so little wine left and the price asked for it is such
> that the number of wine-drinkers in England must be very small
> indeed. But because the War has dried up the flow of poetry and
> wine alike, because it has obliged us to renounce many of the
> amenities of a cultural life, we must not for a moment fear that
> no more poets will be born and no more good wine landed on
> these shores.

There now seems to be a vintage quality of its own in such writing, as there is in Berry's *In Search of Wine* (1935). The conventions of cultural life were still being fully observed by Simon when he wrote *Vintagewise*, although the Second World War had broken many of the continuities. Warner Allen found it more difficult to perpetuate them. In what he called 'doubtful peace' after 1945 he decided not to rely on his own judgement for the assessment of recent vintages of the Bordeaux wines. Instead, he turned to his friends in the wine trade. He believed that they were 'better placed than I am to pass a decisive judgement on the wines that come to be drunk in this post-war period'. Already that period is far away, lost, like the *belle époque* or the pre-phylloxera age, in history and in myth.

12

Post-war Vintages

The sensibility of a wine is similar to the sensibility of a man. There are years that must be forgotten if only happy years are to be remembered.

Voltaire

Vintages since 1945 have been very fully recorded at Haut-Brion, and judgements on each of them have frequently been revised and brought up to date. In the forty years after 1945 there was only one 'very great year', 1961, but there were five 'great years', and there were 'very great years' to follow. There were also eight 'poor years' in the forty, the last of them in 1972, a sign perhaps, as Émile Peynaud has argued, that given improvements both in viticulture and in vinification during the last decade it is now more difficult than it ever was in the past – whatever the weather – to have a really bad year.

Haut-Brion assessments of vintages on the spot deserve to be studied in full, beginning with Victory Year and ending with a 'great year' in 1990. The *température totale, somme des températures*, which is always calculated, is the sum of the average temperatures from 1 April to 30 September each year. Over the forty years it averaged 3,165 degrees. The total for the hottest year (1976) was 3,484 degrees and for the coldest (1972) 2,900, a considerable differential. The rainfall figure, also always calculated, indicates in millimetres total rainfall during the same period of each year. The average was 358 millimetres, and the figures for the wettest year (1984) and the driest (1961) were 550 and 213. Back in 1932 the average rainfall had once been as high as 677 millimetres. A third fact, chronological, not statistical, must always be taken into the reckoning: the date of the beginning of the wine harvest. This has been fully recorded since 1953.

1945 The 1945 vintage has had more *réclame* than any other in the post-war period, except that of 1961, and both vintages were similar in being exceptionally short. Yet 1945 was an odd year in terms of weather, since there was snow in Bordeaux as late as 2 May, accompanied by a dramatic freeze that destroyed 80 per cent of the crop. The summer was very hot and also extremely dry. The sum of temperatures was 3,361 degrees, and the rainfall 253 millimetres. The Haut-Brion of this year deserved the adjectives 'big' and 'majestic': it was felt to have a strong body and a distinguished bouquet. It was deemed without doubt 'the best bottle' tasted at Lockets in 1972.

1946 The year was 'average' for the Bordeaux wine crop, when grapes ripened badly (sum of temperatures: 3,061°; rainfall: 261 mm). No Haut-Brion of this year was *mis en bouteille*. It was a rare year, one to forget.

1947 By contrast, the plentiful year of 1947 was 'very good', the hottest year (apart from 1976) in a half-century, the third in a sequence of four dry years which brought swarms of locusts to the Bordeaux area. During the summer there were forty-two days of high heat and water was rationed in the Gironde. (Sum of temperatures: 3,478°; rainfall: 259 mm.) The Haut-Brion has aged well. Six thousand cases were produced, compared with 5,000 in 1945. The wine was said to have had '*une légère amertume*' (a touch of bitterness), but '*le parfum*' was '*très fleuri*'. This was an outstanding year for La Mission.

1948 This was an 'average year' at Haut-Brion, 'very close to normal', whatever that meant, although the summer was wet (sum of temperatures: 3,126°; rainfall: 315 mm). Many vineyards picked their grapes too soon. There were more hot days in October than in August. The Haut-Brion (7,500 cases) was described a quarter of a century later as '*un vin concentré, tannique, très puissant*'.

1949 Again, by contrast, 1949 was 'very good', dry but above all very hot (sum of temperatures: 3,458°; rainfall: 286 mm). Some wines of the Médoc suffered because of the heat, but Haut-Brion

(4,800 cases) did not: it came to have what was called 'a concentrated and complex richness', and it was hailed by some critics from the start, though not by Penning-Rowsell, as one of the best postwar wines. La Mission was good too, for some judges better than the Haut-Brion. Years later, the 1949 proved one of the longest-lived of Haut-Brion vintages in recent decades, 'tannic', 'big', 'complex'.

1950 The year (sum of temperatures: 3,242°; rainfall: 346 mm) was a good one for the Gironde, when 'very vinous wines' were produced in vast quantities with a high content of natural alcohol. The total output was not matched until 1962. As many as 9,020 cases of Haut-Brion were produced. They were said to be 'dry, elegant and austere'.

1951 In sharp contrast, 1951 was a poor year for the Gironde, relatively cold and rainy, when light wines lacking character and body were produced. (Sum of temperatures: 3,052°; rainfall: 443 mm.) Yet the record production of Haut-Brion (11,500 cases) attracted commentators. This was the first year when chaptalization – adding sugar to the must at the time of fermentation – familiar practice though it was in the Médoc, was formally legalized. The objective was to increase the alcoholic content of the wine.

1952 The year was 'good'. It began with a very hot June (20.5°C) and July (20.6°C), suggesting that an *année exceptionnelle* was in prospect. As had often happened in Bordeaux, however, September made the difference, and on the fourth rain started and lasted for twenty-two days. It was also cold. Surprisingly, the result was an acceptable vintage with a 'lot of style'. (Sum of temperatures: 3,270°; rainfall: 306 mm; 8,600 cases produced.) Bad though they were, conditions were better in the Graves than elsewhere, and this was a very good year for La Mission. When tasted at the château in 1976, the Haut-Brion seemed to have more flavour than the 1953, a great year for the Médoc, when the vintage was said to have been 'made' in the month of August, 'a fabulous month' with little rain (only 15 mm) and great warmth (fifteen days of temperatures above 30°C).

1953 Some people warned in 1953 of the danger of 'scalded' wines. Yet September was uncertain, and it rained during the harvest, which started at the very end of September and lasted until 12 October (sum of temperatures: 3,198°; rainfall: 367 mm). Haut-Brion broke another output record (12,500 cases). In quality it seemed to take longer to 'come round' than some other vintages, in contrast to La Mission, a very round fruity wine with a special reputation from the start. It lasted, and was later judged to be 'rounded' and 'harmonious'. At Lockets it was called 'elegant'.

1954 The year was 'poor', a very cold year, one of the coldest since the beginning of the century, and relatively rainy also. In Bordeaux average temperatures for July were 3°C below normal and for August 2°C below (sum of temperatures: 2,904°; rainfall: 311 mm). The *vendange* did not begin at Haut-Brion until 7 October and lasted until 18 October: only 4,000 cases were produced. Nonetheless, the wine improved with age and came to be described somewhat cryptically as 'interesting for the vintage'.

1955 Contrasts of successive years continued, and 1955 was a 'very good' year, when, according to Daniel Lawton, the vineyards throughout the Graves looked particularly beautiful. For Peynaud, it was the year when oenology first began to be seriously taught and applied in the Médoc. For Peppercorn it was a year of the riddle. There had been just the right amount of rain in July and August, and September was hot and very dry (sum of temperatures: 3,247°; rainfall: 375 mm). Harvest conditions – 28 September to 10 October – were stated to be 'ideal' and everywhere in the Graves and in the Médoc successful wines were produced. Yet, in Peppercorn's opinion, they did not have that 'indefinable spark' which made an outstanding year. Why they did not was for him and for us 'a mystery of wine, which for all our scientific knowledge, remains beyond our grasp'.

This was the first vintage when the prices of the *grands crus* began to rise markedly, a process accelerated by the two poor or short-crop years which succeeded, but which continued subsequently until the slump of the 1970s. The Haut-Brion of 1955 (11,500 cases) was to last well: it had 'more depth than the 1953'. At the time, Daniel Lawton thought that it would be comparable with the 1949. 'This wine is wonderful today,' we read in the Haut-Brion brochure of 1990. This was also an outstanding year for La Mission.

1956 The year was 'poor' (sum of temperatures: 3,083°; rainfall: 441 mm). There had been a severe winter in Bordeaux, and after a mild spell temperatures fell to −20°C in February. A snowfall (80 cm) paralysed the region and the Garonne partly froze over. Many vines died and in general vineyards suffered terribly. In consequence, there was a very late start to the growing season, which was followed by a cold and wet summer (112 mm of rain in July, 104 mm in August). The harvest was late also (11–20 October). Little wine was produced (4,200 cases). The Haut-Brion aged better than most wines of the Médoc: the colour was good and there was a high tannin flavour. Lichine's generalization about Haut-Brion being good when the wines of the Médoc were of poor quality seemed to have been borne out. La Mission had a disastrous year in terms of quantity – but it, too, was judged good.

1957 Troubles were not over for most vineyards at the end of 1956, and while 1957 (sum of temperatures: 3,043°; rainfall: 371 mm) was an 'average' year, many wines were deemed 'acidy'. The harvest started on 1 October and lasted until 12 October. Once again, however, the Haut-Brion (5,400 cases) was judged agreeable, 'more balanced than most', and La Mission was spoken well of also.

1958 The 1958s (8,000 cases) were to develop well, 'supple, fine and soft', but in general this was a poor year for claret (sum of temperatures: 3,142°; rainfall: 497 mm), with a frosty spring and what was described as a 'tragic' August (136 mm of rain, twice the normal). The harvest started late, on 6 October, and lasted until 18 October. Haut-Brion was 'rather light', but La Mission provided a wine in contrast, typically big and 'earthy' with 'lots of nose, body and fruit'.

1959 An uneasy sequence ended in 1959. This proved a great year at Haut-Brion (sum of temperatures: 3,310°; rainfall: 331 mm), with a large yield (12,500 cases). By contrast, Médoc yields were small. Before the harvest was announced, it was already being hailed as 'the vintage of the century', and after the harvest ended informal observers described the result as 'magnificent just about everywhere'. It was very hot (up to 30°) during the harvest itself (it was hot in Britain too) and very concentrated wines were produced. The Haut-Brion was considered 'magnificent' at the Lockets tasting in 1972. One visitor to the château in 1959 wrote in the visitors' book: 'I don't think I will see anything closer to heaven until I die.' It is not recalled what year's wine he drank, but he added in rapture: 'the wine is the best'. The harvest took place from 23 September to 3 October.

1960 In 1960 there was early full-flowering in the Gironde – as early as 30 May – but the summer was cold and rainy, and there were few very hot days (sum of temperatures: 3,130°; rainfall: 459 mm). The harvest ran from 19 to 29 September, and the output rose to a post-war peak at 13,500 cases.

1961 With 1960 only an average year, 1961 was to stand out as another 'very great year', a 'benchmark for fine claret'. Among the vintages 'of the last couple of generations', Coates was to write in 1982, this was to offer all that he looked for in a fine wine: 'ripe fruit, elegance, concentration, "a three-dimensional" quality of flavour and character, and, above all, balance'. The weather pattern, too, was quite different from 1960. In 1961, after one of the wettest winters on record, a short period of intense cold at the end of May was followed by a hot summer, the driest on record, and an even hotter September (sum of temperatures: 3,294°; rainfall 213 mm). The harvest, which took place in fine weather, was a week earlier than in 1960: 12 to 25 September.

The Haut-Brion of this year (only 6,000 cases), the first produced after Jean-Bernard Delmas had become *régisseur*, was deemed 'sumptuous, harmonious, velvety, suave and complex, full of fruit and flower at the same time'. La Mission of the same year was also exceptional, 'a very big, bold wine with lots behind it and plenty of future ahead'. One critic called it 'one of the ten best wines of the vintage'. Its anticipated maturity was set at 1987–2010. Given the small output, prices were high, and they were to reach exceptionally high levels ten years later.

1962 This was another 'good year', although it got off to a late start. The grapes did not begin to colour until 22 August, and the harvest took place from 1 to 15 October. June was dry, July normal, August dry, and September near normal (sum of temperatures: 3,123°; rainfall: 249 mm). Eleven thousand cases of Haut-Brion were produced, testimony to an abundant vintage, not particularly blessed by the weather, of the kind that 'every Bordeaux grower and wine merchant had been praying for'. All in all, the quantity of *appellation contrôlée* wines of the Gironde (3.74 million hectolitres) was the largest since the Second World War, and for red wines was to be exceeded later within the forty-year span only by the 1967 crop and some of the large crops of the 1970s. One connoisseur called the Haut-Brion 1962 'smashingly delicious . . . with an opulent richness that resembles a Pomerol'. It can still be drunk with pleasure.

1963 By contrast, 1963 was a poor year – Peynaud calls it a 'sad year' – cold and rainy, when few (but to Peppercorn too many) wines were château-bottled. (Sum of temperatures: 3,010°; rainfall: 370 mm.) The harvest at Haut-Brion started on 3 October and lasted until 16 October. Eight thousand cases were produced, but in the words of an Haut-Brion brochure, there was no 'sense of nobility and breed'.

1964 Notwithstanding variable weather conditions in 1964, this was a 'very good' year at Haut-Brion, when a record 17,500 cases were produced. There were no spring frosts, and June and July were dry and hot with not a drop of rain. The flowering was over in a fortnight. August had its typical storms, but September was again very hot and dry, while October was to prove exceptionally wet (sum of temperatures: 3,327°; rainfall: 339 mm). In these circumstances the harvest, which began on 28 September, had to be completed quickly (6 October), and unlike most other vineyards, Haut-Brion almost succeeded in completing it before rain fell constantly for three weeks, from 5 October onwards.

The Haut-Brion of this year was deemed 'well balanced and with the authentic Graves nose' and was generally judged better than any of the Médocs of that year. One critic called it 'voluptuous'. La Mission, in one critic's opinion 'one of the three best wines of the vintage', was 'fruity but a little on the coarse side'.

1965 In 1965, a 'poor year', the months of July and August were 'essentially normal, though hot', with the August rainfall (42 mm) lower than the average (50 mm). Yet September (with 212 mm of rain) made the year 'a disaster'. (Sum of temperatures: 3,005°; rainfall: 461 mm.) The Haut-Brion (6,000 cases) was to last well, developing 'character', but it was an exception among the wines: for some the worst vintage of the decade. The harvest started on 1

October and lasted until 10 October. The high prices of 1964 were not maintained, and gloom persisted in 1966.

1966 A 'very good year' if a cooler year than the average, when the season began, like that of a poor year, with heavy rain in June. August was hot, however, and September even hotter (sum of temperatures: 3,161°; rainfall: 359 mm). The quality of the vintage seems to have been determined largely by the good weather in September, a month when there was a terrible fire at the Calvet warehouses. The harvest began in the last week of the month (23 September) and lasted until 5 October. The crop was medium in quality, but huge in quantity (19,500 cases).

While there was some 1966 that disappointed, the general quality level was high, and both the Haut-Brion and La Mission had a rewarding year. Prices soon rose, with Haut-Brion again heading the *premier cru* list, judged this year to be a 'light' wine, 'closed and shy', and with La Mission showing 'great distinction and style, with a long taste – and future'. The white Haut-Brion was to last well too. In 1984 at a tasting at Haut-Brion it was judged 'clean and fresh, with crispness and good body'.

1967 Judged 'good', the year was dry and 'very agreeable' (sum of temperatures: 3,120°; rainfall: 278 mm): wines were produced in most vineyards in large quantities. Red wine output was the largest of the decade. Far less Haut-Brion (7,500 cases) was produced than in 1966, however. The harvest began on 25 September and lasted until 4 October. The price was low, less than half that of the 1961, but in the 1970s Penning-Rowsell could call it 'a big wine for the year' and more than a decade after that it could be described approvingly as 'still very young, harmonious and complex in its aromas and flavours. The quantity of tannin is perfect.' Ten years later, La Mission was best drunk earlier: it had 'a very spicy, earthy, tobacco-scented bouquet, and soft, supple, very attractive flavours'.

1968 The 'late-starting' 1968, 'a poor year', with a very rainy August (161 mm) and a September that was moderately so (97 mm), left grapes in a poor condition long before the harvest, which lasted from 27 September to 7 October. (Sum of temperatures: 3,102°; rainfall: 458 mm.) At 7,500 cases, output was the same as in 1967, but the price higher. Haut-Brion was judged one of the best vintages of the year, 'light but true to character'.

1969 Prices reached new heights in 1969: 48,000 francs a *tonneau* as against 18,000 in 1968. It was only an 'average' year, however, with a hot and dry July and August, followed by an extremely rainy September (206 mm in twenty-three days of rain; sum of temperatures: 3,168°; rainfall: 532 mm). The date of the harvest was 25 September to 4 October and 8,500 cases were produced. The Haut-Brion of this year was pronounced in tannin.

1970 The long-awaited 1970, hailed as another 'vintage of the century', was singled out also as 'the sort of wine to wait for', the product of a perfect year 'without excess' which began with a very late spring, followed by a fine summer and a wonderful autumn. Everything was right. There were only twelve days of very high temperatures, but little rain fell in August and September, and still less over the harvest period, which began at Haut-Brion in the last week of September (25) and lasted until 2 October. (Sum of temperatures: 3,184°; rainfall: 232 mm.)

The 'abundant harvest', which was to produce 18,000 cases, was brought in under ideal conditions, and in retrospect it was very cheap in price (44,000 francs a *tonneau*). The wine was dark in colour and, unlike the wines of the Médoc, notably tannic. As far as the Médocs as a whole were concerned, Peynaud, in retrospect at least, was disappointed: 1970 was 'a false good vintage which was mounted on a pedestal'. I have found it a wine that has kept well and drinks well.

1971 and 1972 Prices rocketed in 1971 and 1972: 75,000 francs a *tonneau* in the first and 90,000 in the second. The years stand out as a pair, but there was a considerable contrast between them: 1971 was a 'good', if slightly early, year with a small crop (10,000 cases) – buying was early, too, and brisk – while 1972, an absurdly over-priced 'poor year', was the coldest in the last forty – with a late start and a low output (7,300 cases). The 1972 harvest (8–14 October), the latest since 1945, began more than three weeks later than 1971's (14 September to 4 October), but by the time it was gathered in there was little confidence in the grapes. In 1971 there was particularly poor weather for the flowering, followed by a very hot July (23°C on average, with eleven very hot days) and an equally hot August. September was rainy (sum of temperatures: 3,269°; rainfall: 496 mm). There was less sun but also less rain in 1972 (sum of temperatures: 2,900°; rainfall: 331 mm).

The Haut-Brion of 1971, which has variously been described as 'big', 'sumptuous', 'oaky', 'spicy' and 'silky', was for more than one judge the best that was produced between 1966 and 1975, and La Mission was also praised. Both are now past their best. The year 1971 was also an exceptionally good one for white wine, but no white wines for sale were produced at Haut-Brion in 1972, 1973 and 1974.

The red Haut-Brion of 1972 was one of the better wines of a disagreeable, discredited year, and it still drinks well. It has a distinctive smoky quality.

1973 and 1974 After its hectic boom the wine trade was in difficulties during these two years, but both were 'good' for Haut-Brion. In both years the weather was awkward, if not bad, and some wines of the Médoc were perhaps prematurely deemed unsatisfactory. In 1973 a very rainy July (14 mm) was followed by the hottest August since 1949, and the harvest was prolific, the record for the Bordeaux area (sum of temperatures: 3,299°; rainfall: 354 mm). The harvest was gathered in at Haut-Brion from 26 September to 6 October, and against the trend was relatively low (9,000 cases). In 1974, as in 1973, June and August were hot and July was normal, but September was rainy (100 mm) and cold (sum of temperatures: 3,124°; rainfall: 301 mm). The harvest was gathered in from 29 September to 6 October, and output was well up (15,000 cases).

In 1973 storms had set in 'at the last moment' – 15 September – with hailstones, rare at that time of year, and the crops at both Haut-Brion and La Mission were damaged. The weather continued cold and wet during the first ten days of the harvest. The wine produced was light and agreeable, however, and reasonably priced (50,000 francs a *tonneau*). It developed quickly: an Haut-Brion to drink soon.

In 1974 both Haut-Brion (15,000 cases) and La Mission were able to gather in the grapes before the deluges that drowned the prospects for an excellent vintage at many other châteaux. The Haut-Brion was rich and complex, but it took time to prove this. It now seems powerful. The price was a bargain: 25,000 francs a *tonneau*, the lowest since 1968. La Mission, which in 1973 had been of poor quality, was also an excellent and low-priced vintage in 1974.

1975 Following a mild and rather wet winter, the 'miraculous' year, 1975, started with severe March frosts that damaged the early-budding Merlot. Uneven flowering led to a small crop (9,000 cases) but as far as quality was concerned it was an *année exceptionnelle* (sum of temperatures: 3,250°; rainfall: 362 mm). Both June and July were very hot, and although in September there was only 'fair weather for the harvest' in the Médoc, there was good weather at Haut-Brion, where the harvest started on 25 September and lasted until 8 October.

The wine of the year is said to have 'tasted good even when it was very young' and when 'drunk blind' to have compared favourably with Latour and Mouton-Rothschild. It went on to seem 'monumental'. It reminded some critics of tobacco aromas, others, inconsistently, of chocolate, but at a tasting at Haut-Brion in 1984 its 'nose' was described as 'quite closed still'. The quality of La Mission of this year, more highly priced than any other La Mission, was thought by contrast to be disappointing. Yet it remained closed longer than Haut-Brion, and both are agreeably drinkable now.

High prices were in jeopardy following the world economic crisis and a 'Winegate trial' in Bordeaux, and initial buying of many clarets, if not of Haut-Brion, which kept its price, was hesitant between 1972 and 1975. Large stocks were accumulated, but by the end of 1975 prices even for lesser clarets had begun to rise again. The 1975 vintage raised spirits even before it raised prices. The 1975 white Haut-Brion, too, was attractive and well balanced.

1976 The next year, 1976, was also 'a very good year' – with an early harvest. Indeed, it came close to being an *année exceptionnelle*; even, some said yet again, perhaps to raise their spirits still further, 'the vintage of the century'. There were record temperatures, the hottest in twenty-seven years, and output was high. There was a drought in June (7 mm), following only 22 mm of rain in April but, after low rainfalls in July (45 mm) and August (72 mm), fierce storms in September (98 mm) disappointed extravagant hopes. (Sum of temperatures: 3,383°; rainfall: 278 mm.) Those *viticulteurs* who had waited too long to gather in their grapes suffered in consequence.

Haut-Brion started its harvesting early – on 13 September – and the vintage of this year (13,000 cases), medium ruby in colour with some amber creeping in at the edges, was highly promising when tasted early in the bottle. It had relatively little tannin, and was soft in flavour. Soon it was deemed 'forward', and by 1981 the question was being asked: 'Will it keep?' It was fully mature in 1983. The white Haut-Brion was full-flavoured too.

1977 The year 1977 was 'average', although it was followed by two 'very good years', 1978 and 1979. A severe frost on Easter night (10 April) heralded a rather cold year with delayed flowering, a poor summer and a late harvest, from 5 to 14 October. (Sum of temperatures: 3,065°; rainfall: 411 mm; 8,000 cases produced.) The average daytime temperature was 18°C compared with 22°C in 1976. This was a year when, again in contrast with 1976, 'cedary, spicy', La Mission won more immediate and lasting praise than Haut-Brion.

1978 In 1978 both Haut-Brion and La Mission were obviously at their best in relation to other *grands crus*. A frosty and humid spring with late flowering was followed by a doubtful summer, a dry and beautiful autumn and, as in the previous year, a late harvest, which did not begin until 5 October and which was completed on 14 October. (Sum of temperatures: 3,029°; rainfall: 327 mm.) The output – 10,000 cases – was considerably greater than might have been expected and the quality was good. The 1978 whites were strong and full-bodied, well suited to be drunk a decade later. The reds, deep in colour, were sweet, concentrated and 'fruity' and contrasted with some of the lighter Haut-Brions of the earlier 1970s. It was felt that they would last longer too, and would be 'ready' in time for the bicentenary of the French Revolution in 1989. From the start they were recognized to be complex in structure. Some called them 'closed'. Ribérau-Gayon thought that they were the only *grands crus* of 1978 that were 'great wines'. The La Mission 1978 was interesting also. It was generally felt to be better than the 1979, and it was considered that it would not mature for ten years.

1979 There was a rainy spring, following a mild and wet winter, and more rain fell in the growing period as a whole than in 1978; twice as much, indeed, as in some years. The vines were in flower in mid-June, when the sun came out for what seemed the first time. Temperatures were lower than the average, and there were only three really hot days (sum of temperatures: 2,937°; rainfall: 366 mm). The harvest was gathered slightly earlier, but still late: from 1 until 11 October.

For some observers the 1979s (14,000 cases), produced from small grapes affected by the drought, seemed likely to prove better in the long run than the 1978s. They were described as 'well structured' and 'supple' five years later and were said to be evolving well. They should now be drunk. The 1979 whites were less promising.

Of the next six years two (1980 and 1984) were 'good', two were 'very good' (1981 and 1983, the latter 'deep' and 'complex' and now *en grande forme*) and two (1982 and 1985) were *années exceptionnelles*. Four of the springs had been poor, however. That of 1980 was cold, wet and windy, and those of 1981, 1983 and 1984 almost as bad. Both in 1980 and in 1981 there were serious problems of *coulure* at Haut-Brion.

1980 The 1980s (10,000 cases), light on the palate, evolved quickly and were best enjoyed when young. The sum of temperatures – 3,051° – was higher than in the two preceding years (September was sunny) and the rainfall was relatively high, at 341 mm. The harvest started late, on 6 October, and lasted until 18 October. In this year 700 cases of white wine were produced. Any of the surviving bottles should now be drunk.

1981 The harvest was earlier (24 September to 8 October) than 1980 and production higher at 12,000 cases. This was described as a very good year (sum of temperatures: 3,157°; rainfall: 292 mm). The wine was more complex than the 1980 vintage and lasted well. It was high in tannin. Tasters spoke of its 'backbone'. Fewer cases of white wine were produced – 500. It was delightful to drink.

1982 The first *année exceptionnelle*, 1982, was a year to remember, a vintage year for clarets of all kinds, including *crus bourgeois*. In the words of an Haut-Brion brochure, 'it is rare to find a year so favourable to wine making'. The spring was propitious – a dry and hot April and a beautiful May – but June was somewhat thundery, and on 8 July the temperature rose to 40°C. There was a fresh but sunny August, and the harvest started relatively early, on 15

September, in hot weather, and lasted until 24 September. (Sum of temperatures: 3,300°; rainfall: 290 mm.) The wine (no fewer than 19,000 cases, the highest since 1966) was wonderful in colour and in taste and from the beginning was compared to the 1959. It was known from the start that it would be a slow developer. High in tannin, it is a wine capable of being drunk with pleasure in 2015. It would be 'infanticide' to drink it before 1992, wrote Robert Parker in 1985. The white wine was superb also – rich and concentrated, and 1,000 cases were produced. It will still be drinkable at the end of the century.

1983 The weather was uncertain. Spring was wet, but June hot and dry. There was exceptional heat in the summer, described as almost tropical (sum of temperatures: 3,351°; rainfall: 442 mm). The weather at harvest time was perfect, however. Picking began on 26 September and ended on 7 October. Production (17,000 cases) was lower than in 1982, but above average. The velvety wine of the year, judged 'a very good year', was well structured, with complexity and depth. It is ageing beautifully and now drinks well. The white wine had a firm structure and developed rapidly. It had an aromatic quality; 1,100 cases were produced. It drinks well now.

1984 The year began with a cold and humid spring, followed by a hot and dry summer with eight days of great heat (sum of temperatures: 3,111°; rainfall: 550 mm). The harvest was relatively late, beginning on 27 September and ending on 12 October. Production, at 11,000 cases, was lower than in the two surrounding years. The agreeable white wine (1,000 cases) drinks well in 1994.

1985 This, the second *année exceptionnelle* in a six-year period, was a dry year (sum of temperatures: 3,185°; rainfall: 325 mm) (the year that holy water had to be rationed to pilgrims visiting Lourdes.) It was characterized by a remarkable autumn when morning mists in late September rehydrated grapes that had dried during intense heat. The harvest, which started on 23 September, was later than in 1982, the other *année exceptionnelle*. Output was high – 17,000 cases – and the Haut-Brion of the year was described as 'velvety'. It is a great wine to drink. In the same year 1,000 cases of a superb white Haut-Brion were produced, rich, fresh and complex.

It is one of the best white Haut-Brions and will drink well between 1995 and 2000.

1980–1985 Seven points stand out in relation to the sequence of six years from 1980 to 1985. First, there was no 'average' year in terms of quality. Procedures both in the vineyard and in the *chai* had been sufficiently improved with the help of science to make it possible to compensate in some measure for relatively bad weather conditions. It was proving difficult to have a really 'duff vintage': the last 'average year' had been 1977.

Second, quantity and quality had gone together no more than they ever had done: both 1980 and 1984 were 'good years' despite relatively low output. Third, quantities were in general greater than they had previously been: there had been better handling of better grapes. Fourth, four out of the six harvests had been gathered in at more or less the same time; differences in springtime weather conditions had proved less significant than at first had seemed likely. Fifth, the very substantial variations in rainfall, whatever their effects on morale, do not seem to have been decisive in their effects on the vintage, although their timing remained important. Temperature seems to have had a bigger influence. Sixth, *terroir* had still counted. The 1985 was as 'typical' of Haut-Brion at its best as the Haut-Brion of any previous *année exceptionnelle*, and the same adjective was to be applied to the 1986, a 'very good year'. Seventh, the financial alarms of the previous decade had been forgotten in a new fit of enthusiasm for claret buying. Indeed, in the following year, 1986, when prices were to fall, a Berry Brothers report on the 1986 vintage noted that what it called 'the fever of recent years' had at last subsided. There was more worry then concerning exchange rates, however, than about recession.

1986, 1987 and 1988 Leaving on one side prices, the subsequent experience of the years 1986, 1987 and 1988 suggests that the first, third and sixth of the points discussed above had become the most important. In both 1986 and 1987 rainfall had been relatively high, but the temperature level of the 1987 'good year' was higher than that of the 'very good year', 1988. In both cases spring had been difficult, but fine, dry weather in the summer and, above all, during the harvest, had made up for this. September 1987 saw ten days of exceptional heat, with temperatures of more than 30°C. The harvests in all three years, the second a 'good year', took place at almost exactly the same time (29 September to 10 October and 28 September to 13 October).

There was a record quantity of tannin in the 1986 red wines, which seemed to be wines likely to last – they are wines to keep and will be drinkable in 2020 – and there was a hint also of caramel. No white wine was produced in this year. The red wine of 1987 was 'severe' but more fruity. It had been decided at the end of August to remove all grapes that remained green to produce a more balanced product. It is a wine that drank well in 1992 and is agreeable to drink in 1993. The 1987 white wine (900 cases) is beautifully balanced – the word 'elegant' has been used to describe it – and it will be drinkable in 2000.

The harvest in 1988, a year which began badly, started on 28 September. August and early September had been very hot and dry following a wet spring, but there was rain at the end of the month when cautious wine producers in the Graves area were already harvesting. At Haut-Brion, however, both the Merlot and the Cabernet Sauvignon were picked in ideal conditions. As for the product, 'there was no doubt', Delmas has written, 'that we had produced a wine superior to that which we had expected to produce before the vintage and superior too to that which we expected after we had gathered in the first Merlot grapes'. The quantity was good also – 17,500 cases. More white Haut-Brion was produced than in 1987 or 1989 (1,200 cases); it is well structured and drinks well.

It was the quality of the vintage of this 'very good' year that encouraged Delmas in his conviction that he was still producing red wines that differed substantially from year to year. While there was a 'typical' Haut-Brion each year, the wine remained 'personalized'. The 1988, very different from the earlier vintages of the 1980s, was closest to the 1966, but these two vintages were different also. This was a conclusion which any *régisseur* or proprietor in the long history of Haut-Brion vintages would have been happy to set down. The wine itself will have a long history too and will be drinkable in the third decade of the twenty-first century.

1989 This, the bicentenary year of the French Revolution, was hailed at the time as a great year with an abundant output. It stands out as *une année très exceptionelle*. There were ideal weather conditions at all important times during the year (sum of temperatures: 3,442°; rainfall: 376 mm). The very early harvest lasted from 29

August to 20 September. The red wine is rich in tannin and will age well, and comparisons can be drawn with the 1959. The number of cases produced – only 15,000 – suggests that the price of the 1989 will rise as we approach 2020, when it should begin to be drunk. The whites too – 700 cases – have a long future: they are full and complex and have been compared to the greatest white Burgundies.

1990 This was also a good year, *exceptionnelle* rather than *très exceptionnelle* in the Haut-Brion ranking. Spring was cold but summer hot and dry and early September ideal for the harvest. (Sum of temperatures: 3,506°; rainfall: 336 mm.) The harvest was again early: from 4 September (for the white) to 28 September. The production of 17,000 cases was higher than in 1989. The white wine (1,000 cases) was excellent in quality, one of the best vintages. It will drink well between 2000 and 2005.

1991 This was a sad year after the outstanding years of 1989 and 1990, although the red (5,700 cases) tastes well and should be drunk in five years. No white wine was produced for sale. The year proved that the rhythm of the seasons remains beyond human control, and if Nancy Mitford was correct in saying that there is always a public for yesterday's weather, this was Bordeaux weather to forget. Frost in spring, a poor spring too for the *courtiers* and *négociants*, was widely publicized. It struck hard everywhere – and not just in patches – at a time when, ironically, the Union des Grands Crus de Bordeaux was carrying out a European sales tour to proclaim the merits of the 1989 vintage. The catastrophe was then followed by a poor summer, and the gloomy harvest started at Haut-Brion on 17 September for what was hoped would be the white and on 23 September for the red. (Sum of temperatures: 3,418°; rainfall: 336 mm).

1992 This was a year when far more wine was produced – 14,000 cases of red and 800 cases of white. The red has a good colour, as has the white, and both show promise. The harvest for the white began on 15 September and for the red two days later. The weather was less good than in 1991 (sum of temperatures: 3,347°; rainfall: 590 mm).

Judging recent vintages can sometimes be hazardous, and there are some writers on wine, for example Pamela Vandyke Price in her

Wines of the Graves, who have expressed scepticism about attempts to include in a book on wine 'such ephemera as vintages, how long certain wines will be on sale or, if they are, be affordable'. Yet these attempts are useful both to drinkers and to historians and they raise important questions about particular wines.

Nonetheless, even for historians, however full, authoritative and evocative reports on particular vintages may be, not least when they are comparative and retrospective, they are no substitute for individual tasting. Indeed, it is often difficult to form an impression from them when they are taken on their own; phrases like 'still good when we tasted them in 1914' – or in 1955 or even 1975 – convey at best the flavour of their author. More seriously, it is difficult to form any impression of continuity from such reports when they cover very long periods of time, and it is within this context that many different kinds of question arise. Were, for example, the Haut-Brions of the 1920s 'ancestors' of the Haut-Brions of the 1980s in anything more than name? Have Haut-Brions changed since 1945 or since 1961? Have they become 'lighter', as several writers have suggested?

Few writers have answered such questions directly. Indeed, there are few classic statements about comparison. In the middle years of the nineteenth century Petit-Lafitte conversed with the Mayor of Bordeaux, 'a competent authority on the matter', about 1784s, 1798s and 1811s. 'How would he compare the wines of his own time with those?' Petit-Lafitte asked. Comparison was out of the question, the Mayor replied, adding vaguely 'between the years there was a gulf'. Petit-Lafitte had himself tasted a 1798 vintage 'in the house of a Médoc resident, who preserved it as a family relic'. He noted as vaguely as the Mayor was to do that while it was 'nothing more than a vinous liquid, it still bore traces of the nobility of its origin'.

In determining which vintages last – and this seems to have been less significant to many wine writers of the 1980s than to their predecessors – tasting, even for the 'passable judge', is infinitely preferable to reading. Moreover, when good and relevant reading is available, it is always necessary to compare verbal records with personal impressions. Doubtless, it takes years to learn how to taste a wine, yet it is because I have drunk Haut-Brion 1924 – the oldest Haut-Brion I myself have tasted – with Bryan Wilson at All Souls College in Oxford that I am sure that there is continuity in the named product from then to now. The *goût de terroir* was there then.

Nineteen twenty-four, three years after I was born, is described in the records as a good year, 'when the flowers dominate the fruit': 'the wines are in general healthy, elegant and endowed with charm'. In 1989 the charm had gone; so too had any sense of youth. What I felt, above all, was the abiding power of the tannin. I would like to have been able to judge the Haut-Brion of my birth year, a wine the Haut-Brion records describe as 'a good year . . . with a woodland aroma and a delicate taste of mushrooms' (quite a recommendation to someone who loves all edible fungi). The weather in the Bordelais at the time of the vintage was so hot that fermentation was said to be difficult, and Haut-Brion was the wine that did best. That was a good omen. Of the 1922, however – and production in 1922 reached a record figure since statistics had been kept, almost double that of 1921 – we read simply in Haut-Brion's 1990 brochure: 'This wine is very old!' The exclamation mark speaks for itself. So, too, does Simon's comment on the whole Bordeaux vintage: 'no good to me'.

The year 1938, when I went up to the university, was only an 'average year', rather like 1939, the first year I visited Bordeaux before war reached it. That was several days before the vintage began, in good weather, on 20 September. The year the Second World War turned, 1943, was 'a very good year', although not surprisingly, we read in Bordeaux accounts of it that 'because of the War, estates were not all to make the most of the vintage'. I have never tasted the great 1945, but I have drunk the 1949, which was still powerful in 1980. It conveyed a sense of brooding concentration. The 1953 I found attractive too – far less intense. I have never tasted the 1955, the year of my marriage. I am glad to know that it was a *très bonne année* – for me it was certainly *une année exceptionnelle*.

I would like to have tasted also the 1934, described in the Haut-Brion brochure as 'very good', 'marvellous on the palate', particularly since Peynaud has described the 1934 as the kind of wine he himself does not like. Here, personal comparison would be particularly useful. André Simon, writing a generation earlier, was certainly of a different opinion from Peynaud. 'The year 1934,' he wrote at the time, 'has given an ungrateful world an enormous quantity of excellent wine, ever so much more than was expected –

and wanted.' Later he recalled how a considerable quantity of wine had been made in 1934, 'and many hours of sunshine stored in the grapes when they were picked . . . A wine made in such a year is like a child with a regular amount of vitality and self-will; whether such a child grows up to be a genius or a criminal is chiefly a matter of education.' Even Simon's metaphors relate personal history to the history of wine. The year was a very important one in his own life. So, too, it was in Haut-Brion, for 1934 was the first year when the Dillon regime had any influence on the wine, which was still Gibert's. In a Christie's catalogue of 1979 Michael Broadbent described the 1934 as 'good for the vintage', although it should be added that he described the 1926 as 'perfection'. That was a vintage that Maxwell-Campbell had called 'hot and unpleasant and entirely unworthy of the name of claret', perhaps the strongest condemnation ever made of an Haut-Brion. I do not have the power to arbitrate. I would like to have been able to do so.

On one memorable occasion while writing this book, however, I had the pleasure of tasting several Haut-Brions as a guest of the Wine Committee of the Athenaeum Club in London, and the occasion lingers in the mind like the dinner in All Souls. They included Haut-Brions 1976 and 1977, drunk with roast veal, and 1970 (in magnums) drunk with cheese soufflé. With an earlier course, pappardelle noodles and hare, there was Bahans-Haut-Brion 1979. The last of these came out well. The 1970 justified the promise made at the time that it was *un vin à attendre*, a wine to wait for. I am still waiting to drink – at the right time – the 1988 and the 1989.

In examining Robert Parker's marking by percentages, I was impressed to learn that he gave the Haut-Brion 1989 his highest mark: 100. By comparison, Margaux received 89 and La Mission 92. According to the Parker scale, wines rated from 90 to 94 are outstanding, and those rated 95 to 100 are 'classic'. With him this word is never overused. It is a word that should be in every wine historian's vocabulary.

Bibliography

Haut-Brion *tout court* everyone is acquainted with.

George Saintsbury, 1920

The bibliography that follows is comprehensive but selective. It places Haut-Brion in the context not of wines but of books. Auberon Waugh, not the first member of his family to be interested in wine – and food – observed at the end of 1984 that production of books about wine had outstripped even growth in wine consumption. Another writer in the same year, Alice King, in an article in *The Field* given the title 'Laying Down a Library', wrote pertinently that the crop of wine books almost made up for the indifferent vintage.

The books I have studied in writing my own are, in fact, of many different kinds. Nor is wine the subject of many of them. To a historian everything is grist to the mill, and since my book covers several centuries the grist is of different kinds.

Likewise, there are various different entry points to the story of Haut-Brion which, despite George Saintsbury's verdict, is not even well-known in Britain *tout court*. I have been surprised by the persistence of the Healy legend even in knowledgeable wine-drinking circles. One of the most interesting entry points is not through oenology but through the law. Documentary evidence from legal records, which survives in scattered, often tattered and moulding papers, is in relative abundance even for periods before the nineteenth century; and it constitutes a major part, if still only one part, of the relevant evidence on which this book has been based. Transfers of property establish dates: lawsuits uncover sus-

224

picions. If Gibert, proprietor of Haut-Brion before Dillon, had not loved litigation, the ancient history of Haut-Brion would have been difficult to clarify. In pursuing every wine-maker who used the words Haut-Brion as part of the name on the label, Gibert turned for evidence, like his opponents, to lawyers – and occasionally to historians – and they obliged him, sometimes at great expense. That particular passion was long since spent, but the material Gibert collected has often been more rewarding to me than it was to him.

There were other clues to the history of Haut-Brion in earlier legal cases of the eighteenth and nineteenth centuries, some involving names, most involving boundaries. The evidence, for example, in one late eighteenth-century case that involved on the one side the then lords of Haut-Brion, the Comte Joseph de Fumel and the Marquis de la Tresne, and on the other the Chapter of the Collegiate Church of St Seurin in Bordeaux, went back to the Middle Ages. It related to the claims of the Carmelites, who had produced wine, Les Carmes Haut-Brion, in Pessac since 1584. There are also maps of the boundary lines.

For the boundaries and what has gone on within them the most interesting remaining evidence is, of course, not documentary but visual. As you walk round the property, scanning the perimeter, peering at the roses at the end of the rows of vines, and examining the slopes, the *plantiers*, and the canalized relics of two streams, you get the sense of 'the lie of the land'. Maps can convey this too, but, alas, there are far too few plans of fields and buildings before the nineteenth century. Surviving implements and artefacts provide evidence also, and doubtless there would be archaeological evidence at Haut-Brion also if the land were not so precious that it cannot be dug up except occasionally to allow it to be fallow. Recent changes in the use of land and the disposition of buildings have been on an exceptional scale, but little that is old has been discovered in the process.

In a different branch of economic history, the quantitive analysis of figures, the evidence relating to Haut-Brion and to most other vineyards is most patchy of all. Details of sales of wine – and customers – are not comparable, for instance, with parallel details of Latour. Nor is there much about labour costs. Indeed, for whole decades evidence is missing. Given this absence of records and the propensity of owners of vineyards to keep things secret, it is therefore necessary to make the most of those samples that *do* survive, and in drawing comparisons to draw them over long periods. There are, however, some interesting details of business in the files of Bordeaux *courtiers* and *négociants*. Whole vintages, including vintages of Haut-Brion, were sometimes sold in advance.

It is sad that the British Consul in Bordeaux from 1856 to 1866, T. C. G. Scott, not to be confused with the Scotts who then owned Lafite as trustees, did not leave any regular records, official or unofficial. According to Paul de Cassagnac, author of *Les Vins de France*, he was said to have been a great connoisseur of wine. Scott's successor as Consul, T. C. Hunt, produced general reports on the wine trade of Bordeaux, some of which, fortunately, were printed in the *Wine Trade Review*, an informative English periodical that was first published in 1863. It showed a disturbing ignorance of history, however, when it remarked in 1878 that while the 'wholesome and refreshing wines of Bordeaux' had come into 'general use among the middle classes of England', it was evident that 'the taste for the higher qualities is also growing among wealthy consumers'.

The statistics of current prices of wine are rather easier to trace – as are exports of wines in general from Bordeaux – and they reflect the changing interrelationships of what have comprehensively been called 'fluctuations of nature, of politics and of the economy'. Bordeaux knew them all. Yet within such overall figures, runs of statistics relating specifically to Haut-Brion are not common or are not available. A longer search might reveal more, but the revelations would not be likely to modify significantly what we already know of patterns of production and sales in the eighteenth and nineteenth centuries from the two volumes of the thorough and carefully footnoted history of Latour.

I have gone back more than once to the general study, based on statistics – prices, wages and profits were the indicators – which was made by the economic and social historian Professor C. E. Labrousse, with whom I sometimes talked, long before the phrase '*révolution des boissons*' had been invented. In his impressive study *La Crise de l'Économie Française à la fin de l'Ancien Régime* (1944) Labrousse traced the long trend (*longue avance*) in the fortunes of viticulture, which had accelerated, whatever official policy might be, between 1710 and 1770 and which ended with a reaction, '*une grande régression*', that was the prelude to the French

Revolution. There were, of course, marked fluctuations in the output of wine – and in its quality – according to weather. There is nothing in Labrousse, however, about 'the demand side' for wine – he is unconcerned with quality – and among the '*grands propriét-aires*' whom he mentions those of Haut-Brion are missing.

Documentary, visual and statistical evidence must always be sup-plemented by oral evidence and, before such evidence is available, by folklore, gossip and tradition. I have learnt more, therefore, by talking to people who work at Haut-Brion than I could have gleaned from any documents or sets of statistics. Some of their memories stretch deep into the past. In the city of Bordeaux, where the clues to the story of Haut-Brion cluster, I was helped at an early stage in my research by M. Henri de Fonroque-Mercié, then Secretary of the Académie du Vin de Bordeaux, who unearthed many ancient documents and many which now have the air of being ancient even when they deal with relatively recent times. Fonroque-Mercié himself played an interesting part in the history of Haut-Brion. He it was, for example, who organized for Clarence Dillon the first great post-war ball there in 1950, an event to prove that at last the austerities of the Second World War were over.

The ball was on a scale that broke with recent tradition. Yet much of the history of any subject that we know – whether social, economic, political, religious, 'technical' or 'cultural' – necessarily hinges on 'tradition'; and in the history of the wine trade of Bor-deaux tradition counts for far more than it does in the history of most subjects. Memory always counts, and folk memory can stretch back far. In the nineteenth century, when so much else was changing, and even tradition itself could be invented, there was much reference in print to it; and in the twentieth century the word 'tradition' still recurs in documents, in speeches, and in books and articles.

When, for example, there was a re-examination of the system of classification for the wines of the Médoc in 1973, the jury noted the existence, as their predecessors in 1855 had also noted it, of 'a very ancient tradition' that linked Haut-Brion with the *grands crus* of the Médoc. 'Taking account of that tradition, and of customs and usages on one hand and of its pre-eminent qualities on the other hand,' the jury went on, 'we have judged that it must figure through assimilation among the *premiers crus classés du Médoc.*'

French historians, rooted in geography, have concerned themselves with *mentalités*, states of mind, and how they change. In that context I have asked myself not only about the mentality of the 1855 jury and why its members were so interested in classification, but about the impact on the proprietors of the vineyards of seventeenth-century domestic disturbances in France which pitted *parlements* against kings. The life of Pessac itself had been violently disturbed by the troops of the Duc d'Épernon in 1649, the 'terrible year' of the *Fronde*. What were the reactions of the Pontacs in the château? Wine and comfort did not always go together, but business had to go on. The Pontacs were trying to build up a business, and there is evidence to suggest that the harvest went on as usual. As in a play, whatever was happening outside they stayed on the stage. And business went on even during the 1790s when there were sale notices both at Haut-Brion and La Mission. Wine was still produced.

In March 1789, on the eve of the Revolution, when *The Marriage of Figaro*, with its disturbing social plot, was performed at the Opera House in Bordeaux, did the comfortable audience feel any intimations of drastic social changes to come? Looking back, Talleyrand certainly did. He once remarked that only those who had lived in France before the Revolution had really experienced *la douceur de vivre*. Surely Bordeaux has never entirely lost it, and the magisterial twentieth-century history of Bordeaux (in eight volumes, one of which is devoted entirely to an index), under the direction of Professor Higounet, deals in depth with all aspects of its life. It is a remarkable product of modern scholarship in the field of urban history. This is a branch of history that has boomed on both sides of the Channel and on both sides of the Atlantic since 1963, and from the volumes edited by Higounet I have learnt much about the fortunes of a European city that over the centuries has retained a quite exceptional sense of its own continuity. It is fascinating to know, too, that Haut-Brion is close not only to the city of Bordeaux but to its university which, unlike some universities, has cheerfully fostered the study of the city in which it is located. Founded in the fifteenth century, in 1441 – before the English kings left Bordeaux – it has a long history of its own, and in recent times it has been deeply involved in the study of wine as well as in the study of the city.

Because I am interested in the history of urban history – how we conceive of it as well as how we write it – I have also studied not only these recent volumes of city history, the product of modern academic scholarship, but far older texts, like Camille Jullian's *Histoire de Bordeaux depuis les origines jusqu'en 1895* (1895), which has much to say about wine in its pages, and T. Malvezin's multi-volume *Histoire du commerce du Bordeaux depuis les origines jusqu'à nos jours* (1892), which argued concisely, if misleadingly, that the dispatch of the English in 1453 was catastrophic for '*le vignoble de Bordeaux*'. Fortunately, the city of Bordeaux, which acquired a splendid new appearance in the eighteenth century, remained 'a city of wine', as Bertall called it in 1878 in his book *La Vigne, Voyage autour des vins de France*.

I have had access also to a beautifully bound copy of a great eighteenth-century work, Dom Devienne's *Histoire de la Ville de Bordeaux*, published in Bordeaux in 1771 '*avec approbation et privilège du Roi*', but apparently without financial support from the Fumels, then proprietors of Haut-Brion. They do not figure in the list of patrons who sponsored it. The *Histoire* belongs to a period in the story of the writing of city histories which is very different both from that of Malzevin and from our own.

It seemed natural for Dom Devienne to quote the medieval chronicler Froissart in his preface before going on to sing the praises of '*la vivacité Gasconne*': after all, the Middle Ages then were not all that far away. Yet Devienne had his own sense of contemporary mission, insisting rightly that history should be written 'neither like a newspaper nor a gazette'. He rightly saw, too, that local and regional history together provide a necessary foundation for national and international history. For him, it was natural to move from Bordeaux to the Graves district, from the Graves district to the Médoc, from the Médoc to the Gironde, from the Gironde to France, and from France to Europe:

> Historians of towns and provinces have formed for long one of the principal branches of our literature. If it were necessary to justify public taste in this respect it would be sufficient to say that it is only through their writing that one day we shall acquire a good history of France.

We are now far nearer to acquiring one. We are also far nearer to getting a good new history of wine. It is interesting that Dion, who wrote the first, was a professor not of history but of geography at the Collège de France.

In recent years there have been big changes in British books about wine, following the publication in 1951 of Raymond Postgate's *The Plain Man's Guide to Wine* and the appearance fifteen years later of a book by a young Cambridge graduate, Hugh Johnson, André Simon's successor as Secretary of the Wine and Food Society. Johnson gave it the simplest of titles – *Wine* – and he later told Jane Macquitty, another well-known writer on wines, that his wine vocabulary consisted then of 200 words. Johnson, still only twenty-seven years old, had already proved himself among the most discerning of 'wine enthusiasts' – and a writer capable of attracting and retaining an immense readership. His *Pocket Wine Book*, the first edition of which appeared in 1977, his *World Atlas of Wine*, which appeared in 1982, and *The Modern Encyclopaedia of Wine*, which appeared in 1983, have reached the widest possible audience. So, too, has the *Which? Wine Guide*, first published in 1981 and edited by Jane Macquitty in 1983 and 1984.

As the number of writers on wines – many of them women – has enormously increased, along with the number of places in which their writings appear (these include excellent – and often delectable – specialized magazines), they have become more adaptable in their style and more curious and expansive in choosing the subjects to discuss. Above all they have brought people into their writing. Jancis Robinson, for example, noted in her *The Great Wine Book* (1982) how 'extraordinarily little had been written about *wine people*'. As she rightly notes, 'the character of a wine, and especially the will to produce really fine wine, is inextricably bound up with the personality, psychology and philosophy of its maker'. In the process, wine writers have had to take increasing account not only of their greatly expanded readership, but of one another. They have tried to be distinctive. They have their own awards system too. Thus, in 1982 Johnson was awarded the *Wine and Vines* 'Perpetual Trophy for Excellence in Wine Writing'. Not even the best of wines could ever be described as perpetual.

An experienced English woman writer on wines – and on the wines of the Graves in particular – Pamela Vandyke Price, introduced her five pages on Haut-Brion with words that would have delighted Clarence Dillon and Seymour Weller: 'The most surprising thing about this property is that there is not already an entire book devoted to it, its wines and its history.'

I have doubts about some judgements of wine writers on their predecessors. For example, in *The Times* of 11 February 1989 in a column headed simply, and economically, 'Wine', Jane Macquitty quoted what to her was an unintelligible passage from one of them, P. Morton Shand. In *A Book of French Wines* (1928, later published in paperback), a study not uncharacteristic of the period in which it appeared, Shand claimed that he found

> the 'scansion' of Bordeaux claret, if scansion there must be, ranges from the Horatian to the Miltonic, from the rippling lyrics of Herrick to the sway and surge of Swinburne in the infinite variety of its scope; the 'rhythm' of its incarnadine burden, the lilt of its splendid majesty, never the din of rant drowning the creaking of the buskins.

'I have no idea,' wrote Jane Macquitty, 'what the author is talking about, and nor did anybody, I suspect, at the time.'

I more than suspect that some of them did, for Shand, who undoubtedly knew a great deal about 'the wines of Bordeaux', was appealing to 'bookmen', to people 'in the know' *both* about wine and about books. In a pre-television, pre-computer culture, wine and books often seemed to go as easily together as wine and food do today. Jane Macquitty was right, nonetheless, to suggest that Shand was overburdened by literary associations. There was also a sense of exclusivity in his approach: he was writing for people who did not need to use a dictionary and/or an encyclopaedia to find the meaning of his erudite references.

In any dialogue between 'wine enthusiasts' and historians – and the terms change – the latter have always had one distinctive advantage. By the very nature of their discipline, they are interested not only in the history of the subject with which they are concerned – in this case wine and, within the world of wine, Haut-Brion – but in historiography, the history of the history of their subject. They seek to discover what previous generations have asked and said, not least when others have cast it aside. For this reason, therefore, I have not been able to dispose of all previous writings on wine and on Haut-Brion quite as easily as Jane Macquitty thought that she had disposed of P. Morton Shand. The history of wine, like wine in the glass, should be studied in depth. The history of the Wine and Food Society, founded in 1933 under the presidency of André Simon, is as interesting to explore as the more recent history of *Which?*

Many remarkable books about the wines of Bordeaux were written long before 1963, and I have found indispensable all the successive, magisterial nineteenth-century and early twentieth-century editions of *Bordeaux et ses vins* by Cocks et Féret: that of 1868, which included details of the first formal classification of clarets in 1855; that of 1881, translated two years later into English 'owing to the demand we have received from England and America', an edition complete with dated pictures of the châteaux, pictures that were to survive the two world wars unchanged; that of 1886, written after the terrible disease of phylloxera (an absorbing subject in itself) had first struck the vineyards; that of 1893, when a German edition also appeared – in the Baltic port of Stettin, which produced wine barrels for Bordeaux; that of 1898, when affairs in the vineyards seemed to be returning to normal; that of 1908, when it was clear that they had not; and that of 1922, after a wearing war, when Haut-Brion was not the only vineyard that had found itself short of harvesters. The later twentieth-century volumes include that of 1929, the year of the Wall Street crash – and of memorable wines; that of 1949, after a protracted German occupation of the vineyards during the Second World War; and that of 1969, on the eve of a dramatic rise in claret prices that was to end in crisis. There was to be more than one kind of crisis, indeed, for in addition to the crisis for the trade, as in 1929, there was a general economic crisis, in this case accelerated not by wine but by oil and not by wine drinkers but by Arabs who were themselves forbidden to drink wine.

I have learned much from comparing what was said in one edition of Cocks et Féret with what was said in another, particularly the second edition, of 1868, which appeared just after phylloxera had first been observed in the Bordeaux vineyards, and the seventh edition, which appeared in 1898, when recovery from phylloxera – and mildew – was almost complete. There is almost as great an interest also in any comparison of the 1969 edition with that of 1949. Indeed, comparing different editions of Cocks et Féret is as revealing as comparing different editions of the *Encyclopaedia Britannica*.

In the course of my research, I have turned also to the many volumes of travel tales written by British and other visitors to Bordeaux, beginning, long before 'wine enthusiasts' developed their craft, with the philosopher Locke whose observations were shrewd and perceptive. There is much that is pertinent also in Charles Cocks's well-illustrated *Bordeaux, Its Wines and the Claret Country* (1846), his first book, the prelude to Cocks et Féret which was long to survive his death; in Cyrus Redding's *French Wines and Vineyards* (1860) and in his earlier *A History and Description of Modern Wines* (1833), the first book of its kind in English; in F. H. Butler's *Wine and Wine Lands of the World* (1923); and in C. W. Berry's *In Search of Wine* (1935), recently reprinted in a Sidgwick and Jackson series edited by Jancis Robinson.

Among more recent 'wine enthusiasts', several, like Berry, have been concerned directly with the wine trade. Michael Broadbent, for example, a Master of Wine, is head of Christie's Wine Department. In my own work I have drawn both information and inspiration from him, from Clive Coates, whose judgements are always well based, and from other recent British writers on wine. I have turned also to the carefully prepared writings of Lichine, who when he was young developed a particular interest in Haut-Brion which he never lost. He dedicated his first book to Seymour Weller and was a consultant to Haut-Brion as late as the spring of 1989. He died at the age of seventy-five while my book was being completed. Lichine had been a victim of revolution. He left Moscow following the Revolution of 1917 and after living in France and in England became a naturalized American. In the words of the Bordeaux newspaper *Sud-Ouest*, which described his funeral at Cantenac in the heart of the Médoc, 'he was the man who more than any other made the American market become aware of the wines of Bordeaux'. For Alain Maurel, he was 'a force of nature with the gospel words of a preacher'.

Another source of inspiration has been the beautifully produced study by Holland's best-known writer on wine, Hubrecht Duijker, *The Great Wine Châteaux of Bordeaux* (1975), one of a series on the wine regions of France, which brings all the resources of the photographer to add to the interest of a compact and readable text. It is a beautiful book, like his *Châteaux Bordeaux* (1988), which is concerned not only with wines, but with 'a unique kind of architecture and a fascinating regional civilization'. Two of Duijker's other books are called (in England) *Wine Discovered* and *Wine with a Smile*.

In reading about wine, comparison is as necessary as it is in tasting wines; and I have found it enlightening to compare the 1969 edition of Lichine's *Guide to the Wines and Vineyards of France* with the French writer Paul de Cassagnac's *French Wines*, translated into English in 1930 – *autre temps, autre pays, autres mœurs*. I have found it equally enlightening also to compare Edmund Penning-Rowsell's thoughtful and wide-ranging book *The Wines of Bordeaux* (first edition, 1969) with the American Robert M. Parker's highly influential book *Bordeaux: The Definitive Guide to the Wines Produced since 1961*, which appeared in 1985.

Penning-Rowsell, who has written about clarets in many places, including *The Good Food Guide*, first published in 1951, never leaves the history out: indeed, he often expounds it at length. At the same time, however, he offers ample practical and up-to-date advice. Parker, creator of a points system for rating wine, has had an immense impact on American taste; and while what he has to say has inevitably been controversial – as much, perhaps, to wine merchants (and other wine writers) as to wine drinkers – his appeal has never been in doubt. As Hugh Johnson put it, when Parker's *Definitive Guide* first appeared, 'Nobody with a bottle in the closet or a wine store on the way home will be able to resist this book.'

I am deeply impressed by the clarity and force of Parker's advocacy. He is an outstanding personality who has guaranteed that knowledge of the wines of Bordeaux is widely accessible in the United States. He judges – and rightly judges – from wine in the glass, and it would be interesting to know what he would have made of the complex *legal* documents which constitute a substantial and indispensable part of my historical evidence on Haut-Brion. He is, after all, a man who gave up a career in law to devote himself to writing about and to evaluating wine. As founder in 1978 of the *Wine Advocate*, a title with legal overtones, he has become in the words of the *Washington Post* 'an ombudsman for the wine consumer'. He has introduced Haut-Brion at American wine-tastings, and he is also an annual visitor to Bordeaux.

Besides general books on the wines of Bordeaux there have been several studies of individual vineyards, varying enormously in range, length, insight and scholarship. Cyril Ray, an Oxford graduate and a personal friend who, like Hugh Johnson, cannot be left out of any historiography of wine, produced his *Lafite* in 1968 and *Mouton-Rothschild: The Wine, the Family, the Museum* in 1974. He was also responsible for revising and editing P. Morton Shand's *Book of French Wines* in 1963, the year of Dillon's letter to Weller.

A year later he was awarded the Wine and Food Society's first André Simon Prize. Sadly, he too died (at the age of eighty-three) while my book, which greatly interested him, was in its final stages. He encouraged me to write it.

More recently, Nicholas Faith has published *Château Margaux* (1982), which had a foreword by Émile Peynaud and which touches on the overlapping history of Margaux and Haut-Brion. Faith has written other valuable books on the subject of wine, including *The Winemasters* (1978) and *Victorian Vineyard: Château Loudenne and the Gilbeys* (1983). French scholarship in this field, incomparable in quality, is represented impressively in the two-volume work edited by Charles Higounet: *La Seigneurie et le vignoble de Château Latour*.

I have left to the last in this introduction to my bibliography the authoritative work *Bordeaux* by David Peppercorn, Master of Wine, which is a key volume, rich in knowledge and in insight, among the Faber Books on Wine edited by Julian Jeffs. First published in 1982, it was published in a completely revised second edition in 1991. The first words of his preface read: 'Writing a book on Bordeaux is rather like the proverbial painting of the Forth Bridge; it is always "Work in Progress".' So, too, within the bigger history is the history of Haut-Brion itself. There can never be a final edition.

BIBLIOGRAPHY

Allen, H. Warner, *The Wines of France*, 1924
– *The Romance of Wine*, 1931
– *Natural Red Wines*, 1951
– *Through the Wine Glass*, 1954
– *A History of Wine*, 1961
Allibone, T. E. *The Royal Society and Its Dining Clubs*, 1976
Ames, R., *The Search after Claret*, 1691
– *The Bacchanalian Sessions or the Contention of Liquors*, 1693
Andrieu, P., *Chronologie Anecdotique du vignoble français*, n.d.
– *Petite histoire de Bordeaux et de son vignoble*, 1921
Anglade, P. and Puisais, J., *Vins et vignobles de France*, 1987
Angot, A., *Étude sur les vendanges en France*, 1985

Babeau, A., *Les voyageurs en France depuis la Renaissance jusqu'à la Révolution*, 1885

Bachelier, L., *Histoire du commerce de Bordeaux depuis les temps les plus reculés jusqu'à nos jours*, 1861

Baker, C. H. and M., *James Brydges, First Duke of Chandos*, 1949

Barrènes, J., *Viticulture et vinification en Bordelais au Moyen Age*, 1912

Barrère, P., *Les quartiers de Bordeaux – étude géographique*, 1956

Baurein, Abbé J., *Variétés Bordelaises ou Essai historique et critique sur la topographie ancienne et moderne du diocèse de Bordeaux*, 6 vols, 1784–86

Beatty-Kingston, W., *Claret; its Production and Treatment*, 1985

Bécamps, P., *La révolution à Bordeaux – J. B.-M. Lacombe, Président de la Commission Militaire*, 1953

– *Bordeaux, 2000 ans d'histoire: catalogue de l'exposition*, 1973

Beer, E. S. de, *The Diary of John Evelyn*, 1955

Behrens, C. B. A., *The Ancien Régime*, London, 1967

Bériac, J.-P., 'Ferdinand Duprat, architecte paysagiste et quelques autres', in *Bordeaux-Aquitaine 1920–1940, Architecture Urbanisme*, 1988

Bernadau, P., *Histoire de Bordeaux*, 1837

Berry, C. W., *Viniana*, 1929

– *A Miscellany of Wine*, 1932

– *In Search of Wine*, 1935

Bert, P., *In Vino Veritas: L'affaire des vins de Bordeaux*, 1975

'Bertall', *La Vigne: Voyage autour des vins de France*, 1878

Betzge-Brezetz, A., 'Les Archives départementales de la Gironde', in *Revue historique de Bordeaux et du département de la Gironde*, 1953

Bidet, N., *Traité sur la nature et sur la culture de la vigne, sur le vin, la façon de le faire et la manière de le bien gouverner, à l'usage des différents vignobles du royaume de France*, 2 vols, 1759

Bijur, G., *Wines with Long Noses*, 1961

Bloch, R., *Le port de Bordeaux, la naissance d'une ville industrielle, ses progrès, son avenir*, 1925

Boutruche, R., *La crise d'une société; seigneurs et paysans du Bordelais pendant la guerre de Cent Ans*, 1947

– *Bordeaux de 1453 à 1715*, 1966

Boyd, J. P. (ed.), *The Papers of Thomas Jefferson*, 17 vols, 1950–

Boyle, E., *The Parlement of Bordeaux and the End of the Old Regime*, 1974

Brace, R. M., *Bordeaux and the Gironde*, 1948

Bradford, S., *The Englishman's Wine: The Story of Port*, 1969

Branas, J., *Viticulture*, 1974

Braudel, F., *Civilisation matérielle et capitalisme*, 1967

Braure, M., 'Quelques aspects des relations commerciales entre la France et l'Angleterre au dix-huitième siècle', in *Annales du Midi*, 1953

Briggs, A., *Wine for Sale*, 1983

Brillat-Savarin, A., *Physiologie du Goût* (1839)

Broadbent, M., *Wine Tasting*, 1968

– *The Complete Guide to Wine Tasting and Wine Cellars*, 1984

– *The Great Vintage Wine Book*, 1980; 2nd ed.: 1991

Brutails, A., *Recherches sur l'équivalence des anciennes mesures de la Gironde*, 1912

Butel, P., 'Grands propriétaires et production des vins du Médoc au XVIIIe siècle', in *Revue historique de Bordeaux et du département de la Gironde*, 1962

Butel, P. and Poussou, J.-P., *La vie quotidienne à Bordeaux au XVIIIe siècle*, 1970

Caffyn, A. and Étienne, R., *Histoire de l'Aquitaine*, ed. under the direction of Charles Higounet, 1971

Campbell, I. M., *Wayward Tendrils of the Vine*, 1947

– *Reminiscences of a Vintner*, 1951

Capus, J., *L'œuvre du comité national des appellations*, 1942

Carling, T. E., *Wine Aristocracy: A Guide to the Best Wines of the World*, 1957

Carter, Y., *Drinking Bordeaux*, 1966

Carus Wilson, E. M., 'The Effects of the Acquisition and of the loss of Gascony on the English Wine Trade', in *Bulletin of the Institute of Historical Research*, 1947

Cassagnac, P. de, *Les Vins de France*, 1927 (Eng. tr., *French Wines*, by Guy Knowles, 1930)

Cassard, J.-C., 'Vins et marchands de vin gascons au début du XIVe siècle', in *Annales du Midi*, 1978

Cavoleau, M., *Oenologie française ou statistique de tous les vignobles et de toutes les boissons vineuses et spirit ueuses de la France*, 1827

Chaix d'Est Ange, G., *Dictionnaire des familles françaises, anciennes ou notables à la fin du XIXe siècle*, 1903

Chambre de Commerce de Bordeaux, *Extraits des procès-verbaux, lettres et mémoires*, 1st series, vols 1–12, 1850–62

Chaptal, J. A., *L'art de faire le vin*, 1807

Charles, A., *La Révolution de 1848 et la seconde République à Bordeaux et dans le département de la Gironde*, Bordeaux, 1945

— 'La viticulture en Gironde et le commerce des vins de Bordeaux sous le Second Empire', in *Revue historique de Bordeaux et du département de la Gironde*, 1963

Charpentier, G., *Les relations économiques entre Bordeaux et les Antilles au XVIIIe siècle*, 1937

Chastaignet, Paul, Vicomte de, *Les vins de Bordeaux*, 1873

Chauvet, J., *La dégustation des vins. Son mécanisme et ses lois*, 1951

Chauvrou, P., 'La formation topographique du quartier des Chartrons', in *Revue historique de Bordeaux et du département de la Gironde*, 1928, 1929, 1930

Chayette, Y., *Le Vin à Travers la Peinture*, 1984

Clarke, O., *Wine Factfinder and Taste Guide*, 1985

— *Webster's Wine Price Guide*, 1986 ed.

Coates, C., *Claret*, 1982

— *The Wines of France*, 1990

Cockburn, F. A. *et. al.*, *Wine and the Wine Trade*, 1947

Cocks, C., *Bordeaux, Its Wines and the Claret Country*, 1846; 3rd ed.: 1899

Cocks, C. and Féret, E., *Bordeaux et ses vins*, 1850, and later editions to 14th ed.: 1991

Communay, A., *Les grands négociants bordelais du XVIIIe siècle*, 1888

Cooper, C., *The English Table in History and Literature*, 1928

Courteault, P., 'Les impressions d'une Anglaise à Bordeaux en 1785', in *Revue historique de Bordeaux et du département de la Gironde*, 1911

— *La Place Royale de Bordeaux*, 1923

— *La Révolution et les théâtres de Bordeaux d'après des documents, inédits* 1926

— *Bordeaux, cité classique*, 1932

Coustet, R., 'Bordeaux ou l'originalité d'une tradition', in *Archives de l'Architecture Moderne*, 1984

Coutureau, E., 'Le pavé des Chartrons, œuvre d'Étienne Laclotte', in *Revue historique de Bordeaux et du département de la Gironde*, 1981

Crawford, A., *A History of the Vintners' Company*, 1977

Crouzet, F., 'Les importations d'eaux-de-vie et de vins français en Grande-Bretagne pendant le Blocus continental', in *Annales du Midi*, 1953

Daguin, F., *L'Aquitaine occidentale*, 1948

Daiches, D., *Scotch Whisky*, 1969

Danflou, A., *Les Grands Crus Bordelais*, 2 vols, 1867

Daniel, B., *Guide Pratique du Viticulteur*, 1935

d'Armailhacq, A., *La culture de la vigne, la vinification et les vins dans le Médoc*, 1858

Davis, C., *English Bottles and Decanters, 1650–1900*, 1973

Davis, S. F., *History of the Wine Trade*, 1969

Delmas, J.-B., *La Collection Ampélographique du Château Haut-Brion*, 1989

– 'La Mémoire Olfactive', in *La Mémoire*, vol. 2, ed. N. Zavialoff et al., 1989

Denman, J. L., *The Vine and its Fruit*, 1864

Derruau, M., *Géographie Humaine*, 1976

Desgraves, L., *L'intendant Claude Boucher, 1720–1743*, 1952

– *Bordeaux au cours des siècles*, 1954

– *Bordeaux, Côte d'Argent*, 1959

– *L'évocation du vieux Bordeaux*, 1960

Desgraves, L. and Dupeux, G., *Bordeaux au XIXe siècle*, 1969

Dethier, J. (ed.), *Châteaux Bordeaux: Wine, Architecture and Civilization*, 1988 (Eng. tr. 1989)

Devienne, Dom J. B., *Histoire de la ville de Bordeaux*, 1771

Dion, R., 'L'ancien privilége de Bordeaux', in *Revue géographique des Pyrénées et du Sud-Ouest*, 1955

– *Histoire de la vigne et du vin en France des origines au XIXe Siècle*, 1959

Don, R. S., *Wine*, 1968

Dormontel, C., *Les grands vins de Bordeaux*, 1934

Doutrelant, P.-M., *Les bons vins et les autres*, 1976

Dovaz, M., *Encyclopédie de crus classés du Bordelais*, 1981

– *Le livre du vin*, 1976

Doyle, W., *The Parlement of Bordeaux at the end of the Old Regime, 1771–1790*, 1974

Druitt, R., *Report on the Cheap Wines of France, Italy, Austria, Greece and Hungary*, 1865

Ducannes-Duval, G., *Inventaire-sommaire des archives municipales – période révolutionnaire*, 1929

Duff Cooper, A., *Old Men Forget*, 1953

Duijker, H., *The Great Wine Châteaux of Bordeaux*, 1975
– *The Good Wines of Bordeaux*, 1980

Dumay, R., *Le vin de Bordeaux et du Haut-Pays*, 1977

Dumbauld, E., *Thomas Jefferson, American tourist: Being an account of his journeys in the United States of America, England, France, Italy, the Low Countries and Germany*, 1946

Dumbrell, R., *Understanding Antique Wine Bottles*, 1938

Dunham, A. L., *The Anglo-French Treaty of Commerce of 1860*, 1930

Dutrait, M., *Dictionnaire topographiqe et toponymique du Médoc*, 1894

Enjalbert, H., 'Comment naissent les grand crus', in *Annales*, 1953
– *Histoire de la vigne et du vin: l'avènement de la qualité*, 1975

Enjalbert, H. and B., *L'histoire de la vigne et du vin, avec une nouvelle hiérarchie des terroirs du Bordelais*, 1987

Ein, J., *Le commerce honorable*, 1648

Escritt, L. B., *The Wine Cellar*, 1972

Étienne, R. (ed.), *Bordeaux Antique*, 1962

Faith, N., *The Winemasters*, 1978
– *Château Margaux*, 1982
– *A Victorian Vineyard*, 1983

Fédération Historique du Sud-Ouest, *Vignobles et vins d'Aquitaine: Histoire, Économie, Art (Actes du XXe Congrès d'études régionales, Nov. 1967, 1970)*

Féret, E., *Le Médoc et ses vins*, 1876
– *Dictionnaire-manuel du négociant en vins et spiritueux et du maître de chai*, 1896
– *Statitisque générale du département de la Gironde, topographie, sciences, administration, biographie, histoire, archéologie, agriculture, commerce, industrie*, 4 vols, 1874–89

Forest, A., *Society and Politics in Revolutionary Bordeaux*, 1974

Forster, R., 'The Noble Wine Producers of the Bordelais, in the
    18th Century', in *Economic History Review*, 1961
– 'The Provincial Noble, A Reappraisal', in *American Historical
    Review*, 1963
– 'The Nobility during the French Revolution', in *Past and
    Present*, 1967
Foster, A. E. M., *Wining and Dining*, 1924
Francatelli, C. E., *The Modern Cook*, 1846
Francis, A. D., *The Wine Trade*, 1972
Francisque-Michel, *Histoire du commerce et de la navigation à
    Bordeaux*, 1867
Franck, W., *Traité sur les vins du Médoc et les autres vins rouges
    et blancs du département de la Gironde*, 1824 and later
    editions to 8th ed.: 1871
Fuisais, J., *Le Vin se met à table*, 1981
Gabler, J. M., *Wine into Words*, 1985
'G. A. K.', *Clarets and Sauternes*, 1920
Galard, G. de, *Album vinicole*, 1835
Galet, P, *Cépages et vignobles de France*, 4 vols, 1956–64
Galtier, G., 'La viticulture de l'Europe occidentale à la veille de la
    Révolution française, d'après les notes de voyage de Thomas
    Jefferson', in *Bulletin de la Société languedocienne de
    géographie*, 1968
Gay, J., *Wine, A Poem*, 1708
Ginestet, B., *La Bouillie Bordelaise ou petite anthologie
    anecdotique et chronologique du vignoble, des gens et du vin
    de Bordeaux*, 1975
Gold, A. (ed.), *Wines and Spirits of the World*, 1968
Goodwin, A., 'The social origins and privileged status of the
    French eighteenth-century nobility', in *Bulletin of the John
    Rylands Library*, 1964–5
Got, N., *La dégustation des vins*, 1955
Goubert, P., *L'Ancien Régime*, 1969–73
Gradis, H., *Histoire de Bordeaux*, 1838
Grassey, R. B., 'Social Status and Commercial Enterprise under
    Louis XIV', in *Economic History Review*, 1960
Greg, T. T., *Through the Glass Lightly, Essays on Wine*, 1897
Grellet-Dumazeau, A., *La société bordelaise sous Louis XV et le
    salon de Mme Duplessy*, 1897
Guillard, M., *Bordeaux*, 1981

– *Medóc, presqu'île de vin*, 1982

Guillaumin, T. A., *Le Parlement de Bordeaux sous Louis XV*, 1878

Guillon, E., *Les Châteaux historiques et vinicoles de la Gironde avec la description des communes, la nature de leurs vins et la désignation des principaux crus*, 4 vols, 1866–9

Guyon, J.-R., *Au Service du Vin de Bordeaux*, 1956

Guyot, J., *Études des vignobles de France*, 1876

Hackwood, F. W., *Good Cheer: the Romance of Food and Feasting*, 1911

Hailman, J., *The Wines of Thomas Jefferson*, 1987

Hawker, C., *Chats About Wine*, 1907

– *Wine and Wine Merchants*, 1909

Healy, M., *Claret and the White Wines of Bordeaux*, 1934

– *Stay Me with Flagons*, 1940

Heckmann, M., *Corkscrews*, 1981

Henderson, A., *The History of Ancient and Modern Wines*, 1824

Heuckmann, W., *The Grafted Vine, European Scions; American Stocks*, 1964

Higounet, C. (gen. ed.), *Histoire de Bordeaux*, 8 vols, 1962–74 (see also the individual volumes Boutruche, Desgraves and Dupeux, Étienne, Lajugie, Pariset)

– *Bordeaux pendant le haut moyen age*, 1964

– (ed.), *La seigneurie et le vignoble de Château Latour*, 1974

Hiscott, W. G., *John Evelyn and his Family Circle*, 1956

Hogg, A. (ed.), *Wine Mine*, 1962, 1972

Huetz de Lemps, C., *Géographie du commerce de Bordeaux à la fin du règne de Louis XIV*, 1975

Hutchinson, W. G. (ed.), *Songs of the Vine*, 1904

Hyams, E., *The Wine Country of France*, 1960

– *Dionysus: Social History of the Vine*, 1965

Ilchester, Earl of, *Lord Hervey and His Friends*, 1950

Jackson, E., *The Diary of John Hervey, First Earl of Bristol, 1688 to 1742, with Extracts from his Book of Expenses*, 1894

Jacquelin, L. and Poulain, R., *Vignes et vins de France*, 1979

James, M., 'The Fluctuations of the Anglo-Gascon Wine Trade during the Fourteenth Century', in *Economic History Review*, 1951

– *Studies in the Medieval Wine Trade*, 1971

James, W. B., *Wine Duties Considered Financially and Socially*, 1855

Jeffs, J., *The Wines of Europe*, 1971
– *The Dictionary of World Wines, Liqueurs and Other Drinks*, 1973

Johnson, H., *Wine*, 1960
– *The World Atlas of Wine*, 1971; rev. ed. 1985
– *The Modern Encylopedia of Wine*, 1984

Joinville, P. de, *Le Commerce de Bordeaux au XVIIIe siècle*, 1908

Jouannet, F., *Statistique du département de la Gironde*, 2 vols, 1837, 1843

Jullian, C., *Histoire de Bordeaux depuis les origines jusqu'en 1895*, 1895

Jullien, A., *Topographie de tous les vignobles connus, contenant: leur position topographique, l'indication du genre et de la qualité des produits de chaque cru, les lieux où se font les chargements et le principal commerce de vin, suivi d'une classification genérale des vins*, 1816; 5th ed.: 1866; Eng. tr. 1824

Kay, B. and McLean, C., *Knee Deep in Claret*, 1983

Kehrig, H., *Le Privilège des vins à Bordeaux jusqu'en 1789*, 1886

Kitchiner, W., *The Cook's Oracle*, 1817
– *The Art of Invigorating and Prolonging Life by Food, Clothes, Air, Exercises, Wine, Sleep, etc.*, 1822

Kressman, E., *Du vin considéré comme l'un des beaux-arts*, 1971
– *Le Guide des vins et des vignobles de France*, 1975

Labrousse, C. E., *La crise de l'économie française à la fin de l'Ancien Régime et au début de la Révolution*, 1944

Lachiver, M., *Vins, vignes, vignerons*, 1988

Lacoste, P. J., *Le Vin de Bordeaux. Ses centres de production, l'art de le choisir, l'art de le conserver*, 1947

Lafforgue, G., *Le vignoble Girondin*, 1947

Lafforgue, G. and Thierry, P., *La Culture de la vigne dans le Bordelais*, 1929

Lajugie, J., *Bordeaux aux XXe siècle*, 1972

Larmat, L., *Les Vins de Bordeaux*, 1944

Laver, M.-T., *Pessac: Étude démographique* (Thesis), 1985

Lawrence, R. de T. (ed.), *Jefferson and Wine*, 1973

Layton, T., *Choose your Wine*, 1940
– *Wine's my Line*, 1955

- *Wine Craft*, 1961
- *Modern Wines*, 1964
Le Magnen, J., *Les goûts et les saveurs*, 1951
Le Roy Ladurie, E., *Histoire du climat depuis l'an mil*, 1967
Leedom, W. S., *The Vintage Wine Book*, 1963
Lelong, M., *Célébration du Vin*, 1963
Lheritier, M., *Histoire des rapports de la chambre de commerce de Guienne avec les intendants, le parlement, et les jurats de 1705 à 1791*, 1913
- 'La Révolution à Bordeaux de 1789 à 1791 – la transition de l'ancien au nouveau régime', in *Revue historique de Bordeaux et du départment de la Gironde*, 1915–17
- *L'Intendant Tourny*, 2 vols, 1920
- *La Révolution à Bordeaux dans l'histoire de la Révolution française: La fin de l'ancien régime et la préparation des États-Généraux*, 1787–98, 1942
- *Liberté: les Girondins, Bordeaux et la révolution française*, 1947
Lichine, A., *Wines of France*, 1951
- *Guide to the Wines and Vineyards of France*, 1986 ed.
- *Alex Lichine's Encyclopedia of Wines and Spirits of France*, 1967; rev. ed.: 1981
Lloyd, F. C., *The Art and Technique of Wine*, 1936
Lodge, E. C., *Gascony under English Rule*, 1926
Loftus, S., *Anatomy of the Wine Trade*, 1985
Lorbac, C. de Cabrol and Lallemand, C., *Les richesses gastronomiques de la France: Les vins de Bordeaux*, 1867
Louberc, L., *A History of Wine in France and Italy in the Nineteenth Century*, 1978
Lough, J. (ed.), *Locke's Travels in France, 1675–1679*, 1953
Lucia, S. P., *A History of Wine as Therapy*, 1963
Macdonald, L., *Bordeaux and Aquitaine*, 1977
McKendrick, N., Brewer, J. and Plumb, J. H., *The Birth of the Consumer Society*, 1982
McNeill, M. F., *The Scots Cellar, its traditions and lore*, 1958
Maffre, P. and Bériac, J.-P., *Le Bordelais néo-classique*, 1983
Malone, D., *Jefferson and His Time*, 3 vols, 1945
Malvezin, F., *Histoire de la vigne et du vin en Aquitaine*, 1919
Malvezin, T., *Histoire du commerce de Bordeaux depuis les origines jusqu'à nos jours*, 4 vols, 1892

Malvezin, T. and Féret, E., *Le Médoc et ses vins*, 1876
Marchou, G., *Bordeaux sous le Règne de la Vigne*, 1947
– *La Route du vin à Bordeaux*, 1976
Marion, M., *L'impôt sur le revenu au XVIIIe siècle, principalement en Guyenne*, 1901
– *La vente des biens nationaux pendant la Révolution*, 1908
Marionneau, C., *Victor Louis – sa vie, ses travaux*, 1991
Marquette, J.-B., 'La vinification dans les domaines de l'Archevêque de Bordeaux à la fin du Moyen Age', in *Géographie historique des vignobles*, 1978
Marres, P., *La vigne et le vin en France*, 1950
Martin, G., 'Les intendants de Guyenne, au XVIIIe siécle, et les privilèges des vins bordelais', in *Revue historique de Bordeaux et du département de la Gironde*, 1908
Masson, J., *La Crise viticole en Gironde*, 1938
Maxwell, C., *Dublin under the Georges*, 1936
Meller, P., *Les anciennes familles de la Gironde*, 2 vols, 1895–6
Mendelsohn, O. A., *Drinking with Pepys*, 1963
Mercier, L.-S., *Tableau de Paris*, 1783
Michel, F., *Histoire du commerce et de la navigation à Bordeaux, principalement sous l'administration anglaise*, 2 vols, 1867–70
Montorgueil, G. ('Monseigneur le Vin'), *Le Vin de Bordeaux*, 1925
Morris, D., *The French Vineyard*, 1958
Morton, L. T., *A Practical Ampelography*, 1979
Mothe, F., *Graves de Bordeaux*, 1985
Mouillefert, P., *Le Vignoble et les vins de France et à l'étranger*, 1891
Mournetas, A. and Pelissier, H., *The Vade Mecum of the Wine Lover*, 1953
Nicolai, A., *Essai statistique sur Bordeaux au XVIIIe siècle*, 1909
Nicolardout, L., *Histoire de la table*, 1968
O'Gilvy, G., *Nobiliaire de Guienne et Gascogne*, 3 vols, 1856–83
Olney, R., *Yquem*, 1985
Ordish, G., *The Great Wine Blight*, 1972
O'Reilly, Abbé P. J., *Histoire complète de Bordeaux*, 6 vols, 1863
Orizet, L., *Les vins de France*, 1985
Ott, E., *From Barrel to Bottle*, 1953

Paguierre, M., *Classification and Description of the Wines of Bordeaux*, 1828

Paillère, F., *La crise viticole en Gironde, 1842–1936*, 1936

Pariset, F.-G., 'Locke à Bordeaux', in *Revue historique de Bordeaux et du département de la Gironde*, 1954

– *Bordeaux au XVIIIe siècle*, 1968

– *Château Margaux et l'architecte Combes*, 1970

Parker, R. M., *Bordeaux, A Definitive Guide for the Wines Produced since 1961*, 1985: 2nd ed. 1991

Pasteur, L., *Études sur le vin*, 1875

Penning-Rowsell, E., *The Wines of Bordeaux*, 1969; 4th ed.: 1979

Penzer, N. M., *The Book of the Wine Label*, 1947

Peppercorn, D., *Drinking Wine*, 1979

– *Bordeaux*, 1982; new ed.: 1991

Perrin, A., *La civilisation de la vigne*, 1938

Perry, E., *Corkscrews and Bottle Openers*, 1980

Petit-Lafitte, A., *La Vigne dans le Bordelais*, 1868

Peynaud, E., *Actualités oenologiques, Conseils pratiques pour la préparation et la conservation des vins*, 1952

– *Connaissance et travail du vin*, 1971; Eng. tr. *Knowing and Making Wine*, 1984

– *Le Goût du Vin*, 1983; Eng. tr. *The Taste of Wine*, 1987

Pierce, C., *The Household Manager*, 1857

Pijassou, R., *Un Château du Médoc, Palmer*, 1964

– *Le Seigneurie et le vignoble de Château Latour*, 1974

– 'Le marché de Londres et la naissance des grands crus médocains (fin XVIIe–début XVIIIe siècle)', in *Revue historique de Bordeaux et du département de la Gironde*, 1974

– *Le Médoc*, 2 vols, 1980

Pinney, T., *A History of Wine in America*, 1989

Pirenne, H., 'Un grand commerce d'exportation au Moyen Age: les vins de France', in *Annales d'histoire économique et sociale*, 1933

Plumb, J. H., *Men and Places*, 1966

Pomerol, C., *Terroirs et vins de France. Itinéraires oenologiques et géologiques*, 1984

Postgate, R., *Plain Man's Guide to Wine*, 1951

– *The Home Wine Cellar*, 1960

Poupon, P., *Plaisirs de la dégustation*, 1973

Poussou, J.-P., 'Les structures foncières et sociales des vignobles de Cauderan et du Bouscat en 1771', in *Vignobles et vins d'Aquitaine*, 1970

Pradel, O., *Le Vin et la Chanson*, 1915

Prial, F. J., *Wine Talk*, 1978

Ray, C., *Lafite*, 1968; rev. ed.: 1978

– *Mouton-Rothschild*, 1974

– *The Wines of France*, 1976

– *Ray on Wine*, 1979

Reach, A., *Claret and Olives*, 1852

Réal, A., *Les Grands Vins*, 1887

Redding, C., *A History and Description of Modern Wines*, 1833

– *French Wines and Vines and the way to find them*, 1860

Renouard, Y., 'Le grand commerce des vins de Gascogne au Moyen Age', in *Revue historique de Bordeaux et du département de la Gironde*, 1959

– *Bordeaux sous les rois d'Angleterre*, 1965

Renouil, Y., *Dictionnaire du vin*, 1962

Rhodes, A., *Princes of the Grape*, 1975

Ribadieu, H., *Histoire de Bordeaux pendant le Règne de Louis XVI*, 1853

– *Histoire des Châteaux de la Gironde*, 1st ed.: 1855; 2nd ed.: 1856

– *Histoire de la conquête de la Guyenne par les Français*, 1866

Ribéreau-Gayon, J. and Peynaud, É., *Traité d'ampéliologie. Sciences et techniques de la vigne*, 2 vols, 1971

– *Traité d'oenologie. Science et technique du vin*, 4 vols, 1972–7

Richard, A., *De la protection des appellations d'origine en matière vinicole; les vins de Bordeaux*, 1918

Robert, A., Cougny, G. and Bourloton, E., *Dictionnaire des parlementaires français*, 5 vols, 1891

Robinson, J., *The Wine Book*, 1979

– *The Great Wine Book*, 1982

– *Vines, Grapes and Wines*, 1986

Roger, J.-R., *Les vins de Bordeaux*, 1954

Rorabaugh, W. J. *The Alcoholic Republic*, 1979

Rothschild, P. de, *Vivre la vigne*, 1981

Rothschild, P. de and Beaumarchais, J.-P. de, *Mouton Rothschild Paintings for the Labels*, 1987

Roudié, P., *Vignobles et vins d'Aquitaine*, 1970

- *Le vignoble bordelais*, 1973
- 'Documents concernant la construction de trois maisons de campagne', in *Bulletin de la Société archéologique de Bordeaux*, 1976
- 'Manoirs et maisons de campagne du XVIIe siècle en Bordelais', *Actes de 104e Congrès National des Sociétés Savantes*, 1979
- *Vignobles et vignerons du Bordelais (1850–1980)*, 1988

Rouher, M., *Sur la viticulture dans le Sud-Ouest de la France*, 1862

Roux, M. P., *A Guide to the Vineyards and Châteaux of Bordeaux*, 1972

Royer, C., *Les Vignerons. Usages et mentalités des pays de vignobles*, 1980

Saintsbury, G., *Notes on a Cellar Book*, 1920
- *A Scrap Book*, 1922
- *A Second Scrap Book*, 1923
- *The Last Scrap Book*, 1924

Salavert, J., *Le commerce des vins de Bordeaux*, 1912

Sayles, C., *The Art of Dining*, 1852

Schama, S., *The Embarrassment of Riches*, 1987

Schneider, S., *The International Album of Wine*, 1977

Schoonmaker, F., *The Complete Wine Book*, 1934
- *Frank Schoonmaker's Encyclopaedia of Wine*, 1964

Scott, J. M., *The Vineyards of France*, 1950

Scott Thomson, G., *Life in a Noble Household*, 1937

Searle, R., *The Illustrated Winespeak*, 1983

Sée, H., *Histoire économique de la France: les temps modernes*, 1942

Seeley, J., *Great Bordeaux Wines*, 1986

Shand, P. M., *A Book of French Wines*, 1928; rev. ed.: 1964

Shaw, T. G., *The Wine Trade and its History*, 1851
- *Wine, the Vine and the Cellar*, 1863

Sichel, A., *The Penguin Book of Wines*, 1965; rev. ed.: 1972

Siloret, G., *Encyclopédie des connaissances agricoles: Le vin*, 1963

Simon, A., *The History of the Wine Trade in England*, 3 vols, 1906–9
- *Notes on the late J. Pierpont Morgan's Cellar Book*, 1906
- *In Vino Veritas*, 1913

- *Wine and the Wine Trade*, 1921
- *The Wines of France*, 1923
- *Bottlescrew Days*, 1926
- *Tables of Content*, 1933
- *Vintagewise*, 1945
- *Drink*, 1948
- *What about Wine?*, 1953
- *By Request: An Autobiography*, 1957
- *Fashions in Food and Wine*, 1968
- *Encyclopedia of Wines*, 1973

Spurrier, S., *French Fine Wines*, 1984
- *The Académie du Vin Guide to French Wines*, 1986

Sumption, J., *The Hundred Years War*, 1990

Sutcliffe, S. (ed.), *André Simon's Wines of the World*, 1951; 2nd ed.: 1981
- *Great Vineyards and Winemakers*, 1982

Thorpe, W. A., *English and Irish Glass*, 1927
- *A History of English and Irish Glass*, 2 vols, 1929

Thudicheim, J. L. W. and Dupré, A., *A Treatise on Wines*, 1872; 2nd ed.: 1894

Trabut-Cussac, J.-P., 'Les Coutumes ou droits de douane à Bordeaux sur les vins et les marchandises', in *Annales du Midi*, 1950

Vandyke Price, P., *Guide to the Wines of Bordeaux*, 1977
- *Understanding Wines and Spirits*, 1982
- *The Century Companion to the Wines of Bordeaux*, 1983
- *Wines of the Graves*, 1988

Vedère, X., *Les allées de Tourny*, 1930–31
- *Bordeaux*, 1953

Viallate, A., *L'activité économique en France de la fin sur XVIIIe siècle à nos jours*, 1937

Vignenux, M., *Aquitaine occidentale: Guides géologiques régionaux*, 1975

Vincens, J., *L'art de déguster les vins*, 1907

Vital, P., *Les vieilles vignes de notre France*, 1956

Vivié, A., *Histoire du terroir à Bordeaux*, 2 vols, 1877

Vizetelly, H., *Glances back through Seventy Years*, 2 vols, 1893
- *The Wines of France*, 1908

Wagner, P. M., *Grapes into Wine*, 1974

Warner, C. K., *The Winegrowers of France and the Government since 1875*, 1960

Waugh, A., *Merchants of Wine*, 1957

– *In Praise of Wine*, 1959

Waugh, H., *Bacchus on the Wing*, 1966

– *The Changing Face of Wine*, 1968; 3rd ed.: 1970

– *Pick of the Bunch*, 1970

– *Diary of a Wine Taster*, 9 vols, 1972

– *The Treasures of Bordeaux*, 1980

Weinhold, R., *Vivat Bacchus, Une histoire du vin et de la viticulture*, 1978

Welles, J. d', *Le Grand Théâtre de Bordeaux*, 1949

Wildman, F. S., *A Wine Tour of France*, 4th ed., 1972

Williams, H., *The Correspondence of Jonathan Swift*, 5 vols, 1963–5

Yapp, R., *Drilling for Wine*, 1988

Young, A., *Travels in France*, 1929 ed.

Younger, W., *Gods, Men and Wine*, 1966

Yoxall, H. W., *The Enjoyment of Wine*, 1972

Index